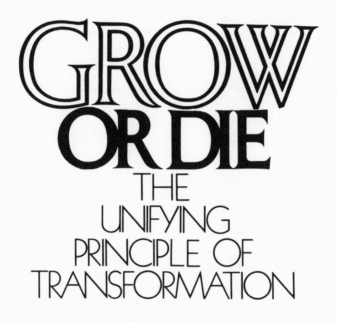

GROW OR DIE

THE UNIFYING PRINCIPLE OF TRANSFORMATION

GEORGE T. LOCK LAND

RANDOM HOUSE   NEW YORK

Copyright © 1973 by George T. Lock Land

All rights reserved under International and Pan-American Copyright Conventions. Published in the United States by Random House, Inc., New York, and simultaneously in Canada by Random House of Canada Limited, Toronto.

Library of Congress Cataloging in Publication Data

Land, George T. Lock.
Grow or die.

Bibliography: p.
1. Evolution.   2. Growth.   3. Man.
I. Title.   [DNLM: 1. Anthropology.   2. Philosophy.
BD 431.L253g   1973]
BD450 L274   116   72-12573
ISBN 0-394-48378-2

Manufactured in the United States of America

The following photographs were reprinted by permission of The Museum of Modern Art, New York:

Willem deKooning, *Untitled Lithograph,* 1960, gift of Mrs. Bliss Parkinson.
Marcel Breuer, *Armchair,* 1925, gift of Herbert Bayer.
Bauhaus: M. Brandt and H. Przyrembel: Adjustable ceiling fixture
                                          Aluminum shade, 1926.
Theo van Doesburg and C. van Eesteren: House for an artist, 1923.

First Edition

DEDICATION

As life can be known
   through living
As growth can be found
   by sharing
For the reality of belief
   and the gift of Love
      to

   My mother, Mary Land
My wife, Catherine

"AS ABOVE, SO BELOW."

- date unknown,

attributed to

Hermes Trismegistus, who may
have been mythical . . .

ACKNOWLEDGMENTS

When a book such as this is finished, or perhaps I should say interrupted long enough for it to be set in print, the author begins to review the thinking, the aid, and the comfort that have enabled him to do his job. At once, he is overwhelmed. To do even the most rudimentary justice to its many contributors is a staggering task. Although it is Nature that painted the great design of life, if it were not for the mosaic drawn by a host of persevering and creative investigators, my task of assemblage could never have been accomplished. A few of these are noted in the bibliography (p. 251); for the rest, I can only hope that the work will answer my responsibility.

For patience and help during the years of gestation there are many—family, friends, and colleagues—who although unnamed here are remembered well. To others who contributed direct nourishment to the theory of *transformation* I must give direct thanks.

From the Turtle Bay Institute of New York, my colleagues Kathleen Murphy, Steven Frankel, and especially Robert S. Weekley I received an unrepayable gift of thought and thoughtfulness. Through their efforts in performing hundreds of studies of open systems in a multitude of settings, the basic postulates of *transformation* have been put to the test of reality. As part of this, my gratitude also goes to those many American companies who are willing to risk dealing with such new ideas (p. 253).

Also to my teachers, especially when they played the devil's advocate, Dr. William Little, Dr. Carol Marcus, and Dr. Charles

Johnson. Their breadth and creativity stimulated my imagination, and their good judgment helped bring my flights of fancy back down to earth.

For interrupting their heavy schedules to review the embryonic draft of this work and for their many contributions and their encouragement, my particular gratitude to: Dr. Frank George, Dr. Margaret Mead, Dr. Karl Menninger, Dr. Oliver Reiser and to the work of Preston Harold (*The Single Reality* and others) as interpreted to me by Winifred Babcock.

My early investigations were considerably helped by my exciting educational experience at Millsaps College in Jackson, Mississippi. In later years my research was further stimulated by such organizations as The Creative Education Foundation, the Menninger Foundation, The Society for General Systems Research, and especially Julius Stulman's World Institute.

The belief and advice of some special people have helped me beyond measure. They include my friend and counselor Ernest Lorch, my first publisher and a continuing stimulator, Barbara Hubbard, and, last but far from least my editor, Toni Morrison, who recognized what I believe *transformation* to be and who saw in me what I did not know was there.

Finally, for serving as literary midwives in the earliest stages of *transformation's* birth, Patricia Earle and Susan Sharp; and for special tenacity and aid my assistant, Eva Rodriguez.

I acknowledge, most of all, my debt to life and to people. The love of both has already given me the rewards of living, a gift that in some small way I hope I can pass on to my readers.

GEORGE T. LOCK LAND

CONTENTS

INTRODUCTION   xiii

PART ONE   **ORIGINS**

CHAPTER

ONE   OVERVIEW   3

TWO   ORIGINS OF BEHAVIOR   17

THREE   SECOND NATURE   35

FOUR   EVOLUTION OF MAN AND ENVIRONMENT   53

FIVE   PSYCHOLOGY FROM BIOLOGY   75

PART TWO   **BEHAVIOR**

SIX   PATTERNS OF HUMAN GROWTH
AND MOTIVATION   111

SEVEN   A GROWTH MODEL   123

EIGHT   ENIGMAS OF MAN   139

PART THREE   **MEANING AND DIRECTION**

NINE   PHILOSOPHY AND TRANSFORMATION   157

TEN   EVOLUTION RECONSIDERED   167

ELEVEN   ACHIEVING GROWTH   185

APPENDIX I—TRANSFORMATION PRINCIPLES   197

APPENDIX II—TRANSFORMATION AND PHYSICS 199

APPENDIX III—A BIOPSYCHOLOGICAL APPROACH

TO CANCEROUS GROWTH   221

NOTES   227

GLOSSARY   239

BIBLIOGRAPHY   251

INDEX   255

INTRODUCTION

Although this book can be considered somewhat "technical" or scientific, for a number of reasons the usual style of such publications has not been followed. In proposing a new theory the tendency to select examples and data that fit the construct and to omit contradictory information is strong. In this work, however, the range of material presented includes both and is therefore very broad. The number of disciplines involved—anthropology, psychology, ethnology, ethology, physics, philosophy, biology, and so forth—are so diverse that the only single language that can be fruitfully employed is general usage English. The audience for which *Grow or Die* has been written is also diverse—including people without the time to read and translate traditional scholarly work. Even so, each reader, depending on his discipline, will surely encounter too much "jargon" in some areas and oversimplification or insufficient background in others. Such is the penalty for compromising between depth and breadth, scientific precision, and general clarity.

The author hopes, therefore, that readers will tolerate a certain degree of frustration with the problems of presentation and nomenclature. Surely a variety of quite legitimate objections can be raised to the semantics employed; a biologist may well object to the use of "homology" in a nonclassical sense, just as a physicist can take issue when what he would call "dynamics" is referred to as "growth." Unfortunately, a sort of Esperanto for science has yet to be achieved, and in the attempt to avoid invention of yet another set of obscure jargon, the use of common words for uncommonly explored phenomena raises difficulties. It is hoped that these difficulties have been resolved and that the departure from accepted academic practices will be justified in the reading.

It is also common practice in a work such as this either to begin with a specific finding and then to proceed to generalization, or to cite numerous and detailed experiments to substantiate verification. *Transformation,* however, is a *general system theory;* that is, it sets out to cover an extremely broad range of phenomena in many interrelated areas with a minimum number of postulates. Over the past five years, although a large number of validation experiments have been conceived to test this theory, investigation has invariably turned up prior research that provided the necessary data. In other words, the breadth of specific findings in each of the sciences to be correlated here has agreed in particulars and substance with the principle and postulates of *transformation.* For practical reasons these thousands of detailed findings are not included. A sampling has been footnoted in the text, and in other cases references and readings have been indicated. The vast amount of correlation, however, suggests that, in cases where a reader wishes data beyond his own area of knowledge, practically any general survey document will provide a plethora of empirical confirmation.

Finally, but most importantly, *Grow or Die* is meant to be a responsive book, one that invites the reader to join activity in the exploration. This is a book to be *used;* to be argued with, to be expanded, and to be exemplified—by you as author-reader. At best transformation theory is a new glimpse of the realities of Life. Its ultimate truth will be that it is but a small part of the great truth of Nature; its transcendence is the task of every thinking human.

PART ONE
ORIGINS

OVERVIEW
ONE

This is a book about Man; a creature who fouls his own nest while flying to the moon, an ambivalent being who grasps the future with one hand while clinging to the past with the other; who does all these things with a mind powerful enough to continually expand his domination of Nature but who is unable to explain why. Subject to seemingly blind and numberless forces, and self-evident but nameless quests, impelled from within and propelled from without, Man continues to seek for answers to his unique enigmas. This book is a part of that endless search for the inner Grail, an exploration from which there is no turning back.

Our radically changing world has resurrected a barrage of questions about our nature and our goals. Proposed answers to our enigmas ranging from "territorial agression" to the "global village" would compile a monumental anthology. Rather than engage in a fruitless dispute of the many theories about our nature, this book outlines a theory on the origin, nature, and nurture of Man that sees apparently conflicting achievements and failures as integral parts of the whole of Man and his mission. It will show that such things as territorial ambitions and hopes for world cooperation are *not* mutually exclusive, but are inclusive and reconcilable aspects of the laws that govern all life and all behavior.

Heretical as it may seem, there is a logical and understandable viewpoint that explains the infinite variety of seemingly paradoxical acts of the human species. Several years ago, Abraham Maslow concluded that there was a scientifically discoverable basis to Man's unique properties. As father of the "Third Force" in psychology, he recognized the urgent need for Man to explain, understand, and encourage such baffling phenomena as creativity, joy, and dignity. He felt that the pattern of relationships between these human experiences and the biological roots of life could reveal a unifying concept of all of life, a concept to help answer many questions that have puzzled Man from the beginning of history.

We call the theory that begins to integrate these relationships "transformation." Through it, we can acquire an understanding of not only the self-actualizing acts of Man, but also his unbalanced and destructive behavior—a dichotomy that has long preoccupied psychology. This theory of Man falls far outside existing ideas of human behavior. As the recent movement toward humanistic psychology and the revolution in psychoanalysis testify, current theories have simply provoked dissatisfaction with and distrust of the sciences. Too much of Man's essence is missing in the present cafeteria of orthodox theories; they are concepts that do not solve Man's problems and that do not fit the facts. As *Science* reported on the 1971 annual meeting of the American Psychological Association, "There is less agreement than ever on the Nature of Man and how to affect it."[1]

Although these facts seem to represent an exacerbating conflict, often described as a "fierce" theoretical battle, among the various schools in the psychosocial sciences, each school has made major contributions to the sorting out of the many elements of Man's extremely complex behavior and has added vital data to our growing picture of ourselves. The word "added" is used here despite the generally accepted judgment that psychology, unlike the other sciences, is not cumulative. Lack of an accumulation is perhaps mostly due to the necessity for developing a concrete and verifiable basis—in fact, for each isolated expression of behavior —before proceeding to speculate on the whole. It is only in very recent years that enough pieces have been available even to start assembling a complete picture.

If we look at the history of how we arrived at our present uncertainty it becomes clear why more widespread attention has not been given to developing more holistic theories of Man. Although centuries of speculation have provided a plethora of hypotheses about the basic causes of behavior, all of them have left large gaps. The so-called instinctivists have offered a wide range of concepts, but even the broadest theoretical views, ranging from Hobbs and Spencer to Freud, do not explain why men strive for goals incompatible with either lineage or the sequestered urges of the unconscious. Environmentalists have attempted to show that, rather than the result of instinctive urges, Man's behavior is a blank slate at birth, a tabula rasa, mediated by experience and resulting in a collection of what are now called "conditioned reflexes" or "operant conditioning." Yet this behaviorist attitude, fostered by Hippocrates and extended by such men as Locke, Watson, and Skinner, cannot explain unrewarded learning or unstimulated striving. The humanistic school has picked up the neglected gauntlet of philosophy and ethics, and investigators like Fromm, Maslow, and Rogers have postulated new and more holistic theories. Although many of their ideas, explained as drives for self-actualization or creativity, work in therapeutic practice, their theoretical constructs leave us with unsatisfactory circular explanations: as, for example, "Man creates because he is motivated to be creative."

Broad theories have always come hard in science. It is particularly true of the sciences of human behavior as they have multiplied into divisions of psychology, anthropology, sociology, and psychiatry, and have further subdivided into such specialties as medical, clinical, vocational, educational, therapeutic, and so on. In addition, there continues to exist in the midst of intensified study and experimentation the "higher nature" school, which historically and continually exhorts us to ignore the base nature of Man and to reach for one that is purely abstract, spiritual, or metaphysical—one that by meditation, drugs, or discipline can be found and followed. The "higher nature" school does not discover Man's nature; it abandons it. Such unresolvability and ambiguity have led some scientists in desperation to advocate simple control of Man's mind through the means of drugs, either mind-expanding or -suppressing.

Like a thirsty man in the middle of an ocean, we are surrounded with knowledge in a form we cannot digest. Although experiments can show how we perceive and learn, how we make affiliations, how we respond in groups, and, to some extent, how we think, notably absent are answers to the question "why?" Why do we bother? Current theories leave us with acts of behavior "beyond explanation," or motived "in themselves." We may know, for instance, how we learn, but we do not know why some choose not to learn or why others use their learning destructively. It is this "why" that is the principal concern of this book.

Transformation is an attempt to reunite the artificial with the natural, philosophy with psychology, psychology with biology, science with art, and emotion with reason. This new union is a part of the revolution of science that has leapfrogged Darwin and re-explained Mendel; that has produced an abundance of new facts in anthropology, paleontology, biology, and ethology; and that has shown that centuries of assumptions about Man's origin and nature are little more than romantic prejudices. Less than a century and a half has passed since the *vis vitalis* concept has given way to the science of physiology, and in our own time the physical and chemical sciences have reformulated our world by demonstrating that the ancient diversity of life is, in truth, unified by a substratum of identical physical, chemical, and organic structures.

As science has extended Man's vision and perception, it has become clear that all matter and life are made of the same materials, albeit in different arrangements. From "subatomic" particles like the deuterons, antiprotons, antineutrinos, mesons, positrons, photons, and neutrinos that make up the electrons, neutrons, and protons of all atoms, the continuum of Nature extends to molecular aggregates, and finally, in huge megamolecules, to the lowest phylogenetic level of life, the cell. With the further penetration of many of the secrets of cellular processes, the patterns of life hold firm. *The diversity of all life depends on the quantity and sequences of only two pairs of four nucleic acids in the hereditary information of DNA in chromosomes.*

There is no doubt that the underlying organization of all living beings conforms in every detail. Beyond that, however, the emerging hybrid sciences of cybernetics, general systems, biochemistry, biophysics, and molecular genetics have confirmed that *all life forms share the same behavioral processes.* Homologous systems of energetics, synthesis, and growth are identical acts of life. These new sciences, made up of unions among older sciences, have begun to remove the inconsistencies and misunderstandings between the claims of sophisticated science and the facts of observation and common sense. They have all pointed in the same direction, making it increasingly more likely that Man is not only biochemical and biophysical, but *biopsychological* as well.

Of late, the discipline of formalized analogy and the construction of analogical models have become techniques whereby new, logical, and profound relationships have been discovered in the physical and natural sciences. It was formalized analogy that

6

revealed the nature of systems to cyberneticians, the structure of DNA to molecular geneticists, and produced a wide variety of discoveries best characterized by Raymond A. Dart's description, "The most poignant discovery in science comes when one suddenly sees the truth that was open to view all the time."

The deep and obviously connective tissue underlying all behavior has been revealed mainly within this last decade of interdisciplinary studies. Linking phenomena in biology and psychology, however, lay outside the orthodox academic syllabus and discovery of them was delayed by the traditional and reciprocal neglect of the natural sciences by the human sciences. Only the cross-disciplinary efforts of such creative investigators as Huxley, Langer, Mead, Reiser, and von Bertalanffy[2] have opened the long-closed portals of scientific parochialism. It is through these doors, laden with the overflowing treasure trove of new facts about Man and Nature, that transformation theory has emerged.

How can a "biological" approach hope to explain the curious behavior of a creature who "lives not by bread alone"? Many believe that biological evolution is a practical process that leads to satisfaction of visceral demands, survival, and reproduction, but hardly to such needs as dignity or aesthetics, liberty or morality, patience or heroism, and contend that such "human-ness" will forever remain unknowable. Yet, the impenetrable mysteries of alchemy have become chemistry, secret incantations and potions have evolved to medicine, and the chasm separating the animate from the inanimate, the unknowable from the known, has gradually been bridged. The leap from the physical to the mental is not as wide as has been imagined. Niels Bohr, recognizing the promise inherent in spanning that gap, commented "The recognition of the limitation of mechanical ideas in atomic physics would much rather seem suited to conciliate the apparently contrasting points of view which mark physiology and psychology." In the human species, following the same laws, the practicality and utility of evolution have produced a phenomenon in form and function more subtle yet identical to all of life's processes.

The goal of this book and of transformation theory is to weave the new facts into an understanding of the complete human being, within the total system of being. Its aims are:

I   To amplify our explanation of how we came to be,
II To help understand why we act the way we do, and
III To aid in the actualization of our future potentialities.

7

TRANSFORMATION

The fundamental premise of transformation theory is that living processes are ubiquitous and universal—that only the absence of facts and the presence of intellectual illusion have separated the physical from the mental. *Transformation maintains that psychological and cultural processes are an extension of and are isomorphic with biological, physical, and chemical processes.**

The single process of Nature that forms the keystone of transformation theory and that unites the behavior of all things is the process of *growth*. Man, as a continuation of the evolutionary process, manifests this universal drive of growth on levels extrinsically different from, but intrinsically the same as his physical and biological forebears. Thinking, communication, socialization, technology, and ethics are all examples of externalized and amplified acts of biological growth: the irreversible transformation of energy and matter into life and life-facilitating products.

For a preliminary view of this principle, we can compare the growth process of two fundamental phylogenetic units of the physical and mental: the simple cell and the single human. In essence, the destiny of a cell, and a human, is to reach out and *to affect the environment*. As Robert D. Coghill has put it, "The organism acts on the environment before it reacts to the environment." *The drive of both the physiological and the psychological process of living is to assimilate external materials and to reformulate them into extensions of the self.* The cell does this by ingesting its environment and transforming it into cells that match its own genetic pattern. The human does it by mentally absorbing his cultural environment and affecting it in ways that conform to his own culturally acquired mental patterns.

---

*Although facets of a biological isomorphism have been alluded to by a variety of investigators, in the main, those views have been confined to analogies of specific aspects of mental and physical life. There have been, for instance, a host of zoology-based concepts that recognize such parallel needs of animal and Man for survival, avoidance of pain, sexual gratification, survival of progeny or the development of greater mastery, strength, dominance, and endurance. While illuminating some aspects of human behavior, these analogical ideas have not shown how Man's unique properties of language and intelligence and their myriad manifestations correlate with animal behavior.

In creating these self-extensions, Man and cell perform identical acts of synthesis, one biologically, the other psychologically. They first seek nutrition, physical or mental. Second, they ingest what they can use, discriminating among materials through screening processes. Third, after ingestion, they digest the material, breaking it down into smaller units. Fourth, this material is then reassembled for use in self-extension. Finally, this total act of growth is reacted to by the environment, and both *the cell and the man modify their subsequent behavior based on this response or "feedback" from the environment.*

In a multicellular relationship or in a cultural group, cell and Man respond in like manner, not only extending the self, but performing acts and making products that facilitate the growth of the organism as a whole. In the growth process both exhibit the traits long considered unique to our human mental process: curiosity (searching for nourishment), learning and memory (digestion, assimilation, and internal growth), creativity (assembling materials in new ways—mutation), growth (affecting the environment through extension of internal patterns), and responsibility (relating to environmental feedback).

Both Man and cell, in their drive to grow, respond to two basic conditions in their environment—the availability of nutritional materials, and the response of the environment to attempts to use it for growth. In their total process of growth, both not only renew themselves and survive, but also grow internally as well as externally, constantly evolving and improving their ability to grow. The nature of a cell, just like what we call "human nature," is not something that *is,* but something forever in the process of *becoming.* It is not wholly determined, but plays a great part in determining itself. As the human recapitulates the same series of events that take place in the life of a cell, his behavior depends on the alternatives available for growth. If the conditions of nutrition and feedback permit new growth patterns, the result will be creative and responsible behavior. If not, the *lack of alternatives result in a regression to more basic growth patterns.*

Thus, to be successful in new forms of growth, all of the activities above must be performed in the presence of a useful, non-antagonistic environment. Of course, not every cell or human is found in that situation; the need to grow is modified by the environment and other patterns for continuing growth activity are established. A cell, as it assumes its position in an organism, develops some of its potentials while suppressing or excluding others. Similarly, when a human assumes his position in a culture, his mode of growth expression is determined by that culture. Human cultures determine the growth of the people within them just as organisms determine the growth of cells. This is not to say that such specialization is forever fixed. Recent biological and sociological experiments have fully demonstrated that in the presence of proper nutrients and feedback cells, animals and humans can be transformed (transdetermined), learning to use previously unexpressed potentials and to behave in new ways.

GROWTH

So far, the abbreviated comparison we have drawn does not penetrate the quality of human life. As we proceed we shall see that current definitions of the process of growth are, in fact, simplistic, tautological expressions, much like a definition of the future as something that lies ahead. *Growth is actually expressed in a variety of ways, on a hierarchical continuum that exhibits behaviors ranging from destructive to constructive.*

One of our very first tasks in understanding the transformative nature of all the processes of life is to redefine the word "grow," for this concept is perhaps one of the most misunderstood. As each science has begun to create descriptions of the phenomena within its boundaries, it has created new terms and definitions for this process. If we consult a modern dictionary, we find "grow" explained as:

> 1. to come into being or be produced naturally; sprout; spring up.
> 2. to exist as living vegetation; thrive; as, orchids do not grow in Cleveland. 3. to increase size and develop toward maturity, as a plant or animal does by assimilating food. 4. to increase in size, quantity or degree, or in some specified manner; as, my troubles are growing. 5. to become; turn; as, he grew weary. 6. to become attached or united by growth; grow on; to have gradually increasing effect on; come gradually to seem more important, dear or admirable to.

In the sciences we might find "grow" also defined as "clustering," "bonding," "synthesis," "dynamics," or any one of hundreds of specialized growth terms. All of these, however, obscure the basic process of growth. Yet, to explain *any* basic process known to Man, from the joining of subatomic particles to the putting together of thoughts into an idea we must use some term, and the word "growth" comes closest to expressing the phenomenon. If we reach down to the basic nature of the concept of growth we find a singular fact: *Growth cannot occur independently—it requires interaction and interrelation between the growing thing and its environment.* Put another way, nothing grows totally from the inside out, something from the outside must be integrated. No matter what word we use, the process requires a joining of things.

As was stated earlier, an organism acts *on* its environment before it reacts *to* it. This is true in all processes; actions produce reactions—neither can exist independently of the other. Things act on each other by their mere presence, and if they join in some way we can see that growth occurs.

Growth, however, means more than interactive joining. There are, in fact, *three distinctly different forms of growth,* each of which merges into the other in a continuum of levels of growth, of interactive joining. The first of these is purely additive—an extension of the boundaries of what already exists. We shall call this form of growth *accretive.* It is characterized by an accumulation of "sameness,"* simply extending boundaries and getting larger without changing basic form.

The second form of growth is *replicative;* it is growth by influencing other things to take on the form of the initiator. Whereas accretive growth is sameness, replicative growth is "likeness." A cell grows and divides; as it grows in its initial stages it takes in the environment and transforms it directly into itself. When it divides, the two daughter cells are no longer within the boundaries of that original organism. They have become replicas of the mother cell. In human terms, children were once considered literal extensions of the parent. They were taught to be the *same* as the parent. Later, children were taught to be *like* the parent and some room was left for individual difference. In the first case we see accretive growth; in the second it is replicative.

The third form of growth is reciprocal interaction; a truly two-sided exchange. This form, which we call *mutual* growth, exists in the parent-child relationship in which we learn as much from our children as they learn from us, a relationship that exhibits the same kind of cooperation found in multicellular organisms. Mutuality is give and take, the equilateral sharing or joining process

---

*Sameness is used in the sense of both identicality or complementarity.

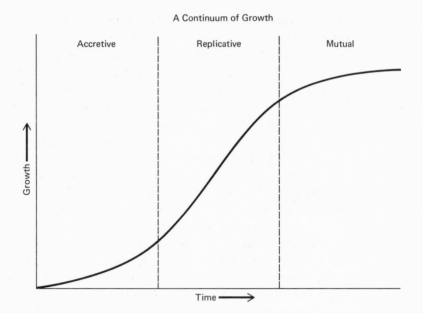

FIGURE 1

that is at the top of the continuum of growth forms. It is the culmination of the success of accretive and replicative growth.

As we proceed we shall see how the process of growth continually transforms itself into ever higher levels of organization. The growth of atoms leads to molecules, molecules proceed to cells, cells join to become multicellular, and organisms recapitulate the growth processes at biological, psychological, and cultural levels. In every natural phenomenon *there is the ubiquitous and irreversible procession from accretive to replicative to mutual growth, at which point, at a new level of organization, the process repeats itself.*

Growth, at this stage of our examination, is defined as a process of joining in which the ratios of interactive effect are continually expressing *higher levels of exchange.*

INFORMATION

Before going further into an analysis of growth, another definition is in order: *information.* Fairly recently, chemicals have begun to be regarded as information—as a specialized sort of "memory." At their most fundamental level, all energy and matter can be regarded as "pieces of data." An atom, for example, accepts only very specific frequencies of energy for its own growth. If a quantum of energy, a photon, is not in agreement, the atom will

12

reject it. On the other hand, if the energy matches the atom's frequencies, it excites the atom to absorb it and move to a higher energy state, referred to as the "excited" "metastable state." The electrons in the outer shell of the atom will expand their boundaries to a new limit. (See Figure 2.) Thus, even at this most basic level of being there is some "meaning" to the different forms of energy available to an atom. This can be defined as *information.*

Proceeding to higher levels of material organizations, atoms will likewise relate only to certain other atoms and molecules. They carry their own meaning to each other for example by the number and type of possible bonds available. A particular set of such physical information determines whether a molecule will be one of, say, sulphur or lead. In each case, the molecule will always be put together the same way. In the formation of a crystal, the axial atoms of the original molecule make up the *language*—the code—that provides the information necessary for other atoms to join the group in regular and specific formations; they experience what is called a "stereochemical sympathy" between each other. Here as elsewhere in our universe, *information determines the probabilities of occurrence of an event.*

This phenomenon is most eloquently expressed in the complex bits of information carried by the molecules of DNA and RNA in the chromosomes of organic systems. Whether one has blue or brown eyes, dark or light skin, long or short arms, and all the myriad of other data needed to construct a living human made up of some sixty billion cells are neatly encoded in the chemical memory of the parental germ cells. For instance, if the internal genetic information for brown eyes is present in sufficient quantity, brown eyes will occur. Otherwise, if a person born with blue eyes wants to change them to brown, by the use of proper external

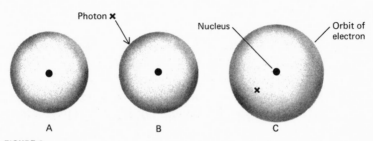

Photon **×**

Nucleus

Orbit of electron

A   B   C

FIGURE 2

Atomic "growth" exemplified in an atom of hydrogen. As energy of the proper frequency enters, the system expands to a higher energy state and the electron moves to a new orbit.

information in "language" available to him and others, he can be provided appropriately with tinted contact lenses so that brown eyes result. In all cases in the phenomenological universe an event can occur only if the proper information is present.

Information in chemical, nutritional, or language form is essential to growth at any level. In the interactive processes of growth, sharing of information provides the possibilities of growth. The more appropriate the available information is, the more growth can occur. If information is absent or inappropriate, growth will not occur. Thus, it is crucial to our examination of growth to regard information as literally a form of energy—the fuel for the engines that carry the processes of life forward to increasingly higher levels of organization. *Growth, in this sense, is a continual joining of larger amounts of information into meaningful relationships, in an "organized" form.*

Man is unique and distinct from his biological precursors, yet he carries forward in his acts the ontology of ancient growth instincts and combines them in new ways with his cultural learning. Man has evolved and is evolving. This we do not question. What we will question is why, how, and in what directions.

PRINCIPLES

As a theory applying to human behavior, transformation embraces basic postulates related to the three central issues of Man: his origins, his nature, and the nurture of his potentialities.

I. Origins. Human behavior has naturally evolved from biological behavior. Psychological phenomena are thus a continuation of the same growth and natural selection processes responsible for biological evolution. All Man's thinking, feeling, acts, and artifacts spring from this source.

II. Nature. Human mental processes are transformed homologues* of biological processes. Psychological processes operate on a parallel continuum with biological systems of growth behavior and are thus isomorphic with them and can be developed in the same ways.

III. Nurture. All organic and human behavior is growth-motivated. The phenomenon of high-level psychological growth,

---

*The expression "homologue" in this case refers to the identicality of *fundamental processes.*

called "mental health," occurs in evolved cultures when more evolved forms of growth are allowed expression. Repression of these higher forms results in substitution of less advanced, but just as natural, growth behavior, and these less evolved forms of growth produce what is referred to as "mental illness."

Transformation theory views every aspect of human behavior, from destructive aggression to creative achievement, as naturally evolved types of growth that are re-statements of observable biological phenomena and subject to the same basic principles and processes. As an evolutionary biology of behavior, human processes are referred to as "transformational" in nature in that at each higher level of recapitulation they are *directed ontogenetic changes, producing higher and more and more elaborate forms, capable of transforming or affecting ever-widening environments.* Transformation relates not only to the expressions of human behavior but to those processes that enable Man to develop, achieve, or lose these expressions; for psychological and social acts experience the same pressures that biological growth encounters with natural selection. From this perspective, human behavior can be studied and explained within the framework of evolutionary theory just as morphologic and biochemical evolution have been.

We shall first explore the origin of human behavior, which includes the sequence of links between our psychologic and biologic behavior that led inevitably to modern Man and modern society. Our exploration will take us into the very deepest valleys of Man's vitality before we ascend to the heights of human expression. In order to provide the broadest correlations possible, our binocular view of behavior will begin at the most basic common denominators of biophysical and biochemical behavior. We shall consider the forms of growth *activity* at the very earliest and lowest levels in order to formulate a holistic model of human behavior.

By the word "activity" we mean the functions, or the acts, of behavior and not the structure or morphology of expression. In life's superstructure, these basic functions are manifested in many ways to meet the challenges of environment. Two animals at essentially the same level of organic organization will exhibit

---

*The directionality of evolution is more fully discussed in Chapter Ten.

distinct differences in structure: organs will be in diverse location, bones will vary, vision will operate differently, and so forth. In each case, however, the *functions* or processes of life will be identical. It is through an examination of functions that we can penetrate the surface of phenomena to find the underlying identity of life. As a subject of *acts,* we shall also consider life as it works, not as what it "is." Like electricity, life itself cannot yet be defined; however, we can understand and explain its behavior by knowing its activities. Similarly, transformation is a study of behavior, the unifying processes of all living things from the simple biological cell to the complex cultures of Man.

ORIGINS OF BEHAVIOR
TWO

The first postulate of transformation states that *human behavior has naturally evolved from biological behavior,* and that the behavior of all living things is *growth-directed* activity. The mandate of nature, as we observe it on every hand, is the same—"grow or die." The imperative of Life is to grow and to reproduce by the assimilation of materials taken from the environment and transformed into either the bodily constituents of the organism and its progeny, or the development of special products to aid growth.[1] The mandate of Nature continues. "Expand, fill in all the possible ecological niches in the environment."[2] This necessary and constant expansion of life can be seen most eloquently in the variety and spread of life and the results of natural selection. Biological organisms are permitted to survive when they can express growth, when they can *reproduce* successfully. This most basic of all causative forces holds true for "psychological" organisms, also. Man is a function of growth. To appreciate the elegance of how Man became the evolved form of growth requires an examination of the workings of some lower expressions of behavior.

Whereas poets may distinguish between the quick and the dead, it is difficult for scientists to select some dividing line between life and nonlife. We shall initiate our search by considering biological evolution and growth behavior from the level of molecular crystal growth, through cell division, and, finally, to animal reproduction.*

PRE-LIFE GROWTH FORMS

Although a certain amount of speculation is required to project a picture of the evolution of the earliest forms of life, sufficient existing growth behaviors are available to provide a reasonably clear idea of the steps in the progression of biological growth processes.

ACCRETIVE GROWTH

The phenomenon most susceptible and perhaps closest to what we can easily identify as a sort of "living" behavior is the growth of crystals. Even the most primitive crystal displays a certain kind of life-likeness. Under favorable circumstances, groups of atoms "grow" into crystals as they reproduce patterns in orderly three-dimensional forms. These patterns come into being through the process of *nucleation*.

The origin of crystal growth that allows it to self-duplicate is the information or memory unit—the ordered formation of atoms within the nucleating molecule. This structured unit, the "gene" of the crystal, can then progressively "order" more molecules to form in the same pattern, allowing the crystal to copy its basic form again and again.** A crystal simply extends its own form.

---

*Although it is beyond the scope of this section to consider growth at atomic and molecular levels, we should point out that these three stages of growth are represented in the normal development of the material world at its very lowest levels. As the ratios of exchange increase at the atomic level from accretive to replicative to mutual, we find the formation of stable compounds, monomers, to polymers, and finally to the carbon-based giant heteropolymeric macromolecules that are the basic building blocks of life. The mutuality function of what we call the "carbon atom" is that which makes possible the joining of large collections of molecules. With its covalent bonds, neither gaining nor loosing electrons, but with four electrons that can "move in any direction," carbon can form an extremely wide variety of hydrocarbons. They thus provide the basis for the molecules of living things. These levels of Transformation are explored more fully in Appendix II.

**Although other materials may be incorporated into the crystal as it grows, they most often occur as impurities and do not affect the basic pattern being repeated. (When materials crystallize together, it happens through *isomorphic* replacement.)

Crystals do not add much new information to their systems as they reproduce; thus their possible forms are limited almost completely to multiples of the chemical information in the basic axial unit of information. The crystal expresses what can be characterized as "self-seeking," "autistic," and accretive growth patterns.

REPLICATIVE GROWTH

The remarkable properties of long-chain "liquid crystals"*— which upon reaching a certain size have the capability of dividing, adding to the divided halves, and dividing again—have tempted many investigators to look upon this activity as a possible precursor of primitive cells. But, like static crystals, liquid crystals are accretions of "sameness" and have no detectable internal machinery by which to add large amounts of new or different information or develop higher growth processes. Even the liquid crystal is dependent upon an environment in flux and the lucky accident of encountering complementary molecules. It is at the mercy of its environment. Nonetheless, the chemical interactions in the construction of a molecular crystal are the same nature as those in living systems.[3]

Higher up the ladder of growth forms we encounter several other "lifeless" amalgamations of chemicals—organic macromolecules and the viruses (most often found in crystal form). Although we shall not delve into the obscure origins of viruses as we move up the ladder of life, they represent the simplest organic form known to "reproduce."**

MUTUAL GROWTH

With the giant organic molecules, what is important in an evolutionary and transformational sense is the diversity of the elements (monomers) that they can incorporate into their carbon-based molecules. Rather than simply accreting like material,

---

*Also called "fluid crystals." An example of these duplicating crystals is para-azo-oxycinnamic acid ethyl ester.

**The organic proteins and nucleotides that make up viruses are isomorphic with the makeup of organic macromolecules in that they both depend on the atomic mutuality function of carbon.

this assimilated, new, and *different* chemical information creates the possibility for the construction of huge heteropolymeric macromolecules that tend to aggregate into film-bound groups called "coacervates," possibly the precursor of membrane-bound cells. Although it is interesting to hypothesize on the origin of cells,* for our purposes what is vital is following the process of information accumulation as it builds with each and every step of growth.

CELL GROWTH FORMS

As described earlier, the basic methods of chemical growth can also be separated into three specific levels of cellular growth forms. These are expressed by:

I. Accretive growth: Extending boundaries and self-expansion ranging from large molecules, to enlarging cell size to vegetative fission.
II. Replicative growth: Organic self-duplication by the asexual mechanism of mitotic cell division.
III. Mutual growth: Cell growth through sexual fusion and gene recombination techniques, for example, conjugation and meiosis.

For a cell to become mutualistic it must first grow through the accretive and replicative stages. Just as it is with cells, so is it for Man and Society. The embryonic cell must enlarge accretively before it can replicate, and it must replicate successfully before the mutualistic society of cells can form the total organism. Thus is a human formed, and just as humans have created society they too must first have created the accretive societies of early Man that gave way to the replicative "imperialism" of colonial empires that, in turn, is now transforming into interdependent mutual relationships.

We can view the hypothetical initial cell form, occurring perhaps three and a half to four billion years ago, as a massive macromolecule, yet a tiny micro-organism—a creature with ma-

---

*The shift from inorganic crystals to organic growth may indicate a change in "genetic" materials, incorporating new chemicals more effective in growth and more easily meeting the demands of natural selection.

Accretive Vegetative (Fission) Growth in Blue-Green Algae

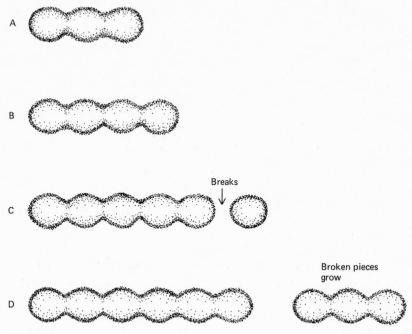

FIGURE 3

Growth in primitive Blue-Green algae shows the accretive character of what is called vegetative or fission growth. As it extends its own form by adding to itself in identical extensions it assumes the form of jelly-like masses or of fibers. In this case we see how this pure self-extension became the precursor to replicative growth, for the organism grows large and unwieldy, unable to maintain its self-connections. As it breaks, in effect, "daughter" organisms are created in the broken pieces which then begin to grow on their own.

chinery for reproduction. In the most primitive forms of life that still exist, bacteria and algae, suspected to be much like those early organisms, we can observe a form of self-extension much like fluid crystals. The blue-green alga, for example, is a unicellular or acellular organism that grows through formation of chains as large as its environment will permit—theoretically, it could grow to unlimited lengths. However, because of the mechanical action of such things as water currents or internal weaknesses, the filaments break. In turn, the pieces of the chain grow longer until they too break. The green alga *Acetabularia* produces a complete organism as a single cell with a single nucleus. Rather than dividing to reproduce, it forms "cysts" of mature germ cells which fuse with each other to produce the zygote that grows into another *Acetabularia*.[4] In essence, like other primitive organisms, it adds to itself, perpetuating sameness.

These primitive organisms can grow accretively by self-extension in a self-fertilized expansion of identical units. They cannot interact as well with their environment as an autotrophic plant which can make its own food from simple chemicals. Thus they do not change a great deal and, although still very much a part of our planetary ecology (the most familiar form of blue-green algae can be found floating on stagnant ponds), they have reached a dead-end in evolutionary terms. Organisms that are primarily accretive forms of growth, that have not developed ways to interact with the environment, are limited to a sort of "autistic" or self-seeking behavior. Because they absorb little new information, their ultimate growth within the total system is extremely limited.*

REPLICATIVE GROWTH

Replicative growth requires the possibility of incorporating larger amounts of *new and different information* in the process of growth to introduce change in subsequent replicas. The evolutionary leap represented in replicative growth is the emergence of externally self-reproducing cells

Although the instructional macromolecule of the nucleus of a mitotic cell supplies the information by which a cell can grow and reproduce itself, it is a significant change from crystal nuclei** or non-nucleated cells in that it contains vastly increased nuclear information that directs its internal machinery and allows both self-duplication and the manufacture of special products. This reproductive process makes it possible, as a cell copies itself, for new information to be incorporated and to produce "mutations"

---

*Although a virus also grows and "replicates," its primary mission is to make more of itself, whatever the cost to its neighbors. The bundle of information (DNA) that makes up a virus can, by invading a living cell, make many more identical viruses. Viruses, as defined today, are parasites; they inhabit their host to multiply and their offspring move on to inhabit other hosts and again to duplicate themselves. The totally self-duplicative behavior of viruses eloquently demonstrates the essentially nonmutual characteristics of such accretive forms of growth behavior, behavior that can be defined as substantially *self-extending* without regard for other organisms. However, the potential exists for the existence of mutualistic and beneficial "viruses." These probably exist but are identified under other names. Bacteriological parasites that have evolved to live in mutuality with their hosts, and not to kill them, have proved mutualism to be the most viable form of growth.[5]

**The nuclear DNA of a cell can be regarded as a "fibrillar crystal"[6] or what Schrödinger called a "periodic crystal" in the Watson-Crick double-helix structure.

in offspring. The tendency of these living cells is thus not only to accrete or to enlarge the self but also to produce independent replicas of themselves.

Although no wholly satisfactory theory of the mutation mechanism has yet been advanced, the observable fact is that unicellular organisms modify their potential for growth through a number of subtle spontaneous or induced genetic information changes. These changes result in an expanded possibility of genetic informational modifications. The changes can occur by substitution, deletion, addition, or rearrangement of the nucleotide code within sections of the DNA or the RNA of a gene. Thus, in the process of growth, unicellular mitotic organisms express in their offspring a variety of alternative growth combinations. Through the sifting process of the environmental pressures of natural selection, some mutated offspring survive and continue to grow and reproduce while the larger number of unfavorable mutations are culled out and extinguished.*

Asexual replication is predominantly a growth technique of primitive plants and micro-organisms. Although it sometimes takes place in some higher organisms, it does not allow elaboration of fundamental and radically new evolutionary devices or paths.[7] Also, with replication, any mutation incorporating new and more advantageous information produces an effect that can be transmitted only to the descendants of a *single* individual. Thus, in time, it can have only a relatively minor effect on the total environment. (See Figure 4.) As Dobzhansky puts it,[8] "Selfing is a form of evolutionary opportunism, which sacrifices the evolutionary plasticity given by gene recombination for immediate and perhaps ephemeral adaptive advantages." To some extent a replicative process is always ill-adaptive; such inbreeding can uncover recessive mutants that may have been concealed, and it frequently results in reduced ability to survive and grow. (See Figure 5.[9])

As illustrated in Figure 5, wide differences exist between the

---

*Other mechanisms in replicative growth involve the use of such mechanisms of partial gene recombination with other cells. This would include the process of *transduction* by which genetic material is transferred from one cell to another by means of a temperate phage, similar to the viral mechanisms, but in this case often does not destroy the cell "host" in the process. Another method is that of *conjugation,* in which cells employ temporary paired union and transfer of genetic material. Both viruses and parasites demonstrate very primitive forms of genetic hybridization.

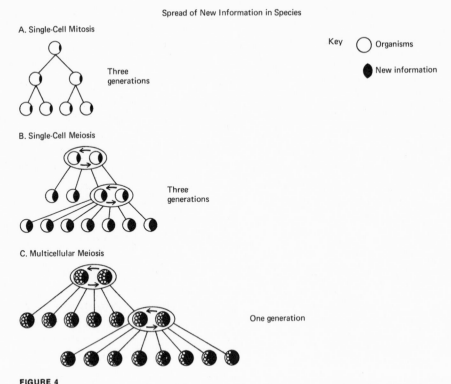

Spread of New Information in Species

A. Single-Cell Mitosis

Three
generations

Key — Organisms

New information

B. Single-Cell Meiosis

Three
generations

C. Multicellular Meiosis

One generation

FIGURE 4
Graphic representation of relative ratios of time necessary for new information to reach members of a species.

viability of hybridization and of inbreeding. Figure 5A shows a comparison over successive generations of heterozygotic, or mutualistic hybrid, populations and, below, the reduced viability of homozygotic, or inbred replicative, populations. Increased information from exchanges creates a vastly more viable population in general, as well, as can be seen in the estimation curves in Figure 5B. As viability moves to the right of the chart we can observe that, although a slightly higher percentage of "supervitals" is produced by inbreeding, the hybrid population is far superior in its ability to survive and reproduce.

MUTUAL GROWTH

Probably about a billion years ago, highly evolved organisms utilized a radically different innovation, the process of meiosis, which allowed sexual fusion and *mutual* gene recombination. In evolutionary terms this sharing method has assumed a progressively larger role; in fact, those organisms in which no gene recombination is known to occur are steadily dwindling.[10] The mutuality of sexual recombination has become the most widespread and successful of the information recombination mechanisms of genetics. With sexual recombination, as shown in Figure 5, A and B, mutual (heterozygotic) information causes changes across a wider range of individuals than in replicative mitotic growth. There is a much greater effect on the total environment as their modified offspring multiply and transform more and more of the environment into themselves. As fossil records show, this exchange of chromosome sections between pairs led to a mixing of different maternal and paternal genetic information and resulted in ever greater variability and viability in succeeding generations.[11]

Crossing over, however, like mutation, does not invariably produce successful organisms in the long run, as we can observe in the metamorphosis of our planet. Almost all the known species that have ever existed—estimated to be over 98 percent—are now extinct. Our planet has been a laboratory of genetic experiments that, through variations in organic and inorganic environment,*

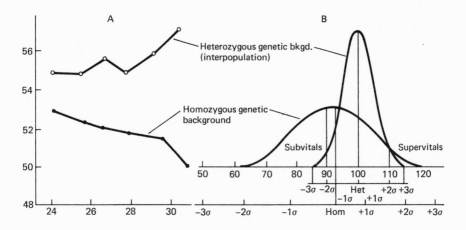

FIGURE 5

Heterozygous versus homozygous viability. A. Relationships in genetic background (Drosophila melanogaster) and viability. (After Dobzhansky, Mukai, et al.) B. Relations of subvitals and supervitals in a technique of estimating frequencies of chromosomes. (After Wallace, Madden, and Dobzhansky.) Both charts represent the increase in viability when different genetic information is combined (heterozygotes) versus the effect of combining sameness (homozygotes).

---

*Changes in the environment, invasions at new environments, or cohabitations occurring by the action of other organisms.

produced organisms that grew and interrelated ever more successfully. Although all the reasons for the hybrid vigor of sexual reproduction have yet to be discovered, practical animal breeding as well as scientific experimentation has shown that mutual, or polymorphic, populations can generate greater growth, biomass, and vitality than can monomorphic replication.

THE DISCONTINUUM

These first manifestations of the progressive development of growth forms set the basic pattern for all the varied mechanisms and structures of further evolution. The development of mutual forms of growth in simple biological organisms shows the root continuum of growth forms as they exist in this single level of development. A *discontinuum* of growth, however, seems to be manifested as this continuum is *re-expressed on another and*

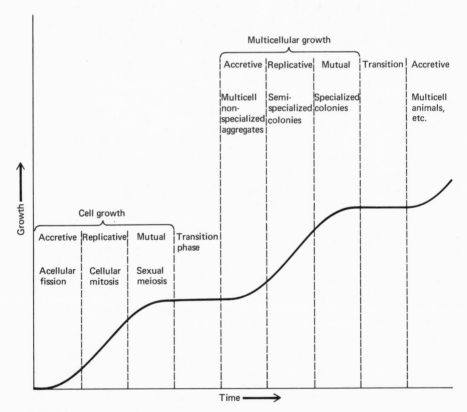

FIGURE 6
The accretive-replicative-mutual continuum is replicated at a much higher level each time a full continuum has been expressed. This produces a discontinuum of form with a continuity of processes of growth.

entirely different level of size, organization, and behavior. Crystal growth in heteropolymeric molecules represents the highest level of mutuality expressed in inorganic terms. At this point the leap was made to the higher information and energy level of simple cell growth. From accretive cell dynamics, these organisms evolved complex replicative fission and then mutual fusion. This new pattern of mutual growth brought life to another leap—to that of multicellular organisms. Thus the development of new levels of growth represents a progressive series of unique leaps, each providing a major advantage in the transformation of our world of relatively inert materials into interrelated living organisms and organized information.

Over eons of evolutionary time organisms became more and more dependent on the harmony of relationships with other organisms in the environment, particularly when multicellular organisms and multiorganismic societies began to emerge. The mutualism evident in gene recombination and the benefits of mutual support between cells began to appear in larger groups that served each other, whether in a multicellular colony, such as a sponge, or in a "multicellular" school of fish. As life reinforced life, cooperation and automatic mutualism generated greater positive feedback and still more successful procreation.[12] An enormous mass of data today records the unfailing tendency of living organisms to thrive in close reciprocal and mutually facilitative partnerships, even among the so-called solitary types. There cannot be found a single triumphant solitary creature.[13] Nature is hardly the "red tooth and claw" of earlier views of evolution. *The tendency to mutualism and cooperation is one of the most ancient and certainly the most vital of Nature's processes.* *

ANIMAL GROWTH FORMS

Looking at larger biological systems, we can easily see how the growth dynamics of unicellular systems are re-expressed by

---

*In unicellular organisms that do not band together, such mutuality and exchange of information for growth have also been observed as, for example, when a non-viable micro-organism that cannot synthesize a single basic amino acid is put in a medium with a different one that lacks the ability to make some other of the basic amino acids; soon, each organism will aid the other so that together they will be able to synthesize the complete range of aminos and both will become viable.

animals. Accretive, replicative, and mutual growth forms are represented as a transformed homologue defined in biology as parasitism, commensalism, and mutualism.[14]

ACCRETIVE GROWTH

Accretive growth occurs in the multicellular organism by simple enlargement of the total animal and between animals in those parasites that, through nonreciprocal self-growth, destroy their host. As with cell accretion, this purely accretive pattern in relationships has been largely supplemented as a form of growth by the emergence of higher forms of interrelationships.

REPLICATIVE GROWTH

Replicative growth patterns, in which either the organism grows larger by absorbing others or by being related to other organisms, are copied by symbionts in a variety of ways. The most obvious is through societies or groups of replicas which reinforce each other's growth, and the interspecies relationships of parasitism in which an organism grows through a nonlethal attachment to its host. This also happens in the *reverse* process, "commensalism." Commensalism is the name given the process whereby one organism becomes related to a larger organism, mimicking the host form in some way and deriving nutrition from their association. In effect, replicative parasites turn their host (environment) into themselves, enlarging at the cost of the environment but not totally destroying it. Commensuals attach themselves to a more effective host and almost become a part of the host, growing through it and identifying with it. (See Figure 7.)

MUTUAL GROWTH

Mutual growth forms occur in symbiotic mutualistic relationships where each organism contributes directly, and often equally, to the growth of the other. The processes of mutualistic symbiosis can be exemplified in an extremely broad range of relationships, from lichens, a cooperative combination of algae and fungi, to more complex relationships, such as that between flowering plants and their insect and animal partners. The universal trend toward mutual, interdependent relationships shows that the organisms involved are always more successful if they retain the flexibility to evolve increasingly mutual relationships.

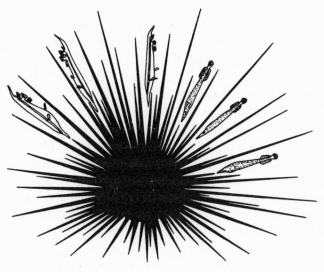

FIGURE 7
Replicative "othering" occurring in a biological commensual symbiotic relationship. Clingfishes and shrimpfishes "copy" or "mimic" the sea urchin, and both grow through the remnants of nutrition captured by the sea urchin and live in its protection. They become "a part of" and identify with the larger, more effective organism and grow through it, just as an individual who practices replication othering will grow by joining a larger human group and identifying with it (cultism). (After Cheng et al.)

A classic example is the case of the mutualism between the Yucca moth and the Yucca plant: The plant furnishes a home for the moth eggs to develop, and the eggs hatch at just the right time in plant pollen development to make the new moth the agent of Yucca plant cross-fertilization.

In both simple and complex animal behavior and relationships, we can observe ubiquitous trends toward mutuality. The hermaphrodite earthworm, which can easily practice selfing, will most often seek out a partner for fertilization. Self-pollinating is often possible in plants as well, but a variety of methods has been designed by Nature to assure cross-pollination. In larger animal societies, even the so-called predators practice a form of facilitative mutualism with their prey. In a recent experiment all wolves were removed from an island to encourage the spread of the moose population. At first, the population did enlarge, but within several years it was almost wiped out by the spread of disease. Wolves were placed on the island when it became clear that they actually served the moose population by removing its weaker, more susceptible members and thereby eliminating the probable carriers of disease. Even plants are not immune to the disturbance of these mutual balances of nature. Parks, for example, have been so overprotected that trees that would otherwise have been destroyed by fire, have been allowed to grow old and become more vulnerable to disease. This alteration of mutual balance has resulted in increasing the probabilities for catastrophic insect blights and enormous unnatural fires.

In all these examples of accretive, replicative, and mutualistic growth, we can observe the constant and unyielding "pressure to mutualism" in natural selection. Within a multicellular organism, constant cellular mutualism is imperative—otherwise the organism could not function as a whole. Early forms of cell complexes dramatically demonstrate how this happens. In the volvox algae, for example, a single organism can get along in life by itself. Yet it tends to gravitate to other volvox and form a "multicellular" community. Unlike the colony of blue-green algae or a bacterial colony, once together each volvox specializes to some degree in order to serve the total organism. In this case, as in all other mutualistic enterprises, the single organism relinquishes some of its broad capabilities in order to make a larger contribution through specializing and amplifying specific potentials to serve as a part of the whole. The cell makes fewer replica "children" but continues its growth through making special products that serve the total group. Also in building a mutual multicellular organism more capabilities come into being. An example of this is the amoeba *Dictyostelium* which alone has no ability to orient itself toward light and heat but when joined with a number of others of the same type develops this skill. This enhanced migration ability is very important for broadening the growth of this soil amoeba to transform wider ecological niches.

This "call to mutualism," from the single-celled organism to the complex relationships of large "multicell" societies, has resulted in virtual domination of mutual growth at every level of life throughout our planetary ecosphere. As time goes by, more and more higher-level varieties of mutual growth-facilitating behavior naturally emerge, not only in the biosphere, but also in our interconnecting social and technical organism—a new and emerging "organism."

EVOLUTION FROM ANIMAL TO HUMAN GROWTH FORMS

Through an ability to form new responses and to learn more complex behavior from experience and example, animals began to add through cognition *new kinds of information* to their internal systems. Thus they increased again their survival and reproductive growth potentials.[15] However, because learned information and behavior did not change genetic information, they could not be passed on from generation to generation. Each infant animal was, in effect, "disinherited" from its parents' learning; over and over again, the same information had to be re-experienced or imitated for each generation to acquire it. Small brain size also limited information storage capacity.[16] Under these circumstances, new information could not accumulate in large amounts; each new generation was largely on its own, adding information very gradually as its society grew.

With the appearance of land-based, warm-blooded mammals and an enlarged brain, learning and adding data to the expanded information system became much easier. In an air environment movement became less arduous than in water, and oxygen was easier to get. More energy became available for new growth. Moreover, the mutualism of better organized social units made learning by imitation more achievable. Internal temperature control made mammals more prolific and flexible reproducers than their cold-blooded reptilian neighbors. Much more importantly, they were better able to transform the environment, because through a remarkable new development—memory—they could pass learned information more efficiently from generation to generation. The innovation of memory, a unique information storage and retrieval device, heralded the appearance of yet another transformation and discontinuous leap in growth processes.

Although the more generalized instrument of the cortex was to give mammals more control over their specialized skills (amplified by the neocortex of primates), mammalian neurons had a unique "disadvantage" which was in time to become the mammal's greatest evolutionary advantage. Unlike its predecessors, as in a reptile, for example,[17] this specialized neuron could not reproduce itself if brain damage occurred. In a remarkable fashion this basic physiological modification produced an outstanding psychological advantage: information learned and stored in the brain was not lost because microscopic memory cells could be constantly replaced and regenerated. Information could now be stored, retrieved, and used *during the total life of the organism.* This new creature could begin to *collect* and to *store* its psychological nutrition, information, in the same manner that it had learned to collect and to store its biological food.

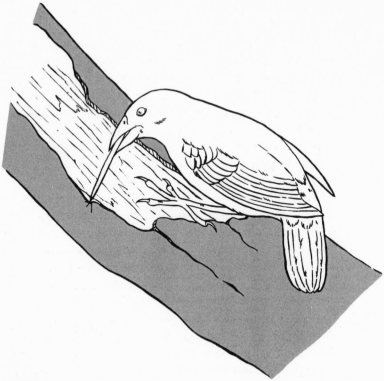

FIGURE 8
The woodpecker finch, <u>Camarhynchus pallidus</u>, uses a cactus spine to pry insects from cracks in trees.

With the advantage of large-scale, long-term memory, the early humanoid began to learn how to extend his capacities beyond his inherited equipment. He could imitate the special advantages of other natural organisms and extend himself in new ways. He created Stone Age "technologies." The pitcher plant became an idea for a trap, the spider-web was useful as a design for both traps and huts, birds' nests were translated into baskets, and poisons were adopted from snakes and dams from beavers. Primitive Man also borrowed skins, teeth, tusks, and horns from other animals to directly extend his own biological equipment.

We can also comfortably speculate that he observed the use of many "tools" by animals and imitated such ideas as a bird's use of spines to dig out grubs, an ape's use of leaf containers for water, and other primates' use of sticks and stones for fighting. This is a reasonable hypothesis, particularly since all the early "inventions" of men were *already in use by animals.* Mimicry of nature allowed emerging mankind to become what has been called

32

"tool-users." As important as this event was in human history, copying the animal's use of physical tools was not what separated Man in a major way from the animal kingdom; it was the new tool that made the difference—the *mental* tool.

Once Man learned that a stone gave his hand new strength, he became a more accomplished hunter, a highly necessary skill because he could then become more omnivorous.* By adding greatly to his carnivorous capacities, he capitalized on concentrated "premanufactured" foods that required less time and energy to satisfy his nutritional needs. Energy once devoted to gathering and eating primitive vegetables could be used to explore more of his environment. His arm-and-stone led the way to the first crude *copy of his own system.* The pebble tool gave way to the hand axe! The discovery by Man that he could actually copy and *amplify* his own sophisticated biological system set the stage for the so-called "technology" that would one day seem to threaten the world he had revolutionized, as we shall see when we consider the evolution of "things."

With increasing energy, socialization, and the evolution of an enlarged neocortex, over an expanse of perhaps three million years, Man developed the power of extended symbolic speech. Once again, because no records provide a history of this great advancement, we must observe the invention of symbolic language in existing situations. Many investigations[19] have now demonstrated conclusively that development of symbolic representation functions occurs quite naturally.** The new evidence available on the communication systems of other animals and on the spontaneous formation of symbolism and language, plus the common form of language basic to all humans, demonstrates that this novel invention, like tool-using, did not represent a break in the pattern of evolution.[20] It is by nature yet another example of the results of the *evolution of information-coding systems.* In fear, for example, adrenalin surging into an animal's system causes bodily reaction and signals that, in turn, cause an observer animal also to translate this external "signal" into outputs of adrenalin in his

---

*Jane Goodall's observations have shown that contrary to popular opinion primates were hunters and meat eaters, however only with small or crippled prey.[18]

**Even in the absence of either a spoken or visual language, deaf-mutes and blind children develop such automatic structures.

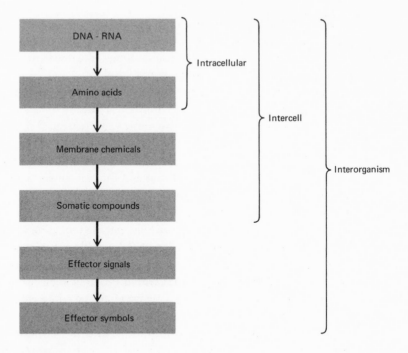

FIGURE 9
Information language translations. Written symbols are to humans what chemicals are to cells. Ultimately, the written symbols are translated back into chemical language for the body to understand them.

own system. Now, with more extensive and powerful vocal signs, a "word" could serve the same purpose. (See Figure 9.)

If we pause to review the history of organic evolution on this planet, we can see that Man's ancient prejudices still paradoxically deny him the perspective to see immediately that emergence of symbolic language codes was a no more "unique" event than, say, cells using nucleotide code information to make protein messages or even of the emergence of sexual information translations in an asexual world! Like those earlier leaps, this new type of coded language was again to transform life and even more of our planet. *It was yet another natural discontinuity in the continuum of growth and transformation.*

SECOND NATURE
THREE

THE GENETIC SHIFT

The emergence of the coding of symbolic language became the primary departure point in separating Man from his less articulate coprimates. It became the dividing line which separated the continuum of physical growth from the new, higher-level continuum of *psychological* growth. Only a symbolic language could make possible the *accumulation of sufficient new information* in the system to cause great changes in basic behavioral patterns.[1] With this capability, whole new forms of "learning" became possible. The enormous "magic" usefulness of such symbols and words to early man was so powerful that protection and preservation of collected information automatically took on the form of such techniques as totem, taboo, and secret ritual to insure that a group always did the same thing in the same way.[2] These ceremonial methods repeated, protected, and shared acquired information and aided memorization as well. With "religious" ritualistic techniques, learned information was recorded in the brains of the tribe and could be re-recorded and thus *passed on,* inherited, from generation to generation, becoming the tribal genetic system.

Even with the advent of socially protected, mentally recalled information, addition to the pool of accreted community data was, at best, slow and uncertain. Rapid fading of vocal signals and overcrowded conscious memories resulted in lost data. In order to protect vital information, cultural and community control of information became critical. Over a long period, the gradual building-up and preservation of tradition became more important than innovation. The risk of forgetting or losing important information about such things as hunting and trapping methods, social rules, or reproduction was too large a gamble to take to experiment with large amounts of new information.

Because "like-mindedness" was strictly maintained within tightly held social communities and identities, the limited way of preserving data through social units automatically produced inter-tribal insularity. "Sacredness" of information became an indispensable aid to holding on to what little information could be accumulated in the emerging social consciousness. Over several million years, primitive human societies naturally took on the pattern of identical duplications of socialized data, maintaining an *accretive* form of social and informational growth.

ECTOGENETICS

Between 50 and 100 thousand years ago an extraordinary new information-preservation method began to shape the creature we now consider human. *Homo sapiens,* the "wise man" of the secret rituals and formulas, gave way as *externally recorded symbolism* replaced the inefficient information-handling heritage of tribal elders. Although many scholars still speculate that primitive cave paintings and the earlier markings on bones and pebbles represented "religious" and "mystical" symbolism or "decorative" art, we now know that what was actually preserved in these works was *that data most critical to life in those times.*

Ancient notation and cave paintings are almost totally dominated by the textbook-like information and record-keeping of complex seasonal changes, flora, animal anatomy, cooperation in the capture and killing of game, the design of traps, fishing, the propagation of animals, and the processes of reproduction in humans.[3] Vital technologies were stored in the externalized memory of paint and stone and were improved and added to without the risk of losing a vital piece of data.

The information-preserving capability of early notations and cave paintings ignited a slow fuse that was to burn for some 30 thousand years, gradually evolving from naturalistic paintings to stylized art and finally to coded symbols. It ultimately reached the primer of the explosive Sumerian, Babylonian, and Egyptian civilizations. These cultures would develop the ability to make permanent marks that symbolized extremely complex information in brief coded notations. The progression of information coding, from the thing itself to a realistic representation, to a stylized symbol, and then to a brief code, is much like the way we have developed increasingly simple codes in computer memories and the like; the result is to enable storage of much greater qualities of data in the same space, whether it is a brain or a filing cabinet. This new information-storage process, which could be reproduced and which *reproduced itself and what it symbolized* in the mind of an observer, led in an incredibly short time in evolutionary terms, to magnified use of the superlarge cerebrum of Man, and to the vast technological society we know today.

Recorded information became the *new genetic construction* that would enable Man to make the vast leaps that characterize our species. Information once stored exclusively in the "endogenetic" biochemical memory system, transferred to new generations by parental germ cells and supplemented by cultural rote learning, could now be carried by and through external genetics, that is, the

FIGURE 10

Genetic Inheritance

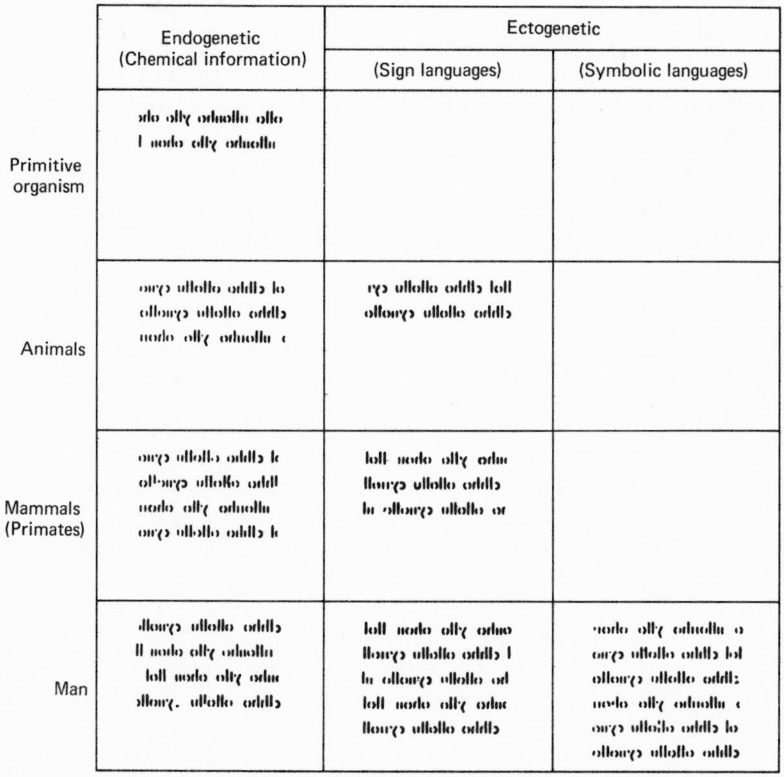

	Endogenetic (Chemical information)	Ectogenetic	
		(Sign languages)	(Symbolic languages)
Primitive organism	ᴐdo ollᶓ od␣oll␣ ollo l ␣odo ollᶓ od␣oll␣		
Animals	o␣rᶓᴐ ullollo oddlᴐ lo ollonᶓᴐ ullollo odidlᴐ ␣odo ollᶓ od␣oll␣ ␣	rᶓᴐ ullollo odidlᴐ loll ollonᶓᴐ ullollo odidlᴐ	
Mammals (Primates)	o␣rᶓᴐ ullollᴐ odidlᴐ k olᵇo␣rᶓᴐ ullollo odidl ␣odo ollᶓ od␣oll␣ o␣rᶓᴐ ullollo odidlᴐ k	loll ␣odo ollᶓ od␣ llonᶓᴐ ullollo odidlᴐ l␣ ollonᶓᴐ ullollo o␣	
Man	␣llonᶓᴐ ullollo odidlᴐ ll ␣odo ollᶓ od␣oll␣ loll ␣odo ollᶓ od␣ ␣llonᶓ. ullollo odidlᴐ	loll ␣odo ollᶓ od␣o llonᶓᴐ ullollo odidlᴐ l l␣ ollonᶓᴐ ullollo od loll ␣odo ollᶓ od␣ llonᶓᴐ ullollo odidlᴐ	␣odo ollᶓ od␣oll␣ o o␣rᶓᴐ ullollo odidlᴐ lol ollonᶓᴐ ullollo odidl: ␣odo ollᶓ od␣oll␣ ␣ o␣rᶓᴐ ullollo odidlᴐ lo ollonᶓᴐ ullollo odidlᴐ

"ectogenetic" system of writing. Memories could be added to and protected in stone, scrolls, and the like and transferred by learning when and if the information were needed. Moreover, the biological role of mutation and recombination that had produced outstanding individuals and tribes could now be broadened to include all who read.

An important result of this ectobiologic revolution was a sudden lengthening of the helplessness and uselessness of infancy and adolescence that was to grow in direct proportion to the increasing ectogenetic load. *To achieve the state of "humanness" it became necessary for man to absorb this ectogenetic heritage.* Because he did not rely on the biologic endogenetics that equipped animals at birth with most of the information necessary to perform their species functions, man became almost totally dependent upon the information supplied by society and culture.

Ectogenetics, the new extension and language of genetics, was a change that made transmission of acquired information yet another profound transformation in information "language" in the history of life, comparable to the enormous shifts of chemical language to DNA nucleotides to amino acid proteins. After this step, biologically programmed, instinctive endogenetic information could be enormously supplemented and shared with ectogenetic culture through *inherited* cultural information.*[4]

An individual born into an information-rich culture became a more successful environmental transformer than his evolutionary ancestors. He could invade broad new ecological niches with the help of the special products he produced. Biologically, Man's survival probability was enhanced by such things as the chemical

---

*This shift in genetic techniques, as a method of passing information on from generation to generation, could begin to pry open some of the secrets of the first life forms. Although inorganic crystals still exist, we have not known if the appearance of organic molecules and their successors did indeed represent a gradual shift from the limited nucleation of crystals to the self-reproducing nucleus of reproduction. Just as the genetic system was reconstructed in Man so that vastly more information could be built up and passed on, the evolution of living cells was also a dramatic change resulting in their ability to pass on accumulated information to successors. Today, in isolated pockets of the world, we can still find humans who are living homologue of the crystal—primitive, nomadic tribes who have no method to pass on ectogenetic information and are almost wholly dependent on an agreeable environment to permit their continued growth. These cultures might yet instruct us about our precursory life forms and how they came to be.

information in medicines, vaccines, and prosthetic devices. The advent of externalized genetics meant that Man, as a species, could grow in totally new ways.

Whereas verbal and pictorial symbolism in earlier times had allowed new environmental transformations (when man needed a warmer skin, for example, he could simply put on the skin of a better equipped animal and use it as he needed it), with the new system Nature no longer had to wait for slow, wasteful, and irregularly successful biological gene recombinations. The ecto-genetic process amounted to *creation of immediate and reversible biopsychologic mutations: in sum, directed and directable evolution.*

The ability to store and to retrieve information on a broad basis, and to build new combinations from generation to generation, made Man the most important natural agent in the formation of new and improved species to transform the environment. Man's records and informative pass-along systems became the new "ectogenetic nucleotide"—a virtually limitless information and growth system in which the inherited "genetic pool" became ever broader. Just as gene recombination was able to produce a broader spread of mutations, writing was to make new mutations of information available to vastly more organisms. (See Figure 11.)

In the phenomenon of writing we see yet another expression of the evolution of a living organism's capability to transform its environment. With the advent of each new level of information growth, from heteropolymeric molecules to gene recombinations, to hormonal and chemical languages, and finally, with Man, to what we term "symbolic language," each progressive leap of adding and using information made the resulting organism more "viable" and "successful"; that is, in each case, the next informa-tion-gathering process became easier. With the process of natural selection, those organisms less capable of growing and reproduc-ing were not just extinguished, they were continually supplanted by organisms that were more efficient transformers—convertors of nonliving materials and relatively unorganized information, either directly into their own organized living substance, or into special products to serve the living organisms and organizations.

Before the advent of this new kind of genetic system, purely biological information inheritance methods left legatees with nothing more than their fixed nucleotide code heritage. If new or changed endogenetic information was not viable, it died with the individual, perhaps to be lost forever. The continuing process of evolution in purely biologic processes did, however, bring about

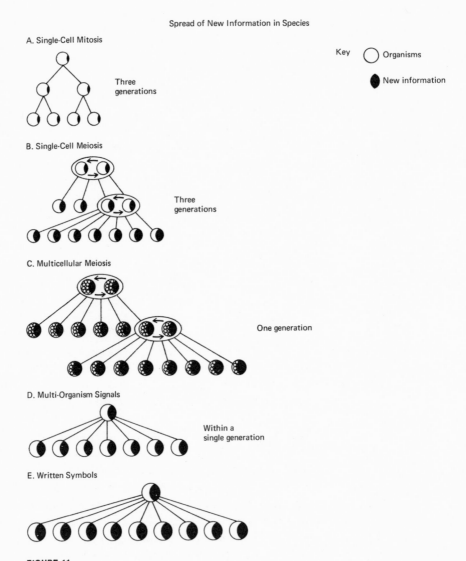

Spread of New Information in Species

A. Single-Cell Mitosis

Three generations

Key ◯ Organisms

⬤ New information

B. Single-Cell Meiosis

Three generations

C. Multicellular Meiosis

One generation

D. Multi-Organism Signals

Within a single generation

E. Written Symbols

FIGURE 11
Graphic representation of relative ratios of time necessary for new information to reach members of a species.

various forms of balancing selection and inventions of even more sensitive endogenetic systems, capable of reacting to environmental changes, without waiting for new mutations to appear.[5] Likewise, the new genetic code, the DNA, of symbolic language enormously extended these mutational advantages; rearrangement, substitution, addition, deletion, and storage of information instantly and "on order" became possible. In this way, mutations that were not favorable were eliminated without great waste and added information made the species more "fit and successfully reproductive." Also, if a new information hybrid did not work, it could be left in storage rather than the grave. It could easily be resurrected "when its time had come" and fit into the system.*

This change automatically decreased infant mortality rates and superabundant wastage of progeny no longer had to occur to ensure the success of life's mainstream of reproduction. "Technological" achievements and idea enrichments inevitably led to such biological effects as acquiring new capabilities and strengths, preventing disease, curing birth defects, and replacing organs and lengthening life, all "technobiologic" effects of externalizing other biologic functions through the use of Man's collective mind.

We can be sure that each substantial change in form and process of genetic systems was, as Dobzhansky put it, ". . . hardly a matter of the superposition of a few lucky mutations; major evolutionary advantages probably always involve reconstructions of the genetic system."[6] The polymorphism that is Man, with its uniquely reconstructed genetic system, goes far beyond the slow process of outbreeding to acquire and pass on valuable new informational "genes." A new idea can be transmitted to any number of living individuals and can be passed on to future generations regardless of their parentage.

PSYCHOSPECIATION

Through the unique new genetic language of multi-organismic symbols and signs, Man was to develop a new form of speciation. Although the definition of what constitutes a "species" even in a strict biological sense has yet to be agreed upon, it is apparent that substantial differences in morphology prevent cross-breeding. In the case of Man's ectogenetic system, the biological process of speciation became psychospecific. Biological momentum, on the other hand, has so canalized Man that despite an almost incalculable number of human blood groupings and crosses, a vast collection of data reveals only a minuscule amount of mortality and fecundity.** Thus, although Man is not biologically separable into species, the fact is that he has become "psychospeciated."

Man sorts out his various species by ectogenetic differences:

---

*Many of us experience this event in the sciences: Mendel's long unrecognized but finally rescued work is a pertinent example.

**Rh incompatibility is perhaps the only irrefutable case.

acquired information, culture, habits, prejudices, attitudes, and knowledge.* If the subcultures of groups are sufficiently different, they can rightfully be classified as distinct species, at least until differences in information can be shared. What we have developed is intra- rather than interspecies differentiation. In biology, we see the testimony of numberless extinct species, a fact that in psycho-speciation is eloquently stated in the equally numerous extinctions of cultures, traditions, and ideas. As we shall see in pursuing our inquiry, the vitality created by "crossing over" in biological hybridization is exactly parallel in the results of psychological hybrids, and the same laws of biological reproductive isolation apply when attempting to make psychological combinations.

SOCIAL GROWTH FORMS

ACCRETIVE GROWTH

As we review the evolution of Social Man, we can see the occurrence of group behavioral modes that follow the same pattern as those we have observed in biological evolution of unicellular and multicellular organisms.[7] The earliest human cultures were fundamentally *accretive,* inasmuch as information and cultures were rigidly controlled and passed to each new generation almost unchanged. Although we can only speculate on the time-frame of those early verbal cultures, the present-day remnants of Stone Age civilization in the South Pacific and in Africa follow this accretive, growth-by-strict-copying pattern. Younger generations are taught to be exact duplicates of older generations, for example, in their dress, speech, and habits.

If possible, *basic* changes in tradition, either generated inside the tribe or from outside, are carefully excluded by the community at large or by those in power. This closed, socially accretive growth system guards old patterns and allows new information to enter the system only very slowly. Even when other tribes with greatly different cultures are conquered, their ideas are not

---

*The sciences in particular clearly demonstrate the process of emphasis upon and elaboration of certain specific features of language and de-emphasis and elimination of others. A scientific language will then evolve into a special jargon which can perform some function better than the mother tongue.

rapidly or broadly assimilated. Accompanying phenomena such as emphasis on breeding for tribal growth and territorial possession are yet other examples of fundamentally accretive growth processes. If these patterns persist over long periods in isolated groups, upon exposure to evolved cultures they have to be maintained by perpetuating their isolation or they become extinct and are replaced by other forms.[8] The great accretive cultures of Man first flourished through the seminal influence of writing about 6000 B.C. as rulers extended themselves, their ideas, their laws and boundaries until the period of 500 B.C. to 1000 A.D. As the civilizations of China, Egypt, and Rome grew beyond their capability to maintain the rigid information controls necessary to preserve accretion, the growing pressures of their heretofore successful growth created the necessity for replicative growth to emerge.

REPLICATIVE GROWTH

When written symbols supplemented the organic information storage and retrieval system, the ability to share and exchange more information, at least between persons or groups of equal status, became more possible. The shift to *replicative* societies began with a gradual dissemination of information during this period, but even so, exchanges of data between social classes took the form of unequal exchanges. The need to replicate the growing "group self" manifested itself in repressive and disciplined education that forced each new generation into archaic conformity and standards. As a group expressing growth, missionary activity, imperial conquest, nationalism, and a host of other techniques were exported so that "others become like us." Wars were fought not to decimate and to seize, but to replicate through colonization of others, in which their thinking and behavior were forced to adhere to the "right" standards. As Christopher Columbus communicated to the Spanish rulers about the peaceful Indians of San Salvador, ". . . there is not in the world a better nation. They love their neighbors as themselves . . ." Yet, he admonished that they should be made to ". . . do all is necessary and adopt our ways." Ideological influence and "psychological imperialism"[9] gradually began to replace the accretive needs for absolute power and territorial ownership.

To guard against invasion of foreign ideas, rigid cultural ideas and institutions were established to assure agreement that old ways continued and were not corrupted by new ideas. A "cultural immune system" was constructed on a massive scale by the mass psychological/sociological organisms. Thus, cultural information standards and norms autonomically become the agent of the natural selection process for ideas and information in human societies.[10]

MUTUAL GROWTH

Mutual exchange pressure persisted, however, and with the advent of large-scale printing and other broad information-sharing and education technology, the pressure to mutuality naturally began to overcome replicative defenses. It was, however, not until the Industrial Revolution that western culture created the new idea of "childhood" and the necessity for broad education was implemented. A gradual shift to mutuality began, exemplified by the early phenomena of anticolonialism and wars of independence.

In quite recent times, principally since World War II, with the advent of more widespread mobility and information-sharing situations, needs for conformity to old patterns were greatly weakened. A new age of social *mutualism* started to gain momentum. The very earliest precursors of this process, however, can be found in the forced recombination of ideas resulting from hybrid colonialism. Examples can be easily seen in the Greek and English islands, the Italian peninsula, and later the conglomerate peopling of the New World. Recombination of ideas in these special environments presented a great opportunity for many cultures to be intermingled and naturally produced ectogenetic, hybrid vigor. Yet, as these cultures enlarged beyond existing information transmission systems, they consolidated and became homogeneous in their own cultural patterns and the initial vigor decreased.

Improved transportation methods in the eighteenth and nineteenth centuries not only brought about new capabilities for colonial conquest, but provided many cultural exchanges and invigoration between alliances, and even more so in conquered cultures. In more recent history, cultural hybridization has been literally forced on the conquered. The result, we have all seen, has been a greater "crossing-over" of cultural ectogenetic pools, in the *conquered* rather than in the conqueror, and extraordinary spurts of vitality.

Over the past three decades, new means of subculturing and

cross-culturing have become widely available. Worldwide travel and more sophisticated communications media have provided a broad new base of common information and created much higher probabilities of combining new and different information, ideas, and cultures. (See Figure 12.) Having progressed in the replicative stage from copying elders and idea exchange between peer groups, we are now experiencing a new mutuality of exchange across many boundaries. Elders, for example, are learning from their offspring who, themselves, are creating their own world, their own morals and music, their own styles and literature.

INDIVIDUAL GROWTH FORMS

In observing the phenomenon of repetition of growth forms, we can follow the accretive–replicative–mutual growth that develops in all processes of organic evolution. In the life of a single individual, the process is replicated in miniature. Just as the fetus demonstrates the organic precursors of our morphological evolutionary heritage, the developing psychological system of the individual manifests each step in the continuum of growth forms.

The early years of an infant's life are devoted almost exclusively to the process of self-discovery and self-seeking growth. *Accretion* through self-growth is observable in the self-interested domination of parents by infants, as they attempt to control, to own, and literally to engorge everything. They are not concerned with or able to empathize with others. Play becomes self-extension through "power games" and the like. This is followed by a *replicative* or imitative phase in which they copy others and are usually obliged to become a "good model" of their elders. In this ectogenetic learning stage, they "become human" as they absorb the conserved information and culture of past generations.

As soon as sufficient information is a part of an individual and relationships with a broader culture are established, the playful imagination of the child can give way to realistic and *mutual* exchanges with others to create new ideas and information to increase his capabilities, not for himself alone, but for the group. In this way, an individual matures, mutualizes with, and contributes to the growth of a larger social organism. How the environment encourages or suppresses this progression of growth is the vital question we shall explore later.

Spread of New Information in Species

A. Single-Cell Mitosis

Three
generations

Key 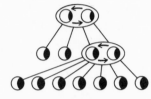 Organisms

New information

B. Single-Cell Meiosis

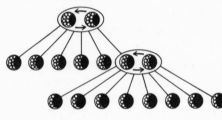

Three
generations

C. Multicellular Meiosis

One generation

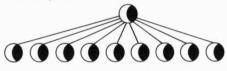

D. Multi-Organism Signals

Within a
single generation

E. Written Symbols

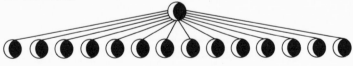

F. Printed Language

G. Television

FIGURE 12
Graphic representation of relative ratios of time necessary for new information to reach members of a species, from unicellular mutations that affect only their own offspring to television, in which information can reach many members of a population almost instantaneously.

COMMUNITY GROWTH

A community of humans develops in exactly the same way a cell community grows and, if we look closely, evolves exactly the same *functions:* manufacturing, circulation, communication, protection, control, and so forth. In an historical sense, as well, we can observe the natural developing mutualism of all organized groups of people. A village, for example, begins as people *accrete* and band together in small groups to form a larger, more defensible, and viable organism. Common pursuit initially unites them—farming, mining, milling. Offspring learn their parents' trades and *replicate* the original (and successful) organism. When they overproduce their own capacity to use the products that they make, new pressures emerge to develop deeper relations with other communities. *Mutualism* is generated through development of specialization, trade, and exchanges of information with others.

As a village grows to become a city, it evolves an intricate network of facilitative mutuality as more special functions and occupations emerge to serve the growing multicellular and multi-organismic society. Such things as "autoimmune" systems evolve to protect the community from general disorders, for example, fire and police protection. As in a biological body, when specific disorders are detected, these immune systems become more complex and specific, for example, narcotics police and sky marshals. The city "nucleus" contains and disseminates the metropolitan ectogenetic codes and patterns, building codes, laws, education norms, and so forth. All these systems maintain and preserve the growth patterns of the city organism as does all genetic information.

As with biological growth, recapitulation of forms of growth occurs with changes in scale and complexity. *The highest form of mutualism begins to transform into a new form of accretive.* When such pure growth in simple enlargement of city organisms occurs, it sets up demands and pressures on the system that start to limit the emerging accretive growth. This limitation tends to stimulate, at first, simple suburban copies of the parent. In many cases, unfortunately, the shift to replicative growth has been hampered as traditional accretive cities attempted to maintain growth by self-enlargement rather than by replication, using their suburbs as

47

self-serving attachments—bedrooms for commuters, for in-stance—rather than as autonomous organisms.

Such attempts at continuous accretive enlargement always fail. No organism's communication and metabolic processes can re-spond to such disproportionate pressures, and the organism's functions ultimately begin to disintegrate (usually beginning with communication and transport). Ignorance of biologic growth principles in metropolitan planning results in a general break-down of these massive, outdated social organisms. A gradual trend toward decentralization of controlling power nuclei, redis-tribution of businesses, and development of more integrated and interdependent communities has naturally evolved toward more organic units, but not without the costs of selection when less fit alternatives have been attempted.

The pathology of extending accretive growth is easily detected in many closed or self-isolated systems; the monolithic organiza-tions of today—public utilities, churches, and multiversities—serve as excellent examples as they also find that bigger is not better. Imposition of increasingly stringent controls, rules, and standards to protect and to maintain accretive growth does not work. In fact, it does just the opposite, for closing a system to new alternatives inevitably results in either radical changes or collapse and extinction.

The effects of these institutional pathologies have naturally forced a major shift in the more responsive industrial manage-ment environments in the past decade. "Participative" tech-niques, mutually involving employees and management, churches and members, students and faculty, and so forth, have had to progress beyond traditional authoritarian, accretive growth. The constant "reorganizations" taking place in many large accretive institutions readily demonstrate these adjustments to the pressure toward mutuality. Responsive organizations that are an integral part of the larger system will naturally mature into more mutualis-tic forms simply as a function of natural selection.

Isolated organisms because of accumulated resources or reg-ulations that do not respond to growth and change pressures often face revolution rather than evolution. Those that do not evolve will be found less fit in the larger response-able environ-ment and will suffer abrupt change. This fact has been abundantly demonstrated in the past several decades by those numberless extinct and virtually extinct companies, churches, universities, and the like that did not shift to a mutualistic "marketing" relationship, one that could consult with and supply their customers' changing needs. Accountability to the real world of transformative evolution is the mandate of Nature and of Man.

ISOLATION AND HYBRIDIZATION

Because the ectogenetic heritage within our many cultures is so varied, it offers both a great problem and a great opportunity. We continually face the crucial problem of *cultural hybridization,* a problem because, like DNA hybridization, new information can be assimilated only when it fits without difficulty into the pattern of existing and accepted ideas.[11]

We can easily see that much of the existing and accepted information in many cultures is quite different from that in other cultures. If we look deeper, however, we find that the bulk of all our intercultural data refers to a single subject—the human situation, one common to all men. In spite of that knowledge, however, we see that superficial differences continually keep men isolated from one another because of the abundant superstructure of cultural traditions and ideas. This phenomenon happens, as well, in biological systems. It is known as "reproductive isolation."

If we look at the biological homologue of reproductive isolation, it can give us insight as to how to create structures permitting more rapid and effective idea "crossings" between disparate cultures and groups of people.[12] Two forms of isolation *prevent* hybridization; the first is that which keeps species from ever meeting at all (referred to in biology as prezygotal), and, secondly, that which prevents viable exchanges once contact has been made (the postzygotal).

Prevention conditions include isolation that occurs for one of four reasons: (1) habitat—location differences that prevent contact; (2) ethological—the attraction between the species or cultures is weak or absent; (3) differences in pollinating techniques—the system or technique of exchanging information is too different; and (4) mechanical—the specific mechanics of individual to individual exchange do not match. These four problems prevent initial contact from occurring and preclude either biological or psychological hybridization.

Habitat isolation in social systems occurs both between cultures and *within* cultures, not only because of geographical boundaries, but also because of the more subtle barriers of status, socioeconomics, and the like. Ethological walls prevent attraction between groups because they lack information to make it appear that either group can offer anything of worth to the other. Instances of this are scientific and vocational specializations that keep groups in one field from attempting exchange of ideas with others in some other field, biologists and theologists, for example.

Distinctive "pollination" or communication systems perform the same sort of isolative function. With the immense proliferation of information, different people and groups tend to use different and specialized media for their information exchanges. Examples of this are such narrowly based media as clubs, journals, convocations, and the like. Mechanical isolation is primarily a more personal function, resulting from the attitude and expectation that even if an attempt were made to exchange ideas, there would be no possibility of understanding one another.

On the postzygotic side, once contact has been made, other influences come to bear in both biological and social systems. There are three primary, post-contact isolating mechanisms: (1) hybrid inviability—the resulting organism has either reduced viability in the system or is inviable; (2) hybrid sterility—the failure to produce a functional offspring; and (3) hybrid breakdown—although a functioning offspring may occur, in the long run it becomes inviable.

As we can see, these identical functions occur in human social and cultural encounters. Inviability can be produced merely as a result of language mixtures not allowing combinations of information to work. Sterility can occur for the same reason, for to accept the notion that it is possible to change your own cultural ideas might endanger your own viability within your own closed culture; that is, there are too many factors working against an idea for it to be viable.

Hybrid breakdown often results even when an idea combination has great initial viability. When an idea is reproduced in subsequent generations within a culture, a single detrimental property can be exaggerated. Because any of the other isolating mechanisms can then come into play to cause extinction, this can be lethal.

To bridge the gaps of isolation between opposing strands of DNA or groups of people, the identical principle applies: *how to produce a beginning of exchange with sufficient commonality of information so that new or different information can be absorbed on both sides.* One of the ways this can be accomplished with groups of people, for example, is by structuring information flow initially to concentrate on common and universal subjects, then gradually to introduce differences. In the developed western nations, for instance, the advent of television as a common medium has created broad opportunity for cross-cultural hybrids, as we can see demonstrated by the ideas and affiliation of young people today. Here visual information content is paramount and common; it is a universal language. The appeal of programs dealing with common, high-interest subjects has allowed for the viable introduction of a wide variety of new and different information.

If we look at very young children who in the past would have been victims of any number of the isolating mechanisms listed above and who today express and act on ideas that are foreign to their limited cultural situation, we can learn how this exchange process works. This fact suggests that the future development of our globe will depend quite heavily on the extension of existing broad-scale media and the creation of new media that will allow for a more ubiquitous, interesting, and common cross-cultural information-exchange process.

Although our concentration so far has been a review of human behavioral origins, except for examples we have not dealt with the character of the new genetic pool itself—ideas and the special products that serve the human organism. The transformation homology in organic, psychological, and social systems is accompanied by *identical* processes as they relate to the evolution of information and of the transformation of our material environment. In the following chapters we shall consider these broad aspects of the processes of growth and evolution.

EVOLUTION OF MAN AND ENVIRONMENT
FOUR

When we survey how information itself grows, we again see the process of transformative evolution and natural selection. The evolution of symbolism is a classic example of transformation from accretive to replicative to mutual growth. In each case of growth the ratios of new or different information change substantially. In accretive growth information is static, with little or no new data combination possible. In replicative growth, although the basic character of the initial information is present there is a greater opportunity to introduce new ideas. Mutual growth provides enormously increased "openings" for new or unique data to be combined. In Figure 13 we see how the mixtures or ratios of information change. Early cave paintings were very representative with little or any chance for the observer to add data. Later, these representations changed to "abstract" the essence of the information, leaving more open for the observer. Finally, with the advent of pure symbols, the observer was free to picture what he desired.*

---

*Symbolism itself plays the homologous role of growth. By combining symbols they provide different forms of growth. Language and symbolic logic provide the functions of growth. In mathematics, for example, accretive growth is represented by addition and subtraction, replicative forms are multiplication and division, and mutual growth occurs as relational operations—proportions, ratios, equations, and the like. In symbolic language we can observe the form of growth represented from such connections of likeness as "John is a Man" to the richness of mutualistic metaphor where joining seemingly disparate ideas communicates far more, as "John's tender strength."

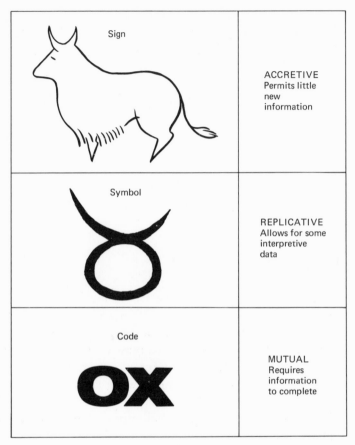

Sign	ACCRETIVE Permits little new information
Symbol	REPLICATIVE Allows for some interpretive data
Code	MUTUAL Requires information to complete

FIGURE 13

Also just as the four base-coding "letters" of DNA produce enormous variation with a very small stock of elements, ecto-genetic coding is accomplished by words and ideas represented by rearrangements of a very small stock of distinguishable sounds and markings. The growth of the body of this recording of information takes the ubiquitous form of all growth. Information and ideas, like organisms, perpetuate and breed; mutate, recombine, and fuse.

To survive, an idea must demonstrate "fitness," or else natural selection will extinguish it, at least until such time as it can be useful. Old and obsolescent information is continually replaced by the new "mutant alleles" and "gene recombinations" of more useful data. Knowledge is linked together into a self-reinforcing, positive-feedback cycle that is, like biological evolution, observably irreversible.

Additions of information or ideational recombinations of our small stock of sound and symbols to the system are not restricted to feasible or useful information, just as gene mutability in biology is not necessarily limited to only those additions that enhance the adaptability of their carriers. A gene cannot "know" when it is good until it has been tested within the system. Just so with information. As one educator admitted recently, "We know that half of what we are teaching is wrong, the only trouble is we don't know which half." Like genes, information surviving in practice in the system is automatically reproduced over and over and, as a consequence, becomes part of the preferred information in psychological systems.[1]

Usefulness for growth is, of course, the chief criterion of viability. Although repeated exposure of information is sufficient to establish a preference, the information must be satisfying and self-reinforcing—useful to the subject for growth—in order for substantial acceptance to take place.[2] Organisms and ideas survive and reproduce only when they serve either the biosystem or the psychosystem. As dinosaurs and dictators can testify, survival does not accrue necessarily to those that intrude most aggressively, but to those that demonstrably work so well that they are repeated and reproduced most often.*

Even so, we must recognize that evolution is an opportunist: It will do anything that "works." The fitness of a given idea at a particular time and place favoring growth will survive the gamut of natural selection, whether or not it is absolutely favorable in the long run. This is particularly true in less flexible organisms or societies such as those mentioned earlier. An idea, like a gene recombination, is less likely to produce new ectogenotypes, or evolve, in closed or static environments than it is in those that are open and in flux.[3] In rigid and isolated social situations, ideas become dogmatized and do not evolve; thus, such cultist phenomena ultimately are greatly changed, often extinguished, in a larger, more flexible environment.

THE PARADOX OF EVOLUTIONARY CHANGE

One essential question of biological evolution is the problem of *substitution of genetic information.* The realization that genetics is

---

*Another case is in the gossip and propaganda technique of "A lie repeated often enough becomes true," and the present-day necessity to dominate and control communications media in order to maintain dictatorships.

no longer confined solely to internal genes solves a paradox pointed out by Haldane as the "costs" of rapid evolution.[4] In biologic systems, the substitution of one variation of genetic information for another always results in genetic deaths; that is, the large majority of mutations are poorly fit progeny that do not survive. Thus, the cost of large and widespread mutations could either slow down the evolutionary process or, at the very least, reduce the vigor of the population (if the substitution involves many alleles at many gene loci, it may require too many generations to complete).

The ectogenetic load of a population operates in quite an improved fashion. As it increases, it does *not* create less fit humans or societies. It does quite the reverse. Rapid substitution of information in human ectogenetic systems provides massive and rapid substitution of increasingly more valid information, improving the optimal fitness of the total species. As a handy illustration of this, review any recent technical or scientific paper and observe how many citations are more than ten, or even five, years old. The tyranny of yesterday's facts does not linger in the social organism of Mankind.

The other premium of ectogenetics, pointed out previously, is that although we may obsolete information we do not destroy it. We do it in such a way that, if necessary, retrieval and use at a later date are still possible. The unique ability to return to and reintegrate old ectogenetic data makes human organisms optimally fit in an extremely broad range of environments.* If the existing examples of some technology were destroyed, for example, even if men had consciously forgotten the data, written documents could be used to reconstruct the technology. Like a cell in a biological multicellular organism, the total information stored in the DNA "library" is not used by all the cells in the organism. But it is available and can be activated, as experiments with cell trans-determination have shown.[5] Man is an efficient transdeterminant organism in that he can use the massive and growing gene pool of his entire species to enhance his fitness in almost any environmental niche—from the vacuum of space to the ocean deeps.

Man is different from all other biological organisms because of

---

*It is possible, however, that the massive overabundance of nuclear DNA in cells may represent such stored data, to be used if the organism encounters regressive environments.

this evolved capacity to integrate and reintegrate massive amounts of new information. Beyond that, his capacity to interact with other men in a super-organism allows new information to contribute to the growth of the species as a whole. Accordingly, *education* as it exists today can be characterized as a replicative act in which we attempt to store in the brain either the available genetic pool of information or knowledge of where it can be found.

Discovery and *creativity* are wholly unlike our traditional concept of replicative education. In these processes an individual or group is able actually to create new data by putting old pieces of information together in new configurations of alternatives so that they may contribute to a larger group. Rather than simply developing himself, in this case Man is contributing toward the group that is developing itself. The mutualistic act of creativity is cooperative evolution that advances the transformation capabilities of the larger organism of which a single organism is a part, whether it be a cell group, a colony of organisms, a man, a discipline, a company, or society as a whole.

With an understanding of the transition of genetic to ectogenetic systems we can reconsider the dilemma of complex moral questions posed by the advent of "genetic engineering." There is a growing fear that, because we have practiced artificial selection on plants and animals, we shall proceed to create a "domesticated man," a man with very little variability and no unpredictability. What the geneticists have yet to realize is that the so-called "genetic manipulation" has been in massive practice ever since the advent of symbolism and culture.

By applying the laws of natural selection to the evolution of ectogenetic information, we have continually "re-engineered" Man and his cultures. We have discarded useless and incorrect information in cultures at ever more rapid rates. And in so doing we have surely designed our future in ways significantly more effective than manipulating small amounts of purely biological endogenetic data.

Besides the elimination of gross physiological defects, the biological genetic experimentation currently practiced can give us many new insights as to the nature of information coding, reproduction, and storage. By supplying the kind of data to enrich "information theory" geneticists can make contributions far beyond the limitations of gene changes. We can learn not how to achieve larger brains, for instance, but how better to use the untapped power of our existing brains, in combination with the external data-handling systems that are now *indivisible* from Man and his culture.

ENVIRONMENTAL TRANSFORMATION

The *special products* to serve human life that Man made out of the raw materials of his environment with his new ectogenetics are, in some ways, an even more effective illustration of organic processes at work in human thinking and the externalization of biological processes. Before the advent of writing, most of Man's inventions were replications of simple animal systems, but, when symbolism made possible the accumulation of information on a larger scale, Man began to *extend externally his own biological life form.* He literally transformed environmental material into products that copied, improved, and enhanced his own functions. He made the world over into his own "image."

A survey of human "inventions" illustrates in a dramatic fashion that, if the pressure of necessity is the mother of invention, evolution is its father. Alfred Wallace, Darwin's great contemporary, provided that insight when he proposed that humans transfer to tools the alterations that take place in animal evolution. When genetics became externalized, the rest of the biologic system was also externalized in short order.

By combining information in new ways, humans took raw materials from the environment and transformed them *directly* into amplified replications of the biological system. As pointed out earlier, the first tools were the most superficial kinds of self-extension—the hand axe, the throwing stick that extended the arm; and the bow, the mutualistic invention that effectively joined two arms to improve projection of a missile. Beyond this, Man built his house—a new "outer membrane" supported by a "skeleton"; used fire and "internal temperature control" to supplement his own energies; and created "predigesters" with cooking implements, a "circulation system" of paths and roads, and, of course, the new "memory system"—writing.

Paralleling the evolution of social development and evolving growth forms, from the time of the development of writing, approximately 10,000 B.C., to the eighteenth century, Man busied himself with extending and amplifying biological functions that he could perceive with his unaided eye. This period is totally dominated by superficial inventions; that is, extensions of *surface phenomena.* Primitive man was at first an inventor of pure self-enlargements—those things that he could add directly to his own body; but, following this long period of accretive technical growth, Man began to copy more complex skeletal and muscular systems with such extensions as levers and cranks. He supplemented his own biological energy with mechanical energy systems using animals, wind, and water. He added simple arterial circulation systems in irrigation and translated muscular contraction operations into simple force pumps. The external eye was copied and brought lenses into being; the nervous system was reproduced with simple signaling devices; and the first crude brain homologues of counting machines were developed during this period. Architectural systems copied not only the functions of the skeletal-membrane system but its form. The truly classic example of this was the "golden rule" of Greek buildings, based on human proportions.

In the seventeenth century, the potential for reinvention of transformed biologic systems was to take a gigantic leap with the invention of the microscope and its extensions of human vision beyond mere surface phenomena. The anatomists Vesalius, Da Vinci, and Harvey began to explore and investigate internal and underlying biological systems in detail. Within the brief span of a century, this new information was spread throughout the known world by the reproduction method of printing, aided by a broad new circulation system, itself enhanced by the amplified "spacial orientation" systems of navigation. As this new information took root, a rash of homologous inventions occurred and climaxed in the Industrial Revolution.

Suddenly, men discovered that they could *make* vast machines that duplicated, multiplied, and combined the effect of ancient "human machines." The interlocking skeletal–mechanical system became the tools of mass production, heat and biochemical energy were transformed into steam and chemical power, vision was extended with the spectroscope, food canning mimicked biological storage mechanisms, the camera added to visual memory, and the telegraph became the first true homologue of the synaptic nervous system. The *in*sights of Man allowed him to duplicate externally the functions of his biological system and thus to amplify his own growing social organism.

Within another century and a half, as Man extended his perception into the microcosmos of molecules and atoms, the

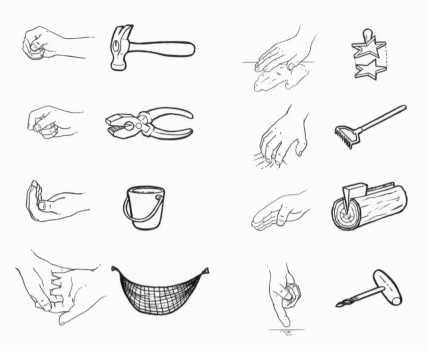

FIGURE 14

human organism brought into being vastly improved combinations when even more basic natural systems at the *atomic and
molecular level* were mutualized. The protective and permeable
shell of the membrane, organs, circulation, and nervous systems
were all transformed in entirely "new" ways. Humans have
created "synthetic" fibers and alloys, friction-reducing mechanical homologues, the nuclear reactor, jets and rockets, electron
microscopy, xerography, television, the concept of automatic
control of systems, and have made simple copies of the brain itself
with computers and data-processing.

What we see around us is a constantly improved and more
true-to-life homologue, in scale and durability, of almost *every
function* of our own biological organism. We can now not only
extend our energy and muscles, but also our minds and perceptions. Imagine a mutation that allows an organism to extend its
vision by bouncing an image off an object in space, or to store its
memories on magnetic tape!

We have literally transformed the environment into amplified
and recombined replicas of ourselves with products that serve and
extend our biological system. Along the way, we have created vast
multicellular interdependent human systems in cities, nations,
and, gradually, world organisms. In each case, we have replicated

the basic design and function of living organisms. Man and his machines, like the conch and his shell, have formed a new and higher type of organism, indivisible and still growing.

As we look again at a city organism or colony, we recognize the identical biological and somatic functions of: nerve center control, energy and nutrition transport systems, circulation systems, protection and excretion methods, manufacturing organelles, and food synthesis. In each and every detail, the systemic development of our ectobiologic technology system verifies our total unity with all Nature.

If we focus our view on a single unified social organism—a manufacturing company, for instance—we can observe that it, like any species, changes its environment with its effects and in turn adapts itself by changing its own characteristics to meet that environmental change. It responds to feedback and it supplies feedback to other organisms in its environment. The factory, in fact, breeds. It begets progeny in the form of products, services, and subsidiaries, some of which live and some of which die. As a productive organism, it must continue to improve its own processes, or within the broad society of growing corporate organisms it too faces extinction.

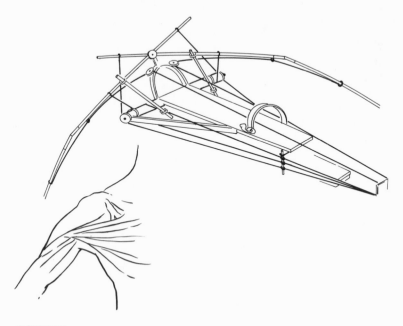

FIGURE 14A

A Da Vinci design for a flying machine shows how arm musculature was copied in mechanics.

FUNCTIONS & ORGANIC SYSTEMS AND THEIR TECHNOLOGIC EXTENSIONS

Ectogenetic Period (Yr. Apprx.)	Boundary Protection	Mechanical & Support	Energy	Transport	Communication	Perception	Processing & Control	
	Skin, hair, etc.	Bone, skeleton, cartilage	Food, Muscle	Circulation Systems	Nerve Systems, Signals	Senses	Brain	
5,000,000 B.C. Pre-writing & Notation	Animal skin tents fences huts armor	hand axe wedge lever drill throwing stick bow	fire human group-effort	paths rafts boats	messengers verbal & sign language notation drum horn paintings			surface phenomena exploration
10,000 B.C. Writing & block printing	bricks cloth fortified villages buildings	crank wheels pulleys looms force pump molds valves	animals wind water gun-power agriculture mills	wheel roads carts carriages ships irrigation canals and locks	writing paper scribes block printing books relay stations towers navigation	spectacles telescope clocks		
1500 A.D. Movable type printing	iron structures cement glass cities	gears lathe machines bearings	steam agricultural implements electricity food-canning fertilizers	steamboat railroads bicycle	movable type printing camera typewriter	microscope spectroscope thermometer barometer	automatic valves tabulators	substructure exploration anatomy chemistry biology
1900 A.D. Electric & electronic communication	synthetic & alloyed materials plastics, etc.	cantilever machine tools factories mass production	internal combustion turbines nuclear power	automobile aircraft rockets	phonograph motion pictures telegraph telephone radio television xerograph holography	X-rays electron microscopes remote cameras sensing instruments	automation cybernetics computers	infrastructure exploration

FIGURE 15

The information in both organic and organizational systems generates a large number of different transformations over time; the company changes its production machines, its employment practices, its raw materials, and, most of all, the *information* necessary to keep the whole running smoothly. The purely biological organism instructs us as it undergoes exactly the same kind of transformations in its internal machinery, use of raw material, and so forth, and finally changes the data bank that makes up its gene pattern.

The social organism of the company controls its biological wastage in new ways, however. Rather than tolerating the immense waste of the precursory biological system in which only an extremely small proportion of the total progeny survives and grows, the industrial company uses the equivalent of internalized "prebirth" testing procedures so that only those progeny with the greatest chance to survive are allowed to be reproduced. Like information evolution, the process of making things has evolved in parallel, isomorphic processes.

This principle is aptly described by the cybernetician Stafford Beer:

> In the animal this process is actually called "natural selection." The adjective "natural" is there to indicate that the selection mechanism is self-operating; the right mutations for survival are found because the wrong mutations are vetoed by death. Therefore, whatever lives on is right. In industry the wrong mutations are vetoed by management. They are not indiscriminately embarked upon, as in Nature, and allowed to work themselves to self-destruction. Management foresees that a particular mutation would have this effect, and vetoes it. Management also foresees that the right mutation is likely to have survival-quality, and selects it. So, foresight and selectivity are key attributes of management; they are also the major characteristics of intelligence. Now foresight is a matter of constructing a behavioral model of a situation: the model is filled out by experience, and this is a learning process. The methods of operational research in assessing the probabilities of various possible outcomes, together with cybernetic methods of inducing a system to learn, will between them simulate the factor of foresight.[6]

These natural methods of control and evolution have formed much of the discipline of cybernetics and general systems in today's world. By continually understanding more of natural processes, we can more accurately copy and *improve* on basic biologic systems. The study of cybernetics and general systems, while formidable-sounding in title and language, is actually nothing more than the study of *relationships* and their application in broad perspective. It is a matter of identifying the complex interactions of one part of a system with another and attempting to see what will happen when specific changes are made. As we can see in the analysis of human and social systems, one thing can be instructive of these relationships: the study of their biological basis.

As we added the ectobiological extension of things and ideas and systems, we progressively continued to affect our pure biologic system in parallel: improving health, lowering the rate of infant mortality, remedying biological defects, and extending the span of life, in some countries doubling life span in several decades. We have carried our own biological capabilities far beyond their origins, just as the first social colonies of cells extended their capabilities far beyond the solitary and independent cell. With the study of more homologues, we can begin to grasp that a division between "technology" and "biology" is also, like the separation of biology and psychology, nothing more than an outdated intellectual illusion. A tool or process that extends and aids life is as natural as a tree. Good technology is just good biology.

A very apt illustration of the importance of understanding the homologous nature of human systems has been given to us by many of the world's great inventors who have referred time and time again to their use of analogy to receive inspiration. Da Vinci is, of course, a preeminent example, but even more interesting is a case of directed use of analogy that occurred in the 1920s at the Bauhaus School. As can be seen in Figure 16, the influence of their seminal ideas dominates the form of a vast number of today's "contemporary" products.

Much of this influence is due to the insights of men like Laszlo Moholy-Nagy and other Bauhaus teachers who utilized the device of biological memory. "We are striving toward those timeless biological fundamentals of expression which are meaningful to everyone . . . we observe art because of its basic and common roots permeating life."[7]

ART AND TRANSFORMATION

Art intuitively follows the course of biological evolution. Just as scientists unearth hidden analogies to make discoveries, the artist

FIGURE 16

Bauhaus designs originated during the early
1920s. Theo van Doesburg and
C. van Eesteren, House for an artist, 1923.
Marcel Breuer, Armchair, 1925.
M. Brandt and H. Przyrembel, Adjustable
ceiling fixture, Aluminum shade, 1926.

uses extensions of our perceptual system to penetrate and to
reveal the mysteries of life. Teilhard de Chardin noted,

> Success has been most readily achieved in the visual arts with a
> naturalistic approach, but this does not invalidate abstract and
> impressionist approaches; indeed, it may explain them. Perhaps
> these succeed only to the extent to which they evoke, somewhere
> along their passage to the brain of the viewer, psychological
> changes that parallel, or contrast with, those evoked by natural
> forms.[8]

In point of fact, Chardin was far more correct than he stated. Abstract and impressionist approaches, just like modern technology, have followed the course of introducing us to nature at progressively deeper and deeper levels. Impressionist art, for instance, "invented" the separation of color into base components exactly as the human eye does. Art actually became more "naturalistic" by going beyond superficial phenomena to reveal underlying truth. In traditional African art, for instance, we see the intermediate step between representation and coded symbol. In fact, this "art" is actually a language that carries the vital information of philosophy, morals, legal codes, and the like. Evolving beyond depicting nature in a representational way to convey more information and ideas, such art taught European representational artists how to evolve their own art to new levels of growth. The "abstract" art of today can be seen as we look at nature through a microscope; it too reveals the new beauty of infrastructures of Nature by extending our eyesight beyond the boundaries of naked eyes and visible light. The comparison of art and nature in Figure 17 dramatically illustrates just how close these phenomena really are. At an even lower level, subatomic phenomena are mimicked in the "uncertainty" of today's random interactions in "found art" and "happenings." Art is a vital way we learn about nature—and ourselves.

Whereas we can use experimental evidence to provide cross-linkages between much biological and psychological phenomena, because art is substantially a subjective, personal experience it is revealing to know how some great artists express their union with Nature and how art is used to extend the self. Eugenio Rignano, in 1925, postulated that the artist "needs to transform outer reality according to his own pattern." The artist, in fact, joins himself with external materials to produce that product which, in itself, is a medium by which others can experience that same joining. The observer of art mutualizes with the artist through his work.

The artist uses himself as the natural model by which to reveal Nature. As Goethe put it, "Here I sit molding creatures in my own image." Bacon reflected this in his ironic statement, "The vision of Christ that thou dost see has a great hook nose like thine. Mine has a snub nose like to mine." Not only can we deduce the evolution of music through the "heartbeat" of drums, the "vocal cords" of strings, and so forth, but in sophisticated mutualized contrapuntal music it is as Casals said, "Composers can use any

FIGURE 17

Willem deKooning, Untitled Lithograph, 1960.

material as long as they make a complete whole of it, a whole which will express true life in music."

As Chardin noted, it is not just parallels that serve the purpose of revealing Nature, but contrast as well. It has been said that much art is a lie in the service of truth. An artist will take the most common experience or object and distort it so that the observer can be awakened to the usually unobserved and deeper beauties within it. A Picasso bottle becomes something else, something that strips away the superficial commonality to reveal dormant differences and new information. The common object provides the strong connective links that make possible the discovery and acceptance of these new pieces of data.

The organic nature of art prompted Arnold Schoenberg to declare, "The world of art is like every complete organism. It is so homogeneous that in every detail it reveals its truest, inmost essence . . . When one hears a verse of poem, a measure of a composition, one is in a position to comprehend the whole." Art in this sense is truly a living thing. It is a psychological "seed" that grows within the observer, a nuclear life form that not only reproduces but holds the promise of mutual growth.

Because art brings us together with ancient biological fundamentals and provides new growth opportunities, it becomes beautiful and meaningful. The roots of great art are so deep in the historical continuity of Life that it reveals the profound reality of the self. The task of the artist can be seen as creating mutuality, reproducing parts of his own pattern that are so common or contrasting to our species that they can be recognized and experienced by others. The artist is not alone in this growth activity. He is joined by all those—the craftsman, the architect, the engineer—who create the useful artifacts of Man. A constant use of biological synthesis penetrates reality to psychologically and physically extend Man and his effects.

The mystical process of "creativity" can now be understood as simply another manifestation of the primary drive of growth. This understanding allows us deliberately to tap both the insight and outsight skills of creativity. No longer must the creative person be as Carl Jung described him: "A creative person has little power over his own life. He is not free. He is captive and driven by his daimon." Today it becomes possible to understand where the daimon growth is driving us; to know more of the ultimate goal we can better develop and use its power.

FORM VS. FUNCTION

The ubiquitous processes of growth can be observed to manifest themselves in all the acts and artifacts of Man, representing yet another ontological recapitulation of Life's most basic function. Once we pierce the shrouds of form, identical *functions* emerge. We can see why the principles of transformation have remained in relative obscurity for so long.

The dominance of structural or morphological evolutionary approaches has stood in the way of understanding how natural processes are joined with the empirical human activities of art, technology, and socialization. They are all evolutionary creation. They are the extensions of nature with a second nature—the flow of intrinsic to extrinsic function that supplies the continuity of accumulated genetic energy. Instinct and intelligence are distinct developments of one and the same principle: One remains within the self, whereas the other steps out of itself to achieve union with the whole.

TRANSFORMATIVE EVOLUTION

As we begin to understand more about biological systems, we can see that Man continually creates interacting systems with more mutually beneficial potential, for example, recent developments in such things as ecology, social responsibility of corporations, extended world relationships, and crumbling social barriers. The use of such processes as those occurring in molecular biology can be the formation of homologues to aid us in the further illumination and growth of human systems.

A particularly meaningful illustration of this is the understanding we can gain from simple cell dynamics. The logic of these systems is quite beautiful. In a cell, a particular potential exists in a latent or "repressed" state until its "repressor" is inactivated by an "inducer" chemical in its environment; two negatives combine to form a positive. Once the potential is "derepressed" it can proceed to manufacture products for use by the cell and for export to other parts of the body. As long as the inducer is present it will continue to manufacture the particular product; *but* if it makes too much

69

product, the excess product will now *depress the inducer* and manufacturing stops. It is like "too much of a good thing"; a surfeit of anything will act to limit itself.

Human systems respond identically. A farmer who produces more corn than he can use and export will start to cut his production. The "inducer" of his own needs and the marketplace will be saturated and become depressed. This fact is aptly illustrated by problems in urban development; the availability of abundant "inducers": light, air, water, and energy derepressing the repressors of the potentials of social organisms. The resulting production of manufactured materials has now, in many cases, begun to *repress* these *inducers*. Light, air, water, and natural resources have been eaten up and the human organism is now responding by beginning to re-repress its potential for those manufactured forms of "terminal metabolites" of growth. Artificial overavailability of such inducers as housing, transportation, and raw materials also often leads to community development that is not balanced. Adjustments that have been costly in the past can be avoided in the future by use of biopsychologic homologues in planning systemic growth.

Although mistakes, misuse, and repression occur in biologic and psychologic systems, even in these circumstances, they do not cause the total system to revert to a condition of "homeostasis" or "equilibrium." Transformational growth is a ubiquitous and irreversible growth state process. We literally *re-create and amplify nature* with technology and sociology whether we realize it or not. This fact, of course, contradicts current ecological theories that, we might add, had they been around at the time, would have contravened almost any major evolutionary advance, not to mention such conservationally unsound ideas as the invention of agriculture.

The most important function in this irreversible process in biology and psychology is the *interaction* of mutation and change with selection. Although Darwin did not believe we would ever be a witness to evolution, with the things we make, natural selection occurs all around us every day in the form of the continual turnover of products and services. Dobzhansky expressed succinctly the essence of the modern "marketing process" when he said, "A favorable mutant allele will increase in frequency and eventually will displace and supplant the original allele."[9] As soon as the process of systemic natural selection and evolution is better understood by producers, the failure rates in new products and services are reduced substantially. Today, the processes that create these products are like primitive organic systems, in that even now many of these experiments do not meet the criterion of "fitness" in the biopsychological system and are thus doomed to extinction.

The mechanics of directed animal, idea, and artifact evolution and "artificial selection"—superabundance of alternatives, obsolescence, and selection of those that best "fit" our living systems—are such an identical process to biological systems that the resemblance can by no stretch of imagination be considered accidental. The definitive nature of these phenomena is further emphasized as we see that Man's inventions have been shaped by his capacity to observe and to understand his own biological system and create extensions that are more effective transformers of the environment. The ratio of energy needed to transform the external world versus that required for survival is constantly being improved. As the energy necessary for simply staying alive becomes increasingly easier to obtain, more of Man's energies can be spent on adding and linking new information to the system, which in turn provide the opportunity to evolve improved machinery for affecting and transforming the environment, *ad infinitum*. The process inevitably results in new and more flexible information handling, more "crossings" of data, and more new ideas by which once again we can multiply our use of energy and improve our transformational capacity.

Nature has demonstrated the ability to translate these information-handling processes from one coded language into another that is substantially different in form and degree. Just as Man uses coded tapes and cards to handle masses of numbers, letters, and words, sensory inputs of vision, hearing, tastes, and so forth, are transformed into neuronal signals and finally into chemical substances (such as acetylcholine and noradrenaline) to communicate information to the peripheral nervous system and to activate certain genes in cells. With an organic perspective, we can observe this process at work in the basic translation of the four-"letter" language of DNA into an incredibly large number of proteins. In this translation process, nonliving matter is transformed into living material. This "miracle of life," in which nonanimate turns into animate, represents a transformation on an order and scale similar to that which took internalized endogenetic information and transformed it into unique human symbolic expression and ectogenetic language. We can now see that this major transformation converted biological growth patterns into what we have long called "psychological behavior" and that these patterns are also the patterns of social and cultural growth.

GROWTH AND THE FUTURE

Numerous and eminent authorities maintain today that the human condition can be improved only if our growth rates can be balanced, slowed down, or stopped. In their projections of the future, they cite such things as industrial growth, increasing pollution, and decreasing resources to verify the contention that the reins on our spiraling growth must be tightened now. If we do not stop and balance our efforts to achieve equilibrium, they assert, starvation, suffocation, and stultification of our species is the inevitable result. Open and free development, they claim, is not the answer, for, rather than providing solutions, this activity intensifies science and technology and only multiplies problems. The only solution, therefore, is to stop where we are, cure our failures, and fall back on past and present successes. Thus, by controlling growth we can avert imminent disaster and bring about a return to more halcyon and hopeful days.

To look into our future and to imagine that the result of continued growth is the inevitable collapse of civilization, is to miss the central point of the evidence of prehistory and the findings of the recent past. Unfortunately the past data used to program both minds and computers for foreseeing the future are comprised of the obvious *products* of growth, not its underlying *processes.* Put another way, the "whats," the things in life, stand in the way of seeing the more vital "why." An example of this fallacy occurred in the early part of this century with a forerunner of today's projectors of progress, Henry Adams. He was the first to set out the now standard mathematical forecasting tool, the "Law of Acceleration." Using the world's coal output as a basis, Adams demonstrated that use of power would double in ten years and multiply faster thereafter. Extrapolating this information, a few decades of growth would exhaust raw materials and cast a massive bituminous pall over the earth. We know today that he was wrong. Yet who could have foreseen the explosive growth of hydroelectric power, atomic energy, discovery of new resources, or the parallel amplification of energy efficiency: Only a Wellsian imagination could have envisioned new energy forms, electronics, air travel, or any of the thousands of creations that have taken us so far so fast. Past products as a foundation did not help Henry Adams nor do they in today's world aid others to predict the future.

History, in the breadth in which we have considered it, tells us clearly that a blind conservation of the past is a setting not for survival but for extinction. We have seen that the process of growth is the very definition of life itself. As life expanded, Nature also instructed Life to continually invent new ways to grow, growth that goes considerably beyond simple physical enlargement. It involves the processes by which organisms learn to grow through and with each other.

There is no evidence of any successful return to a past or balanced system. The pressures of growth actually create constant disequilibrium in environmental and life systems, and these inevitably result in the dynamism that some now see as uncomfortable and threatening. Yet, human life itself, with its intelligence and amplification, has come about just because of such "uncontrolled and unbalanced growth." With only a smattering of historical perspective we can see the oscillation of forces that make our lives fuller, healthier, longer, and more interesting than were those of our ancestors. We can see that it is a natural characteristic of human behavior to accept these advances as natural and to press to move ahead, no matter how we idealize the past.

As we became Nature's evolutionary agent, we too have continually learned how to practice the process of evolution, selection, and growth at ever more efficient rates. We do not wait around for the slow and uncertain processes of primitive biological evolution; we create our own imbalances *and* the counterbalancing improvements. Surely we still make mistakes, but unlike our primitive ancestors thousands of eggs are no longer necessary to produce a single successful progeny—or *idea.* Mankind's ratios of successes to failures constantly increase as he evolves himself, his thinking, and his environment. The momentum of change creates a present that Man inhabits only briefly in his Faustian quest for an evolved future.

Anything we produce, whether concepts, products, or complex economic, political, and social systems, will ultimately suffer extinction at the hand of our own selection mechanisms if it is not allowed and helped to grow. This is the good and natural reason why we see so few of yesterday's products and ideas around today. Those that tried to hold the line were "selected out" as Life moved forward.

Attempts to pass on "unchangable" truths become pressured out of existence. As we consider the records of history it is vital to note the problem of *information balance*. Positive or "agreeable" information preserved and presented with the exclusion of negative data often leads to the repetition of past mistakes: the only way false books of history can be balanced. It is unfortunate that well-meaning historians have created such accounting practices, for they leave new generations with the dynamics of these unbalanced facts. It is, however, encouraging that as we enter today's age of mutualism many of these errors are being brought to light. Our mistakes as well as our successes are now becoming a more important part of our ectogenetic pool.

In this sense it is well to recall that a purely "positive thinking" approach provides little true growth if it is not nutritive—accompanied by information. Feedback given in a mutualistic way is far more growth producing than empty positivism. Transformative growth always requires valid information. One example of this in United States history can be made when we consider the question of today's "drug culture." A hundred years ago a variety of dangerous addictive drugs were available to everyone at any drug or grocery store. Opium growing thrived in such states as Florida, New Hampshire, Vermont, and Texas. Tincture of opium, laudanum, was even given to babies in Mrs. Winslow's Soothing Syrup as well as being used by adults for everything from rheumatism to insomnia. Opium was also sold as a "cure" for cocaine addiction, an ailment acquired by multitudes of soldiers during the Civil War—while at the same time cocaine was sold openly and legally as a catarrh remedy.[10] This sort of *negative* information is not generally found in history books and the neglect of such negative facts often creates a false perspective of today's problems.

Growth is, after all, an irreversible phenomenon, and undeniable. As we study our planet and ecosystem, we find that Nature has never been content to settle for merely the successful. History, in every sense, from the biological to the social, demonstrates that what we really have to fear is not so much the perpetuation of our growth failures; *much more dangerous is the deliberate attempt to repeat our successes*. Today's successes become tomorrow's failures. The idea of "limiting growth" is anathema to Nature and to Man. Not only that, but just to "balance" growth would deny the very influences that created the ascending and achieved values and ideas most vital to our species. Life in its very manifestation is growth and change. Not to grow is to die.

PSYCHOLOGY FROM BIOLOGY

FIVE

The second postulate of the theory of transformation is that human mental processes are transformed replicas of biological processes; and that psychological processes are on a continuum with biological systems of behavior and are isomorphic with them. To examine this postulate, we shall review the system of behavior in each process and then examine in detail the function within each system.

BIOLOGICAL GROWTH SYSTEMS

In reviewing the functional nature of biological systems, we are concerned with the process and system that the basic unit of life, the cell, follows in its cycle of protoplasmic life—in particular with the growth activities that are invariant in *all* cells.

In its most rudimentary form cell dynamics is a system of self-renewal, growth, and duplication. It is a protein-nucleic acid based organization that can ingest its environment's molecules, break them down, and reassemble them into either its own likeness, through cell-division, or into specialized products that serve and become a part of the organism. This activity of the cell differs from chemically *reactive* macromolecules in that it is, first and always, an *active* and growing system.[1] Even in its most static form, any cell is in a constant state of activity with at least part of its system—in a state of growth, development, and self-renewal.[2] On this very basic difference between life and nonlife lies the cornerstone of the isomorphism of transformation. The unique prerequisite of life is *growth*—stasis is death.

When we look more closely at the growth *system* of living organisms, we can see the phenomenon as a number of discreet and interrelated functions. (These steps are outlined graphically in Figure 18.) All organisms convert and transform their environments into living and life-facilitating substances in seven basic and orderly steps.

1. The first of these is the very act of *searching* or probing for nutritive material in the environment, the act of a "hungry" cell. This search is the primary manifestation of what we can describe as an intrinsically open system, the restless "growth state" of an active search for growth material so characteristic of all living things.

2. Once an organism has encountered material, the second step, a regulatory substep, is to react to this material by the *screening* or discriminating processes of its selectively permeable membrane. This determines whether or not contiguous substances should be accepted or rejected. These mostly growth-serving substances enter the system through the membrane.

3. Inside the cytoplasm of the cell, the third step, *digestion,* takes place. Raw materials are broken down into their chemical components and are once more screened to determine which can or cannot be used for growth. Useless residues or waste products are eliminated.

4. In the fourth step, usable components are distributed within the cytoplasmic system and are recombined or *synthesized* into new compounds (often joining with previously stored materials).

5. The fifth step is the actual *use* of this recombined material, either for growth and expansion of the cell, for reproduction, or in the case of certain cells, for specialized products to be used by the organism of which it is a part. Not only does this process of growth cause a changed cell, but it creates a changed environment, one that substantially affects subsequent actions by the cell.[3]

6. The next two steps are vital to the continuation of all growth processes. This open system approaches the definition of a steady-state model as it allows the opportunity for both positive and negative feedback to open or to close the loop of systemic activity. Because no single cell, even a free-swimming protozoan, lives in independent isolation from some form of environment,

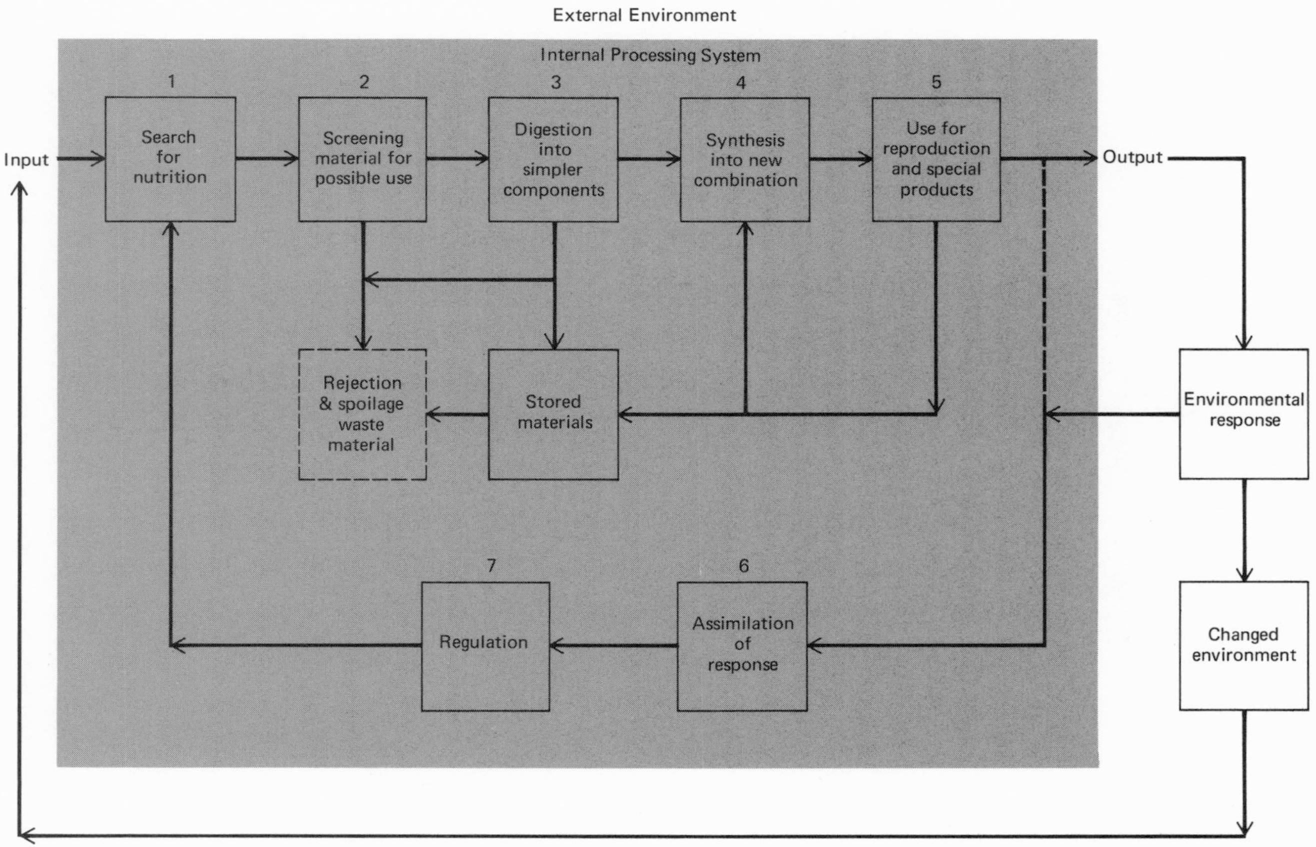

External Environment

Internal Processing System

Input

1 Search for nutrition

2 Screening material for possible use

3 Digestion into simpler components

4 Synthesis into new combination

5 Use for reproduction and special products

Stored materials

Rejection & spoilage waste material

6 Assimilation of response

7 Regulation

Output

Environmental response

Changed environment

FIGURE 18

77

the sixth step turns to *assimilating the environment's reaction* to the cell's activity.

7. Finally, the seventh step of the cycle is use of that information to *regulate* or to mediate subsequent growth activities. Unlike cybernetic systems that depend almost exclusively on self-corrective *negative* feedback, in organic systems the realization and development of potentialities depend on the possibility of responses of a positive and *nutritive* nature. An example of the effect of response at the cellular level has been pointed out at the cell "psychology" level by D'Arcy Thompson, who has shown that the rate of asexual reproduction can be observed to be many times as great when two cells are in the same drop of water as when they reproduce separately.[4] Thus, the loop of the living feedback system provides opportunities for responses to open the system and continually to enhance growth.

PSYCHOLOGICAL GROWTH SYSTEMS

In considering the basic psychological system, the homologous nature of the growth process returns us again to the basic diagram in Figure 18. To see how psychological systems replicate the observable growth phenomenon of biological systems, we shall shift our perspective to that used by natural scientists as they follow the phenomena of biology from physics, to chemistry, to life. To do so our adjustment to changed conditions, scale, and complexity requires a type of "quantum leap" of conceptualization.

We can easily see, for instance, how a young human infant copies the physiological growth processes of a cell as he actually tries to "eat his environment," attempting to incorporate each new object into his system by trying to engulf it. We can also observe such "drives" as withdrawal from pain and need for sleep. Our perspective changes when we follow the growth processes duplicated in the more subtle psychological mechanisms of curiosity, learning, and personality formation. These and other mental phenomena carry forward psychologically the complex dynamics of biological growth.

In the psychological process, as in the biological, the organism is a creature who adapts reality to his own ends, who transforms reality into a congenial form, who attempts to make his own reality.[5] Thus, we see the human organism intaking his environment through the faculty of his senses, disassembling it, and remanufacturing it in a form that fits his own internal pattern—a pattern far richer than the genetic information that guides biological behavior—his *ectogenetic* pattern. Man literally remakes the world "in his own (culturally acquired) image."

1. The first psychological function to occur in all normal infant behavior is that of a "hungry psyche," curiosity. Beyond early psychological demands, there is in all healthy children an active, cognitive *search* for new information.[6] When deprived of the nourishment of varied information in a child's environment, normal human development cannot occur.[7]

2. Data presented to the senses are *screened* for their usefulness. That information judged to be most useful is absorbed, while that seen as harmful or useless material is rejected in the process of "selective perception."[8]

3. The third step in our processing of cognitive nutrients is the *digestion* and analysis of the information, breaking it down into acceptable and manageable bits.

4 and 5. Step four is reassembling or *synthesizing* the material into new arrangements. This step is followed by that of *use,* step five. Recombined materials, ideas, can be stored as memory for later use; they can be used for an act of behavior or they can be used for the making of an artifact, a specialized product, either for use by the individual or for use by others.

6. As with the cell, no individual lives in isolation from his environment—human or otherwise. How that environment responds to the human's attempt to grow is vital. The sixth step is *assimilation* of that response.

7. *Regulation* of subsequent acts of growth is critical to the development of potentialities. In the very simplest terms, if something does not produce a positive effect, if it does not work, we try something else. Regulation of growth, expansion, or contraction of Man's mind is very much a function of environmental response; feedback either closes or opens the loop of the human psychological growth system.

As illustrated in Figure 18, *the basic growth system of any living physical or psychological being is the same,* whether it is expressed physically at the simple level of the single cell or in the transformed and complex level of human mental acts. *It is a case of basic drives to express the full potentialities of accretive, replicative, and mutual growth being mediated by nutrition in, and feedback from, the environment.*

SYSTEM FUNCTIONS

For any model to go beyond mere analogical allusion, it must correspond in detail with the facts as they are known. It must also account for phenomena previously unexplained and it must have predictive value. We shall examine each of the functions of the total process in some detail to reveal the unity in biological and psychological systems, and to point out applications of transformation in varieties of human behavior.

SEARCH

The fact that biological organisms are open systems and, even without external stimuli, are intrinsically active can be supported by any amount of biological and physiological evidence.[9] Any living organism acts *on* its environment before it re-acts *to* its environment; even the quiescent autotrophic plant sends out "searchers"—the roots and branches of its ever-broadening search for nutrition in the environment. In plants, for example, a spore, the organism can often exist in a "lifeless" state until nutrition is available, but the aggressive search of an animal cell for nutrients is obviously fundamental to its life. A "timid" cell, if there is such a thing, will not find food and, undernourished, will regress and ultimately die. In psychological terms, this function is verified by many experiments demonstrating that both animals and people do not try to avoid stimulation, but actively try to attain it.[10]

The evidence shows that human beings find low levels of stimulation and variation in their environment not only unpleasant, but actually disruptive.[11] Lower animals also "actively seek stimulation of various kinds . . . Sights, sounds, smells and other sensations that have not led to or been associated with physical satisfaction seem to be interesting, attractive and sometimes demonstrably rewarding in themselves," and "this appears to be a universal motive among animals and especially man."[12]

This searching process prompted Pavlov to declare, "There is a reflex which is still insufficiently appreciated and which can be termed the investigatory reflex. I sometimes call it the 'what is it? reflex.' The biological significance of this reflex is enormous."[13]

Whether we call it the "what is it? reflex," the "investigatory reflex," or use Thorpe's term of "anticipatory arousal,"[14] this active search for the psychological nutrition of information is the vital and unconditional initiating act of growth.

The insatiable searching function can now begin to clear away the misunderstandings that have described this phenomenon as being motivated "in itself." The child's "Why?" the term *curiosity,* can now be defined within a biopsychological system of growth and transformation. *The first prerequisite for psychological growth is the availability of sufficient mental nutrition.* How this nutritional information becomes transformed into growth depends on how it is processed in subsequent steps.

SCREENING

It has been generally observed that the cell discriminates between useful and harmful materials and allows only certain things to enter its internal system. The cell, acting as though it had chemical senses, absorbs what it chooses, when it chooses, through the selective permeability of its membrane.[15] This frequently overlooked fact is particularly striking when we relate it to the mechanics of human perception. Information permeation can be observed and even measured in humans in specific and gross physiological changes that correspond almost precisely to those occurring in the cell. The outer membrane of the cell opens or closes to permit entry of nutrients in the same manner that the human eye lets in only certain information; the nutritional receptor membrane—-the pupil—opens or closes, depending upon the nature of the material presented.[16] Because it is estimated that the majority of human cognition is achieved through visual perception, this homologue is particularly significant.* Domination by the optic receptors probably prompted the emphasis in our language on such sayings as "I'll believe it when I see it."

As with a cell, only a small portion of the available information becomes a part of the organism. That portion, like selective

---

*Linguistic patterns and metaphor in speech emphasize the power of vision over all the other senses. We say, we shall wait and *see.* We use our mind's *eye,* we admonish to *see* for yourself and not accept anything *sight unseen,* we have a *vision,* a *viewpoint,* or *outlook* on things, and even the blind man says in the classic pun, "*I see.*" In information terms the modern cliché sums it up, "What you *see* is what you get."

permeability in cell dynamics, does not simply admit a random sample of what is available. In hearing, this is often referred to as the "cocktail party" syndrome—selecting at will to hear or not the various conversations occurring around us. The organism is never merely a passive receptor or reactor to stimuli; it is an active selector among stimuli.[17] Mental nutrition is in fact determined as acceptable or unacceptable by what a person wants or needs to see or not to see. Mediated by experience, people will selectively ignore irrelevant, useless, or harmful information.[18]

Because both cell and man screen nutrients based on the *usefulness* of environmental material, we can safely deduce that cell "psychology" is motivated by whether material can be either growth-producing or -inhibiting. Experiments have demonstrated that human responses regarding the attractiveness or repulsiveness of stimulus material are *not* determined by the stimulus itself, but also depend on internal signals that indicate the subsequent or anticipated *usefulness* of the material.[19] *The human sensations of pleasure and pain are the accompanying cues that determine perceived usefulness or uselessness of environmental materials for growth.*[20]

Use, in the case of the human being, can be described as that material representing not simply the information itself, but what growth can subsequently be achieved with it, what it can be connected with, how it can be changed, and so forth. The need for usefulness is such that if cognitive material is substantially nonuseful for growth, the uneasiness and pain produced from such dissonance is often reduced by distorting or changing the perception of the material.*[21] All in all, we are observing an organism's contact with the environment and subsequent reaction on the organism's own terms, that is, based on what kind of growth the organism wants or has learned to practice.

DIGESTION AND ASSIMILATION

Once information has entered the system, the subsequent and almost simultaneous process of digestion takes place. Materials taken into the system are broken down and then reassembled so

---

*In human development, information distortions are "useful" to certain types of internal regressive growth as we will see when mental problems are considered later in this book.

that they are complementary to the genetic pattern of the organism. Again, the internal information, physiological genes, or psychocultural ectogenetics determines whether or not new material will be successfully assimilated. As in endogenetic recombinations, if the new ectogenetic information presents stimuli to a person that are similar to information already existing in his system, high positive recombination or "transfer" usually results, and learning progresses more rapidly than if the material is totally new or different.[22] If the new material is similar to the old but requires a use or response that is new, there is only a slight positive transfer. In fact, if new information is similar or identical but the learning situation demands dissimilar or opposite uses, negative transfer results.[23] In both endogenetic and ectogenetic systems, existing information patterns persist and must be connected with in order to acquire new data. This fact is particularly true of information that must be stored for later use. Meaningful material is easier than nonmeaningful to learn and once learned it is retained longer.[24]

USE

An understanding of an individual's possibilities for growth and his expectation of useful information is critical. These possibilities and expectations affect the screening, digestion, and assimilation processes of all materials encountered in the environment. At the level of the cell and even in primitive bacteria, many examples of elementary life forms will actually modify their genetic makeup when confronted with unusual food sources and will produce new and stable lines that are able to grow successfully.[25] Like the behavior of a human stranded in a strange environment, the normal growth behavior of cells can be modified substantially if the recombined information is conducive to growth in the new or altered environment. In single-celled organism, the pragmatism in growth is relatively easy to detect and measure. Usefulness in human terms is a more subtle phenomenon.

Growth in a psychological sense is the process of internal and external expansion–absorption from the environment and projection into it. This ability to live an effective life—to *affect* one's environment and be *effected* by it, in however a minute way—is the psychological equivalent of biological growth. It is the making and expanding of one's own reality. As Paul Tillich suggested, to be creatively alive, one need not be what is called a creative artist, scientist, or statesman, but one must be able to participate meaningfully in one's own original creations. Such participation is a growth phenomenon if it changes that in which one participates, regardless of whether that change is great or small, external or internal.

The meaning of growth, as defined in transformation theory, was offered also by one of the now unfashionable forerunners of Freud, Jung, and Adler: Levy-Bruhl. In his "Participation Mystique" concept he said, "The mental activity which by virtue of an intimate participation possesses its object, *gives it life and lives through it,* finds entire satisfaction in this possession."[26] The basis of this satisfaction is pleasure as it was defined earlier, that is, use—becoming a *part* of the environment, the *people,* and *things in it;* incorporating parts of the environment into our system; and extending ourselves into it—creating an interrelationship. In this way, we experience psychological growth; we have made the environment part of us and made ourselves part of the environment. As Spinoza put it, "We have created extent." In a very real sense, in psychological growth we *are* the extent we have created. It becomes as much a part of us as our physiological extensions. There is good reason why Man is so extremely facile at this so-called "adapting" behavior—at doing or learning to do things that allow him to manipulate and to modify his environment for his own purposes.[27]

Creation of environmental effect can manifest itself in a wide variety of ways. For example, active recitation of verbal materials leads to much more efficient memorization than does reading without producing *any* observable external effect.[28] On a more subtle level, thinking on difficult materials which produces subvocal speech often facilitates understanding.[29] On a more participative level, anticipating the subsequent use of material to affect others has been shown to increase memorization markedly.*[30]

It is vital to recognize at this point that, as with biological forms of growth, psychological growth and self-extension include all

---

*Learning and anticipating the effect of subsequent use have been demonstrated in a number of experiments.[31] People tend to remember what will be most liked by an audience they are to talk to. In one case, experimental subjects were to make a talk on teachers' salaries. Those told they were to address teachers tended to recall arguments for increasing salaries, whereas those told they were to talk to a citizens' group interested in economics recalled the opposing arguments.

forms of growth. The evolution of psychological growth mechanisms follows the same pattern of biological ones: Accretion, replication, and mutuality all occur. As in biologic systems, the most successful forms of growth in "psychosymbiotic" relationships are those that are *mutualistic* in character. *The process of effecting and being affected by others, in a sharing of information and growth, is the highest level of organic development.* As Karl Menninger described it in *The Vital Balance*, "Thus he begins to give and take, earn and spend, work and play, live and let live—all with a favorable trade balance and an increasing *Joie de Vivre*."[32]

FEEDBACK—ASSIMILATION AND REGULATION

The process of feedback is so fundamental to all of the other growth functions that regulation can be observed to occur almost simultaneously with the very first ingestion of external material. In cells, this takes place through communication mechanisms such as allosteric effectors.* In a culture medium, for example, cells automatically mediate their growth behavior when they come in contact with one another.[34] Although even without perceivable "contact," as noted earlier, varieties of protozoa increase their asexual reproduction when two cells are simply placed together in a medium. In the development of multicelled organisms, feedback from contiguous multiplying cells sets off the highly complex processes of cell differentiation.[35] Hormones and other chemical substances play a critical role as messengers in intercellular communication and this regulatory activity produces physiological influences parallel to that which organisms psychologically exert on each other in a "multicelled" society.[36]

At many phylogenetic levels, the process of biopsychologic feedback effects has been pointed out in cases ranging from tadpoles, whose injuries heal more slowly in isolation from other tadpoles, to mice, which grow more slowly in isolation.[37]

Living organisms do not exist in isolation. Each modifies its immediate environment and creates new environmental conditions for others as well as for itself. Group dynamics, a network of interacting growth inhibition or stimulation, operate for

---

*The coordinating and regulatory functions of interactions between cells are known as "allosteric interactions" and correspond to the existence in animals of large-scale intercellular coordination through the endocrine and nervous system.[33]

all organisms. We find these homologous principles at work at various structural levels. *The basic forms of growth are set up in the instructions of the genetic code, but the particular rules observed at any time by a single organism are determined by messages from its environment.*

In human psychological phenomena this same type of regulatory mechanism determines the form and character of growth strategies. We never approach an act of perception with a totally blank mind; rather, because of past experience, we are in a constant state of preparedness or expectancy. It is clear that normal human development can occur only through relationships with other people.[38] The expression of human potentialities is determined primarily by the intraorganic feedback supplied by contiguous humans. This is particularly true for the infant; the less positive feedback and affiliation he receives, the less developed he will be in his subsequent personality, independent action, and sense of identity.[39] Early influences that provide ambivalent or uncertain feedback, in which an activity is sometimes rewarded and sometimes punished, produce so-called neurotic behavior.[40]

The nature of the form of exchange enjoyed in interpersonal transactions is critical to growth and development. Whether feedback is accretive, replicative, or mutual influences the conditions and patterns of future growth. Mutuality or equivalence in psychological terms is somewhat more complex than, say, exchanging goods or labor for money, but human value systems are becoming clearer.* (See Figure 19.) The fact is, however, that a psychological exchange such as returning "information" for "status" does not reduce the amount possessed by either party,

---

*The character of these psychological exchanges has recently been studied by Uriel Foa to determine some of the relative values in this process. The level of equivalence has been studied in the cross-relationships of exchanges of "love," "status," and "information." In this case, *love* is defined as an expression of regard; *status*, as an expression of evaluation judgment; and *information* as advice, opinion, instruction, or enlightenment. Thus in restructuring this data pattern, both "love" and "status" can be seen to be evaluative feedback functions; "information" represents the other critical parameter of psychological nutrition. In psychological feedback the combination of evaluation and nutrition determines the mutuality of exchange. Although not represented in Figure 19, one of the vital observations in this study was that the significance of the person who provides the resource changes the values. The "rate of exchange" varies with our regard for the other person. On the other hand, a positive response from a "negative" person may actually result in negative feedback.[41]

Resource received	Resource returned					
	Love	Status	Information	Money	Goods	Services
Love		65	10	0	2	23
Status	62		20	10	3	5
Information	17	34		11	24	14
Money	0	16	8		60	16
Goods	6	5	21	55		13
Services	41	18	7	16	18	

FIGURE 19
Representation of the percentage frequency distribution of psychological exchange transactions. Love is defined in this case as an expression of regard; status as a positive or negative evaluative judgment; and information is defined as advice, opinion, instruction, or enlightenment. Thus, in pure psychological terms love and status are the positive-negative aspects of feedback, whereas information is nutritive. We can see that in all cases the resource received from a person, regardless of whether it is purely psychological or not, requires a return or exchange that includes either love or status and information.   (After Foa.)

which is quite the reverse of traditional concepts of physical exchange, whether in economics or thermodynamics. *In ectogenetic mutual exchange, both parties not only profit, but keep what they started with!* Rather than producing entropy, information exchanges are syntropic; that is, the whole *is* greater than the sum of the parts.

In both "feedforward" and feedback, human mental organizations reflect the evolutionary origin of *adaptive immunity*. Once basic internal patterns have been established, the natural tendency of any organism is to respond favorably to self-recognition or "likenesses" and to reject foreign influences. Like cell behavior that controls its own potential in order to cooperate with the organism in which it functions, a "hungry psyche," in order to assure itself of positive feedback, will often manipulate information to fit its larger organism: a man will perceive what he thinks others want him to perceive, will remember what he thinks others want to hear, and will frequently act the way others expect him to act.[42] When given the opportunity, humans will press to satisfy their own growth needs when they encounter differences in others, attempting to change others rather than themselves.[43] Cells and men *attempt to convert to their likeness anything distinctly foreign to their internal information.* When this is not possible, they make an effort to *eliminate* the alien element from the system or, when too much foreignness is present, they attempt to destroy it.

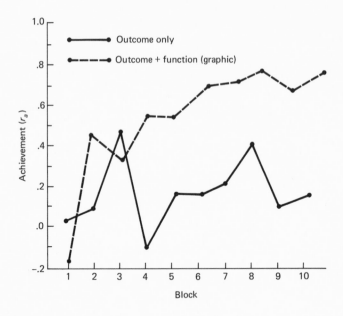

FIGURE 19A
Learning achievement improves substantially when nutrition (function) is added to evaluation (outcome). The figure shows a computer-aided results analysis where students in one case receive only evaluation in an outcome –only response, versus another case where outcome is supplemented with functional information about the subject.[44] (After Hammond.)

As in our microcellular example, feedback is not simply a binary "yes" or "no"; it is variable and flexible. In cellular biology, these phenomena are, for all practical purposes, invisible, seen only by embryologists, for example, in experiments with such things as transplantation and grafting. In the human situation, we are able to see and anticipate the various types of feedback that affect growth. Yet, as with cells, human feedback does not merely determine the form of primary growth activities; it is also often the primary source of *information nutrition.* (See Figure 19A.)

Although every individual is affected by his biological genetic makeup, in the absence of major organic defects, his primary load of genetic information is ectogenetic. Ectogenetic "cultural" information in Man comprises a ratio of data in his total inherited system so much greater than genetic data (biological supplements and information) that in modern cultures humans previously considered unfit, born with even relatively large biological defects, not only can become fit, but can make great contributions to our total system. Thus, if a human is born with less than optimal vision, hearing, musculature, etc., his ectobiological heritage can correct, supplement, or supplant these purely biological deficiencies.

The most critical variable in human growth, therefore, is our ectogenetic inheritance. This is a function of the broad information culture into which a person is born and, even more so, his very specific relational culture. Even if an immense ectogenetic information potential is available in the environment, a person will absorb only that which is *permitted* to be useful to him. More importantly, the *way* he is allowed to use this information determines the *forms* of growth potential that he develops. The rules laid down by feedback patterns to which an individual has become accustomed, provide the most important growth function—*the determination of the form of growth process that will be used by the growing person in future acts*—whether growth will be permitted, and, if so, whether it will be growth through accretion of *sameness* or assimilation of *differentness*.[45]

The process of feedback, the response to growth by the environment, and subsequent mediation of acts based on this response, are fundamental to the processes of organic growth at all levels. The concept of using feedback in machines for self-control originated many decades ago and its first application was in the classic water closet. In that mechanism, a simple float valve communicator directed the system's output related to its input. This type of response system simply tells the machine when to stop. The basic cycle can be seen in the figure below. Thus, when the output of water increases, the input valve closes. The extension of this process to what is called a "homeostatic" system was inspired by the body's internal temperature control system, which always maintains temperatures within desired operating limits. The general assumption that this process of achieving equilibrium is a fundamental characteristic of living systems has fostered a basic misunderstanding of living processes, as we shall see.

As the science of *cybernetics,* or control, evolved, the idea of automatic temperature control was implemented in thermostats

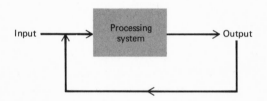

FIGURE 20

and in many other applications. In these applications regulation was carried much further than in our example of the float valve. Here, desired limits such as high and low temperatures are set in a temperature-detecting and -measuring instrument. When the temperature approaches the high limit, the furnace is shut down. When the heat subsides to the lower limit, the furnace is started and will run until the high limit once more shuts it down. The temperature is thereby kept within the desired limits. This process inserts a feedback control between output and input as diagramed below. This system corresponds not only to such organic systems

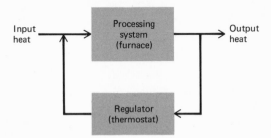

FIGURE 21

as bodily heat control, but to acts such as picking up a pencil from a table. In that act the eye acts as the regulator while the hand approaches the pencil. This motion is not one continuous act, but a series of discrete steps. In each segment of motions, the eye informs the arm and hand just where they are in relation to the pencil and keeps each small motion within the desired limits of motion. As the pencil is neared, the limits are narrowed so that the target is reached with precision. Studies of this process have shown that if the hand went too far in one direction, it was compensated for by being carried back too far in the opposite direction until it was stabilized on its course. In an improperly adjusted feedback system, this phenomenon can cause violent oscillation and result in loss of control. This type of compensatory process helped cyberneticians achieve the concept of self-correcting *negative* feedback. If a system were to go too far, certain data could introduce an input exactly the reverse of the primary one and thus achieve a continual operating system always in perfect control. In the furnace example, both a heater and cooler would be in parallel connection so that each could correct for the other. In electronic terms, this development brought about the idea of high fidelity. Previously, the major effort in reproducing sound was to remove distortion of an amplified signal by continually perfecting the amplifier and removing error. For a variety of reasons, this goal was difficult to achieve. Negative feedback was to solve the frustrating problem with an elegant simplicity. It merely introduced a regulating feedback device that took the output signal and turned it upside down, reintroduced it in a very short time into the input, and canceled the reciprocal error. A perfect output resulted. The diagram below illustrates this process.

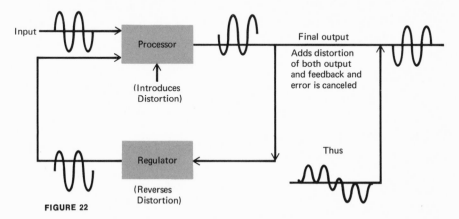

FIGURE 22

Although all these feedback processes compare well with natural or organic systems, they have created the general idea that positive feedback can cause instability in a system and even cause disintegration of the system itself. It would only increasingly magnify the original distortion. This is true in examples such as the electronic system illustrated; however, *it has practically nothing to do with organic growth systems.* If a process such as this existed in the growth processing system of even the simplest living thing, it could not grow; it would always maintain itself in a balanced state. This is observably true, in experiments and by all the rules of common sense.

The basic causal machinery of a living organism is not homeostatic. It is, in fact, quite the reverse, it is *heterostatic.* In the absence of *positive and nutritive feedback,* it can slow or lose the essential character of life, growth.

In considering the concept of feedback in a growing system, its potential to contribute to growth depends on two fundamental functions:

1. The affirmation of existing growth (information)
2. The introduction of new information

By supplying positive feedback we provide a *foundation* by which new information can be added. Affirmation of another also sets up the conditions for mutuality in the sense that such acceptance allows for new information to enter the responder's system as well. To see just how various kinds of feedback nurture or deny growth we can construct a model representing the mixtures of affirmation-negation and presence or absence of new (useful) information.

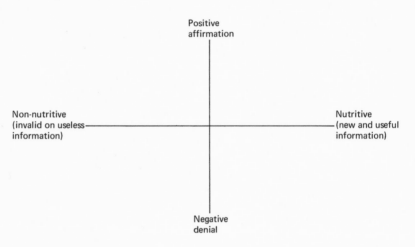

Positive
affirmation

Non-nutritive
(invalid on useless
information)

Nutritive
(new and useful
information)

Negative
denial

FIGURE 23

In this diagram we can divide feedback into eight categories:

A. Positive/Nutritive

B. Positive/Non-Nutritive

C. Negative/Nutritive

D. Negative/Non-Nutritive

E. Positive/No Nutrition

F. Negative/No Nutrition

G. None/Nutritive

H. None/Non-Nutritive

In defining the terms we are using in this feedback model it should be understood that "positive" does not mean a sort of total acceptance of all acts of behavior. It means that in responding to an act of another person *something* in that act is seen and responded to in a positive way—that the "tone" or character of the response is positivistic. Then, in supplying "nutrition," information, this can contain data that actually serve to correct the non-useful parts of the perceived act. A child who brings his mud pies in from the yard and puts them on the living-room rug might be complimented for his pies and then informed that mud pies most properly belong in other places. This can be considered a Positive/Nutritive feedback.

To this list of responses we can add one more category, that of *no* feedback at all.

I. None/No Nutrition

To appraise the results of these types of feedback we can visualize the initiator of an action or communication as a person with an elastic rope in his hand, the other end being held by the person responding (feeding back).

FIGURE 24

Initiator (*I*)   Responder (*R*)

If one flips such a rope up and down rapidly it sets up what is called a *sine wave* pattern, as below.

FIGURE 25

I   *R*

Depending on how the responder feeds back, this wave will take on different characteristics which dramatically illustrate the effect on the initiator.

Key—Initiation act or communication = solid line
Responder's feedback = dotted line

FIGURE 26: A. Positive/Nutritive

Mechanically, the responder picks up the rhythm of the wave action and adds new energy, stretching the rope and following the basic pattern. In this case the information going out, the existing growth, has been not only maintained but has been amplified by new information. A close look at one segment shows how.

FIGURE 27

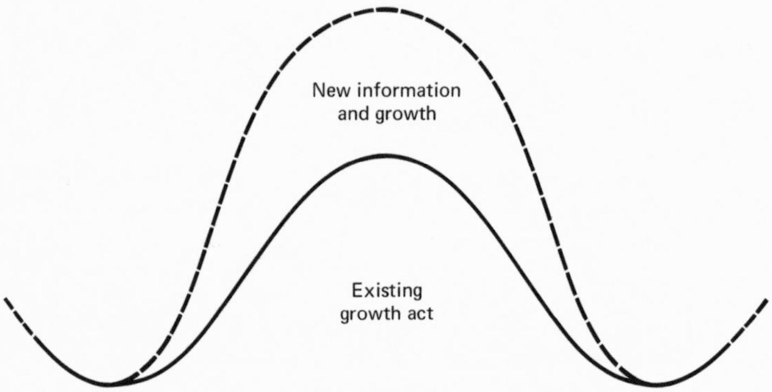

New information
and growth

Existing
growth act

Thus, growth has been affirmed and supplemented. This is the very highest level of growth feedback possible. What is not represented on the chart is the potential synergism of positive/nutritive responses. The content of the combined data is *more* than the sum of the information content of the separate messages.

FIGURE 28: B. Positive/Non-Nutritive

Here, the responder has simply reacted by supplying enough energy to keep the rope stretched in the same pattern and has introduced a force that distorts the pattern with invalid information.

While we can see that the responder agrees with and affirms the existing growth information, no real growth is evident. The presence of non-nutritive (invalid) information most often detracts from growth as it changes existing growth data. This is often the case of a nonmutual response by a person who would like the initiator to change to his pattern: to one employed by the responder.

FIGURE 29: C. Negative/Nutritive

The responder's act de-affirms, or negates, the existing growth of the initiator. "That's wrong, do it this way" is the common response. While this introduction of nutritive information serves a corrective function, just as it does in mechanical/electronic systems, in the case of *growth* behavior, since it reduces the foundation of growth, it becomes more difficult to add to the system. Every one of us has probably experienced this in a traditional schooling situation. The responder finds absolutely no "redeeming value" in the message communicated by the initiator.

FIGURE 30: D. Negative/Non-Nutritive

Self-denial is added to here in the sense that non-valid, non-useful information is also present. "You are wrong," this says, "do it this way." In this situation, however, "this way" turns out not to be useful in later growth efforts. Much ridicule is based on such a response; the foreman sends the new helper for a monkey wrench and then admonishes him and sends him back for a "left-handed" wrench, at which point he enjoys the negative growth effect of having belittled another person—seemingly—growing larger by comparison.

FIGURE 31: E. Positive/No Nutrition

This response simply affirms the growth act and helps maintain its momentum, but it adds nothing new. It provides a sort of yes-man effect, reassuring but not augmenting.

FIGURE 32: F. Negative/No Nutrition

A purely negative response with no information at all is an abject denial of growth. The initiator's act or message is "amputated." The signals of pain tell the initiator that this is a growth-threatening situation. Most commonly we hear this in a dialog: "Don't do that"; the initiator then asks "Why?" and receives "Because I say so." Nothing has been gained in this exchange and much has been lost.

FIGURE 33: G. None/Nutritive

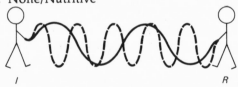

This transaction really indicates an act such as attending a lecture, reading a book, and the like. If the information received does not in some way support what the initiator is (and knows) it only provides information which can change the growth pattern but not build *on* it. Effective growth-stimulating communication of this sort must contain connective "hooks" so new information builds on what has gone before, and in these cases it is positive/ nutritive.

FIGURE 34: H. None/Non-Nutritive

Similar to the negative/non-nutritive, this response tends to distort subsequent growth with non-useful data. In that it does not de-affirm existing growth, its negative effect is less than the negative/non-nutritive. Usually this is a well-meaning response and is not aimed at ridicule or "cutting down to size."

FIGURE 35: I. None/No Nutrition

To sustain any effort with no feedback of any kind requires enormous effort. After a period of this, an individual will begin to imagine feedback, talking to himself, hallucinating, and so forth.* In extreme cases, in order to merely affirm existence, a person will even turn to self-mutilation to prove to himself that he can have an effect. Looked at this way, to ignore a person is perhaps the most destructive interrelationship that can exist.

Returning to our simplified model of feedback we can detect "zones" of growth effect.

---

*In a typical experiment, subjects were isolated in a cubicle, wore translucent goggles, had their fingers separated by cotton, etc., to reduce tactile stimulation. During and after a two-to-three-day isolation, subjects suffered impaired intellectual ability. Twenty-five of twenty-nine subjects reported hallucinatory effects and exhibited greater susceptibility to propaganda.[46]

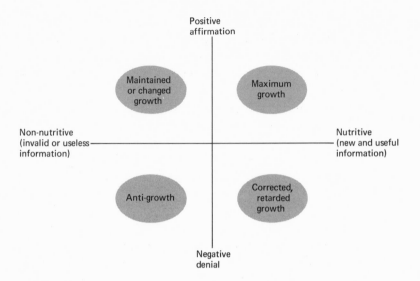

FIGURE 36

Like all models of complex human behavior these general descriptions are simplistic. Every response is a mixture of various kinds of feedback and change from minute to minute, from response to response. We can see, however, that the basic form or character of feedback and its potential effect on the other person can be identified.

There is, as well, a *cumulative* effect of feedback. If a person receives a great deal of one kind of feedback or another early in life, it sets up a dynamic balance in subsequent behavior. If, for example, a child receives consistent positive and nutritive feedback he will be able to tolerate high levels of negative response later in life. This is the common denominator of all great men who have worked many years on unpopular ideas. They have had enough early accumulation of positive growth that they can sustain many years of scorn and ridicule. Negative feedback works the same way. We see this in the cases of a relatively minor thing "setting a person off." Accumulated negativism can erupt into violent and destructive behavior with the final straw of another negative response. This is particularly true when a person has finally begun to achieve some minor growth and is trying new growth behavior. In this way, both information and feedback provide our ectogenetic pool for growth.

The cumulative process works in many different ways, in a relationship, for example. Over time, in person-to-person or group-to-group interaction, a pool of feedback effects will grow in positive and negative modes. A positive relationship can tolerate the occasional, and seemingly inevitable, negative reactions. They are offset by an effect much like a charge in a battery built up over a long period. Negative accumulations are also like the battery; if the battery has been drained for a long time, a short positive charge will not build up enough energy to start the engine. People who have had long periods of negative living require very long periods of consistent positive and nutritive feedback to be able to reach their potentials for growth.

To be a growth agent in life requires that our relationships with others be positive and, when possible, nutritive. This is not to encourage a form of false positivism or "permissiveness," for this can be non-nutritive indeed—it can supply responses that reinforce behavior which will be useless or damaging in later situations. What positive/nutritive, mutualistic feedback implies is the constant discovery of useful growth in all people, even in those cases where only the most primitive growth behavior can be found. By employing this growth as a foundation we can then facilitate it by supplying additional nutrition. In our every act of interrelationships, with people, with environments, with systems and things we can facilitate or repress growth for others and for ourselves.

In organic systems, the process of "feedforward" exists as well as feedback. In the furnace example, the furnace does not exist independent of the environment: Feedforward is the ambient temperature of the room when the furnace is first activated. This initial interaction condition sets up the alternative for the furnace; it can heat or not. In a living system the range of alternatives is much greater, and it controls the initial act of behavior. If a person is brought into a room, tied, and gagged, his range of alternative action is very limited. If he is not constrained, the room and its contents will set the limits: How many elements are available for processing, for combining, rearranging, and so forth? Thus, the possibility for alternatives itself has an effect on the organism. In social culture this exists mostly as "rules" or "laws" that operate as constraints to the creation of alternatives. In growth systems, the concept of freedom is an expression of broad alternatives in feedforward conditions. A feedforward alternative without the response of feedback, however, produces anarchy, that is, a loss of responsibility.

While in biologic terms the varieties of feedback so far described serve as a guide for diagnosing conditions of growth, in human, or psychological terms, even this description of feedback still does not fully characterize the relationships that inhibit or facilitate growth. In the mentally heterogeneous human population, *feedback is directly related to the form of growth being expressed by the person(s) supplying the feedback response.* It will be either accretive, replicative, or mutual. In other words, the form of growth in practice by the responding person adds another dimension to the evaluation and nutritive mix. A person conditions the acts of growth around him by his own place on the continuum of growth.

An individual born into an information-rich culture, but who is only allowed to use it in accretive or replicative ways, will develop only these limited growth processes. This situation produces a more limited human than does one resulting from a less information-rich, but a more mutualistic, culture.* The mutualistic person can be easily subcultured and grow with new information. The replicative-patterned person will be limited to his rigid and prejudical patterns regardless of exposure to new cultures and data. He will carry the scars of early growth experiments and their "amputations" through his life.

The environment's response to alternative attempts to grow quickly teaches a child which forms of growth work and which do not. True growth feedback is more than positive and nutritive. It acts in *mutuality* with the originating organism in a give-and-take model; *both* grow as a result. If feedback is only positive and nutritive, it may reinforce only a replicative form of growth. It may provide encouragement and information that merely reinforce the established pattern of the responder. It does not mean that the *responder* has grown in any new way. Just telling someone that an act is right and providing reinforcing data, without mutually growing by receiving and transmitting new information yourself, does not open the system to growth. Thus,

---

*Numerous studies now verify that behaviors from autistic to feeble-minded are the result of environmental deprivation. Experimental groups that receive higher levels of attention, love, and information—feedback and nutrition—consistently spurt far ahead of control groups.[47] In one such study under way at the University of Wisconsin it has been found that children of mentally retarded mothers who have been exposed to sensory and language stimulation over a period of years now (at age 4) exhibit average IQ scores of 128, approximately 35 percent higher than control-group children.[48]

in dynamic human relationships, feedback should be mutually enriching, providing evaluation, informational nourishment, and *reciprocal ratification.*

The varieties of feedback mentioned above fall easily into the patterns of growth described earlier: Accretive, replicative, and mutualistic feedback. Whether it affects growth in a positive or negative way, whether it opens or closes the growth form of the human receiving it, or whether it is repressive or destructive depends upon which *form* of the following categories of feedback is supplied.

    I. *Accretive* (enlarging the self). Here, the correction supplied is totally on the terms of the responding organism. Feedback is supplied to dictate the "copying" or enlargement of the responder, not to enhance growth of the initiator. No empathy or sympathy exists at this level; it is autistic.

    II. *Replicative* (multiplying the self or copying others). As with accretive, the aim of the person supplying feedback is to influence the initiator either to be more like him, *selfing,* or the reverse, to mediate his own response so that he becomes more like the initiator, *othering.*

    III. *Mutual* (joining with others to produce a shared effect). In this form of feedback, the response is facilitative and provides not only evaluation but *nutrition* for growth in the form of new information. In face-to-face relationships, the initiator and the responder both contribute to each other in a mutual transaction.

Depending on the form of feedback received, an individual or group's behavior will tend to follow the pattern of responses provided. Wide differences in forms of feedback result in vacillating behavior. The type of response generated by the environment causes a behavioral cycle to re-enact itself, repressed or encouraged, degenerated or regenerated. As we proceed to other chapters dealing with the questions of human psychological growth, we shall examine in more detail just how different types of feedback affect growth.

INTERNAL SYSTEMS: THINKING

Referring to Figure 37 we can observe once more the function of biopsychological processes and systems as they occur within

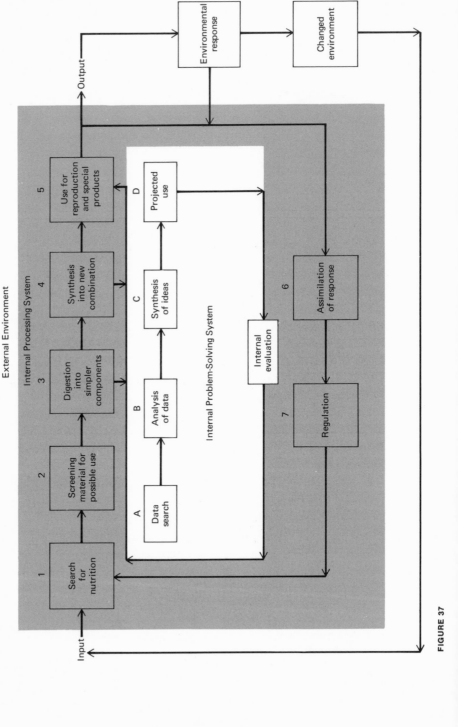

External Environment

Internal Processing System

Internal Problem-Solving System

Input

Output

1 Search for nutrition

2 Screening material for possible use

3 Digestion into simpler components

4 Synthesis into new combination

5 Use for reproduction and special products

A Data search

B Analysis of data

C Synthesis of ideas

D Projected use

Internal evaluation

6 Assimilation of response

7 Regulation

Environmental response

Changed environment

FIGURE 37

human thinking and problem-solving processes—yet another homologous system. The sequence of functions in the stream of consciousness that accompanies mental processing of a "problem"[49] is represented by the same steps living organisms follow:

I. *Searching* for available knowledge and information.
II. *Analyzing,* breaking down, and *digesting* the data.
III. Manipulating that information through imagination into new *synthesis,* into a hypothesis or idea.
IV. Internally projecting the *use* of the idea.
V. Evaluating the solutions for their "fitness," that is, their potential effect and value and the probable *feedback* that will be received.

Once this internal system has processed a problem to our satisfaction, we put it into the primary growth system and try it out in the external world. Although we do not know the details of all the internal processes of the cell, we can speculate that this creative internalization confers to the activities of Man a unique advantage—being able to submit a wide variety of growth alternatives to an *internalized* simulation of evolutionary natural selection process *before* actually applying it in the real world.*

Although we have so far considered the process by which the ectogenetic system of Man came about and how it operates, some of the parallel steps in the growing organization of information may indeed have created a reconstructed system even more fundamental than the ectogenes or culture. Because the primary mechanism of biologic endogenetic information accumulation has always occurred by creating mutated nucleotide codes and testing their fitness through natural selection, it is reasonable to imagine that both the external replication of the system through Man's tools and ideas, and the internal structure of the human system operate in an identical way. Man's brain may be, in fact, a miniature evolutionary laboratory.

---

*This ability may not be unique to humans; it may exist in cellular dynamics in a sort of internal "testing" of mRNA within the cytoplasm (regulatory enzymes). In this way, an unsuitable form of growth or product may be inhibited prior to its expression in an external world. Lack of such "evaluation" might result in damaging cell behavior.

To take a closer look at this concept, imagine that the brain is a colony consisting of 12 billion cells or so. If an "idea" is formed in the mind, it can actually represent the rearrangement, addition, or subtraction of codes among neurons. The neuron does not duplicate itself in the usual way, however. Its propagation and self-verification come about when it is subjected to the environment made up of *the other brain cells.* The nuclear data making up the coded pattern of these cells are the facts, opinions, and perceptions of the external environment, a condensed replica of that believed world. It may very well be that, like the transfer of DNA in such operations as temperate phage transduction, the idea attempts to grow in the "culture" by transmitting its code to other cells.* In this process it encounters normal environment pressures. If it fits, it is allowed to grow and affect many parts of the brain. Thus, by successfully propagating in the replica culture, it has been "pretested"; it can change, mutate, and even die within the cerebral system without incurring *any* gross biologic waste. The brain and the process of thinking may be, in effect, a miniature, accelerated, and magnificently more efficient evolutionary instrument—in quite real organic and biologic terms.

As an automatic and autonomic "laboratory" of testing reality, the enigma of the unconscious state of dreaming can also be explored within the conceptual framework of transformation. Although we may temporarily sever the connection of our link with external reality in sleep, the process of mutation and selection continues. Deprived of external effect and feedback, however, the brain may react unconsciously in the same way that consciousness operates in sensory-deprivation experiments. After a period of no perception and feedback, even while fully awake, a person will begin to fantasize and hallucinate. The unconscious, while it is attempting to perform normal "problem-solving" or what can be seen as evolutionary activity, may be greatly affected by loss of connection with the outside world.

---

*Recent research supports this hypothesis in that it shows that learning affects many cells and is not localized, as previous theories have suggested. These large ensembles of neurons in broad regions of the brain constitute a "population" or "colony" of specific memory(s). Thus, if stimuli do not evoke internal neuron growth (interrelationships) it is not learned.[50]

In a practical sense, by applying individual experience each of us can observe the evolution, mutation, and selection processes as they go on in our own minds at any time. The process we call imagination generates mutations with "novelty and diversity"; the function of natural selection or "judgment" is observed as the pressure of facts buffets an idea, allowing it to grow or die inside the mind.*

INTERNAL SYSTEMS: NON-THINKING

In each of the steps of information growth we can observe what might be called the principle of *redundancy*. Just as crystal lattices and DNA occur in repeated patterns, the rituals, mores, and traditions of cultures repeat information to ensure its being carried forward. The more redundancy in a system, the less "thought" or information manipulation is required to perform certain acts—those activities most necessary for survival. In somatic terms, the autonomic nervous system is just such a manifestation of redundancy. As we descend the ladder of organisms and cultures we encounter higher levels of redundant information and less diverse data. Insects, for example, have an extremely large amount of DNA, almost all of which is merely the same data repeated millions of times. Their "instincts" are thus highly programed and fixed. In primitive cultures we can observe the same phenomenon on a programed ectogenetic level. Behavior is rigidly controlled by often repeated rituals, totems, and taboos.

We can speculate that the function of redundant information makes up the most basic or habitual growth behavior of any organism, biological or psychological. As organisms mature, they develop increased ectogenetic "autonomic" behaviors and are more capable of tolerating increasing amounts of diverse information, thus providing more alternatives for growth. The *effect* of this process of redundancy is our concern in a study of behavior. Such patterns of information lead to habituated behavior, acts

---

*Though the ideas above are submitted here as a speculative hypothesis, a number of recent experiments have demonstrated that nucleotides do increase in the brains of animals when they are subjected to a psychologically and culturally enriched culture.[51] Today, the mechanics of memory more and more seem to conform to the basic means of biological and genetic memory—the nucleotide codes.

performed literally as "second nature," without thought. The building up of traditions provides mores that act accordingly for cultures. Accepted or normative behavior makes up the "rules of the game." Thus if any organism experimented with new behavior and was unsuccessful, behavior would autonomically fall back on redundant data. It becomes the basic repertory of behavior that fits the system and ensures survival.

We repeat again and again for our children those behaviors, habits, and values that ensure their doing those things most acceptable in their cultural environment. In this process of repetitive acquisition this information forms those behaviors that are so spontaneous and unthought as to be classified as "emotional," producing what we often call "thoughtless" acts. In such cases, logic or reason—active thinking—is unnecessary because the system is responding automatically. A threat to life, an act against conscience, or an instant liking or anger can be a response to environmental situations that are so fitting or unfitting to this redundancy that spontaneous recognition of foreignness or likeness occurs.

The magnified effect of emotion as redundancy can be likened to the difference between what happens when one suddenly stops a single automobile compared to the effect of stopping a string of cars. The "telescoping" of a chain accident, in which many autos, or effects, are traveling in the same direction at the same speed in contiguity, is much like the experience or learning that, occurring time and time again, collects momentum. It is difficult to alter such a collective effect; it is as difficult as breaking a habit or trying to change a person's basic beliefs. Any system becomes "emotional" when accumulated redundancy is confronted with change.

Nowhere is this better illustrated than in science itself. A scientific theory grows until it becomes implicit, creating a "second nature" of its own. When time and time again an idea is reinforced it becomes a rule or "law," operating automatically.[52] Thus, an objective scientist becomes "emotionally" attached to it. If evidence is presented in contradiction to the belief, it is often misinterpreted or even rejected. The history of science reflects the bitter emotional battles fought with every major advance that threatened past beliefs. Ectogenetic redundancy acts with the same blind instinct as does the endogenetic.

Whether Man thinks or acts based on logic or intuition, reason or emotion, he is governed by the fundamental laws of growth that express themselves in complex interaction with this total environment. Although the laws of growth are simple, behavior is indeed complicated by the mixture of forms operating simultaneously. In the application of such laws to a specific behavior we must be wary of oversimplification. In the following section we shall begin to examine some of the complexities of human growth and behavior in the light of transformation theory.

PART TWO
BEHAVIOR

PATTERNS
OF HUMAN GROWTH
AND MOTIVATION
SIX

The third postulate of the theory of transformation is that *all behavior is growth motivated.* The phenomenon of "mental health" occurs only when individual forms of growth are congruent with those expressed in the contiguous culture. Repression of these forms results in regressive growth behaviors and produces what is called "mental illness." Recapitulated, the continuum of biological growth forms—accretive, replicative, and mutual—is manifested in the psychological behavior of human beings and is carried forward to new levels of growth.

GROWTH MOTIVATION

Each human receives *two* genetic "pools" of information. The first, biologically bound DNA, not only determines the morphology of the human organism, but contains within it the legacy of a universal set of growth drives. Our "nature" and primary inheritance, therefore, are a set of physiological-psychological equipment *and* its impelling forces of growth.

Our second inheritance, the acquired second nature, is ectogenetic; it consists of the available information in our subculture and provides through its responses the possibilities for the expression of growth. Just as the determination of a cell occurs as a result of the phenotypal influences on the genotype, so it is with the emerging human psychological personality. The contiguous human beings and other environmental materials provide the basic ectogenetic information and create the feedback that determines how this information can be used. Regardless of the quantity of information present, the quality of the culture and its prevailing growth form set up the possible range of accretive, replicative, and mutualistic growth behaviors.

Psychological growth behavior is expressed by the way the organism absorbs, processes, and uses environmental nutrients in some act that affects the environment. All behavior, in this sense, is reciprocal: a dynamic balance of internal affect and external effect.

In each probe at growth, the human organism receives internalized signals of pleasure when growth is successful and signals of displeasure or pain when these attempts are met with no effect or with antagonism.[1] If the human cannot achieve mutualistic pleasure as he descends the continuum of growth, *he will receive pleasure through the other forms*. A destructive act that represents displeasure to a mutualistic person may indeed be producing pleasure in the accretive person effecting the destruction. Although we can be sure that there are qualitative differences between the "joy" of mutualistic growth and the "pleasure" of accretive growth, the difficulty of objective discrimination between these differences is such that a pleasure orientation, or "hedonistic philosophy," can hardly serve as a guide to behavior, not, at least, in mutualistic societies.

Growth at *any* level, however, creative to destructive, does serve the goals of organic life, just as a mental "disease" serves the patient. Obviously, if *no* growth can be achieved, we have stasis and death. The physical disintegration that we can observe under a microscope when a cell is confronted with a no-growth culture is aptly described by mental patients who say they are "coming apart" or "going to pieces." The final act in a static situation is the elimination of massive signals of pain, or death. The psychological mechanism will not allow for a condition of no-growth and, in effect, as in our example of the overloaded antibody, is self-selective. In extincting itself, it actually serves the total force of evolution.

In developing a model of psychological evolution, our concern will be mainly with the fruition of a complete range of behavioral forms as they relate to any and all ectogenetic information heritages. If the form of psychological growth develops to the mutualistic state, the integration of available ectogenetic information is facilitated, regardless of content. Obviously, if mental nutrition is denied, growth will be affected, but the achievement of mutuality allows an individual to deal creatively with the various

112

new subcultures that he may encounter throughout life. Thus, although we shall consider the diagnosis of growth repressions, the central objective is to expose means to detect opportunities for growth so that higher forms of growth may be deliberately evolved.*

PSYCHOLOGICAL FORMS OF GROWTH

We also carry the acquired redundancies of our ectogenetic pool as we have seen. Like the redundant DNA of cells the human system also builds up such repeated data, described as "habits" and emotions. These can also consist of what are referred to as "hidden drives": acts of growth formerly denied. When given an opportunity of experience, they will frequently emerge in unexpected outbursts—as acts both *for* growth and *against* forces that suppress growth.

Of all the alternatives for growth we are offered, we can experience only a few. Of all the repressions of growth we can never overcome all. These residues of denied and threatened growth linger in our memories and may accumulate over long periods. When this occurs, the internal pressure of the growth system cries out for either expression or remedy. It can provoke frustration, confusion, anxiety, and depression. Thwarted growth, however, is the universal condition of all living systems. There can be no completely expressed growth for, as we grow more and more, new ways to grow will always be found. In this sense, perhaps the greatest tragedy of Man is the lost opportunity when he himself turns away from exploring a new avenue of growth. Of all life, Man became a kind of ambivalent yet dynamic creature, fearful of the unknown, afraid of what new threat to growth may emerge, yet ever eager to build new extent.

In attempting to construct a useful model of behavior, we shall start by reviewing the various forms of growth in both biological and psychological terms and then go on to a more detailed example of an analytical technique. First, let us review the three basic forms of growth in psychologically descriptive terms:

I. *Accretive.* Biologically, forms of self-expansion and enlargement. Psychologically, an expression of the "me" or the

---

*What Dr. Halbert Dunn calls "high-level wellness."[2]

"you." It includes the need for absolute possession and control of either an external or an internal world. It is self-seeking and autistic. In its reverse, or complementary, form, it is the need to be totally possessed and dominated.

II. *Replicative.* Represented biologically by self-duplication. Psychologically, this is the "mine" or the "yours"; a result of either influence of, or identity with, the external environment. It involves both modifications of the outside world to copy the internal, and the reverse, changing of the inside world to mimic the external.

III. *Mutual.* Biologically, characterized by recombination and fusion. Psychologically, this behavior represents itself in the "our." It is behavior that is self-extension through sharing— reciprocal exchange of growth with the outside world.

We can represent these three forms of growth as a spectrum of behavior, ranging from accretive selfing on one end to accretive othering on the other, with mutualism in the center.

Accretive (selfing)	Replicative (selfing)	Mutual	Replicative (othering)	Accretive (othering)

At the left we see growth by extension of the self while at the right growth is by attachment to others. It is important to note that *all growth behavior is a mixture of these various forms.* A cell, person, organization, or culture, for example, that has achieved mutualistic growth has done so *by building on accretive and replicative behaviors.* Thus, mutualism is founded on lower forms and cannot exist without them. A total abandonment of the self in an attempt to achieve "pure" mutualism leaves nothing to be exchanged; it would be nothing more than an accretive othering. *Lower forms of growth provide the self-maintenance needed for mutualism to be successful.**

These growth forms of accretion, replication, and mutualism correspond to a great extent to the ancient Greek behavioral description of Eros, Philia, and Agape. *Eros,* or accretive growth, is the existence of nothing but the "I," *Philia* recognizes the existence of another and "outside" I as a replication, and *Agape* is seen as a total sharing of love, the "we." In more modern terms,

---

*A more detailed exposition of this phenomenon is covered in Appendix II.

we can see that all of the fragmentary theories of psychology easily fit into the various patterns and manifestations of growth. Drives and compulsions for such things as power, possession, and dominance, as well as the lower biological urges, are ones of self-expansion through production of offspring, emphasis on sex, and so forth; thus they are accretive in their nature. Needs for manipulation, as well as being manipulated—dependent and counterdependent modes of behavior—are basically replicative. Mutualistic patterns are found in empathic and creative behavior—drives for self-fulfillment and self-actualization. The existence of an inherited "collective unconscious," as proposed by Carl Jung, demonstrates the potential and power of the ubiquitous ectogenetic heritage, whereas environmental forces and stimulus–response–reinforcement models show basic parts of the functional interaction of growth and feedback. *It can be observed as one reviews the catalogue of motivational theories that there is no human behavior that cannot be subsumed and explained under the fundamental drive to grow and to transform.*

Although the descriptions that follow will trace the observable course of expressed behavior, it is important that we reflect here on the question of latent drives. As an individual or a culture evolves to higher levels and manifestations of growth, the potential for regression or atavism is always present. In other words, if a human is not allowed to grow *with* his cultural environment, then he must of necessity grow *against* it. If he cannot incorporate it into his system in such a way that he can extend himself as part of *its* system, then he will automatically regress to an emphasis of lower growth form. Descending the ladder from mutual behavior, he will attempt to influence the external world to be more complimentary to his relatively static internal system and thus will produce a replicative form of growth. If replication does not work, the drive to grow will then manifest itself by calling on a lower level—accretion—*forcing* the environment to be an extension of himself and, if necessary, eliminating or "extincting" those parts of the environment that are "nonself." In this regressive process, we see a human de-evolving into an "antibody" that destroys foreignness represented by what is perceived as external cultural "antigens." As in biological systems, if there are too many antigens, the system destroys itself in the process of attempting to assimilate too much. It becomes self-destructive.

Freud described higher growth forms as "sublimated"; however, rather than being a sort of artificial replacement of what

Maslow described as the "deep, dark, and dirty" urges of Man, they are, in a very real sense, completely natural evolutions of behavior. The lurking "unconscious" is simply the collection of the heritage of growth we carry with us. Like the outgrown inner shell of a sea animal, they serve their purpose by supporting and maintaining growing life.

Let us examine a general and simplified narrative description of the three basic forms of growth behavior. Although it may be true that a single individual seemingly fits one of these broad descriptions, it is important to recall once more that *each person deals with his environment, human and otherwise, in a mixture of mutual, replicative, and accretive growth.*

MUTUAL BEHAVIOR

The "healthy" *mutualistic* person can be characterized by an empathic, give and take, creative attitude. He is interested in his environment, deeply involved in his outputs and work, innovative in his contributions, deep and open in his relationships with other persons, and derives not only satisfaction but joy in many experiences in life. He feels that he is a "natural" for the kind of work that he is doing and will often sacrifice immediate pleasure and, at times, would even risk his own survival to achieve what he feels is a contribution to a greater cause or organism. There is little separation between him and his environment, for he both absorbs it and projects himself into it. The characteristic of mutuality is evident in his consideration of the things and people about him, and his ability to respond in kind and mutuality to any kind of behavior. He listens to other people and is willing to be affected by them as well as having effect on them, at their own level of growth. When frustrated by circumstances, he turns problems into opportunities and challenges, and the result is heightened input and output. He loves both himself and others.

REPLICATIVE BEHAVIOR

The *selfing replicative* person wants things to be basically "like" him. Responses other than habitual ones are geared to bring things "into line" and to influence them to be more "his way." He has a relatively limited scope of interest and associates principally with those who share his own feelings. In some cases, his needs for power and influence are represented by "neurotic" distortions

116

and behavior that tend toward the envious, the authoritative, and the compulsive. His work is more a means rather than an end in itself, and it creates neither great joy or sorrow: Money and possessions can become growth ends in themselves. His loyalty and devotion are to "his group": those which he builds as extensions of himself. He will protect these extensions from any intrusion by foreign ideas or persons and thus is defensive and discriminatory in his relations with others. He changes little as new information is made available to him, desiring to change others rather than to exchange with them. He likes himself and those who are like him.

The *othering replicative* individual can be described by his tendency to attach himself in dependent relationships with others, and to derive his strength, identity, and growth through them, their organizations, and their ideas. The normal replicative phase of infancy is manifested in hero worship and emulation. The adult "otherer" will devote himself to others in self-effacing and negative ways, often submerging himself in the sea of "followers." Passive vicarious pleasures often dominate his interests rather than participative ones. His greatest pleasure is derived from belonging and the positive feedback that he gets from fitting in. Because identity and growth can be constantly threatened by the whims of others, much anxiety can occur in this form of replicative behavior. The replicator relates well to other replicators, but he can be frightened by relationships that call for high-level exchanges in which he feels too much may be expected of him. Like the selfing person, he becomes a creature of habit and will not change easily except when his group membership demands it, and then he will change abruptly. He does not like himself and looks for others to imitate.

ACCRETIVE BEHAVIOR

In considering the phenomenon of purely *accretive* growth, we are dealing with a case of either substantial deprivation of information and feedback, or massive amounts of negative, nonmutual, nonnutritive feedback—a person, for example, who has been reminded at every turn that he is a worthless person or that there are very few (or no) alternatives open to him. With othering accretive behavior, because his relationship with the outside world is characterized by failure, his internal self begins to disintegrate. He manifests the symptom of being cut off or alienated from the rest of his environment. Being thwarted in his attempts to grow externally, the symptoms of rationalization, projection, obsession, and so forth, are magnified to such an extent that most, if not all, feedback loops become closed. The classic symptoms of compulsion can become regressed to creating an inner world, as in "schizophrenia." Here, one symptom is a total disruption of the information process which results in such frantic attempts to absorb new data (perpetually screened from his system) that attention cannot remain focused.

Ultimately, othering accretive growth can result in either flight into total withdrawal from reality in order to achieve a state of imaginary internalized growth, or in selfing, an urge totally to possess or to destroy external reality. The individual can experience this "destructive growth" through relative enlargement by destroying the nonlikeness around him or through such reality-distorting methods as drugs or alcohol. In these cases, the projected fantasy world becomes real; it can be made to be "like" the individual. This becomes a world that he can control and in which he can *grow*.

MENTAL DISEASE

In aggravated cases of repression, represented by low levels of replicative as well as in all accretive growth, we encounter the phenomena variously described as neurotic and psychotic.[3] These behaviors are entirely *normal*; however, they are natural pleasure-producing expressions of low-level growth that occur when higher levels have been denied. The subpotentials for these so-called "illnesses" exist in all biological organisms, all humans, and cultures. An amoeba that has often been amputated, for example, will learn never to reach full size; it will never progress to the level of growth by replication.

As we descend the continuum of growth from mutuality, we encounter the symptoms prevalent in the "pathologies" of Man: rationalization, projection, obsession, and loss of connection with others and with reality.* These symptoms represent a return to

---

*The lack of mutuality in some cases has resulted in expressions of exaggerated or false altruism; i.e., most philanthropic organizations were begun by "robber barons" and "exploiters." It is the case of getting more than you give or vice versa that can produce feelings of guilt or insufficiency.

such basic self-growth preoccupations as external selfing growth through sex, possessiveness, control, and dominance, or internal othering growth through exclusion of external reality and creation of a fantasized internalized reality. Mutuality is denied in an inability to take help, as in counterdependence, or, the reverse, not being able to give help, as in exaggerated dependence, total self-love or self-hate.*

How destructive growth can result from purely accretive or low-level replicative growth patterns can be observed in a biological cancer or virus, or, for example, in biopsychological terms, in the case of an "undifferentiated, unspecialized" organism such as an uneducated, poor, ghetto-born child, convinced by his parents (who didn't want him), his neighbors (who don't need him), and other environmental responses, that he is "no good." He finally attempts to grow by extending his negative self to the environment which has frustrated him. Accretive growth often destroys by attempting to force the outside world to be like the ruins of the internal one. Another manifestation of these destructive types of growth is the "belittling" or "cutting down to size" technique that provides ephemeral sensations of *growth by comparison.* Ridicule as a distorted form of humor is one manifestation of this.

"Affective" emotions such as anger, hate, or fear, are all results of growth negation. These can be exemplified in a broad spectrum ranging from the frustration of being denied perceived new growth opportunities (such as in the civil rights movement) to actual amputation of an existing extension generating hate. Growth is such a powerful and overriding motivation that when achieved growth is cut off catastrophic results can occur. Murderous rage can be directed against the person or group perceived as responsible, particularly if the lost extension is accretive or replicative. In those cases, it is difficult for the injured party to imagine how he might regain this part of his lost self.

Punitive emotion can also be expressed by withdrawing growth from someone who has negatively affected self-growth. Cutting

---

*In some instances, a particular and narrow "mutualistic" type of skill—painting, entertaining, or dancing—will be exaggerated in a distorted compensation for denial of mutualistic growth in other areas. These specialized growth areas reveal a mutualism that is, in fact, accretive. This paradox is evident in the exchange process this type of person employs. His relationships with individuals are extremely limited; his mutuality with faceless audiences provides positive (non-nutritive) feedback.

one's self off or sulking is a typical response. In some cases, this act degenerates to hurting the self in order to affect negatively a parent or friend. If you are an extension of someone you can hurt him by self-destructive acts. This may be the penultimate act of the child of an accretive parent. Hate for someone who has totally denied another's growth can cause suicide.

A FUNCTIONAL DESCRIPTION

In all the above cases, transformation theory takes the position that new growth in repressed areas can often be transdetermined and developed with techniques of incremental and facilitative mutualism. Certain types of group therapy, for example, can create the conditions for a recognition of commonality with others and can provide the opportunity for mutual growth as the participants discover their own growth and value by aiding one another. Of course, as in biological transdetermination, behavior will autonomically revert to lower growth forms if this mutualistic environment is not incremental and is substantially changed. New self-extensions (internal and external) are amputated if new behaviors that produce successful growth in an artificial situation are not realized when practiced in the real world.

Each of the behavioral modes and forms of growth described can be related to the series of *functions* that a person performs in his ever-recurring cycles of psychological growth. The following chart represents many of these behaviors as they relate to this functional pattern.

Obviously, even the chart is a very simplistic description of the complexities of human behavior. Such approximate models or "labels" deter the true identification of human personality and potential. To avoid the pitfalls of such conveniences, we shall outline in the following chapter a somewhat more comprehensive model designed to identify the expressed and repressed areas of human development.

GROWTH SYSTEM FUNCTIONS	ACCRETIVE	REPLICATIVE	MUTUAL
SEARCH FOR NUTRITION	Apathetic, listless, or frenetic Disoriented Rejection of all conventional Much is seen as threatening	Interest in common things and people Boredom toward unknown areas Serious, on guard, intolerant Denial of ignorance	Eager curiosity and exploration Strong interest in many ideas, people, and things Interest in differing viewpoints Playfulness and zest
SCREENING	Accepts everything or nothing—arbitrary Distorts perceptions grossly to match own thoughts "Closure" either extremely rapid or not at all	Simplistic rejection of nonagreement Cynicism, mistrust of new information Tentative acceptance of changed data Reduces cognitive variables	Open to wide variety of inputs Absorbs freely Uses priority system to discriminate Tolerance of ambiguity
DIGESTION	Sees wholes—black and white Polarization Confusion Makes useless connections	Matches analysis with existing classifications—interchangeable Uniformity	Analysis of material into many parts under a variety of analogous classifications
SYNTHESIS	Mechanical sameness of assembly Disconnectedness with stored data No recall or rigid, repetitive memory No ideas or all fantasy	Assembles parts into matching configuration with preformed opinions Low recall of stored data that are unfavorable or new Few new ideas Accepting conventional solutions	Attempts to put new information together with different stored material, looks for wholes High recall of stored data Many ideas, imaginative Good (empathic) judgment
USE	Self-centered "What's the use?" giving up Nothing to work for or at, or everything to do and no way to do it No use for others	Perpetuates sameness, safety Sometimes careless Works "on" others, expands self through others—copying-imitation Rushes into action	Courage—working with others to create mutual effects on environment Willing to take detours if they can further his goal
ASSIMILATION OF FEEDBACK	Little interest (see search for nutrition)	Positive accepted, negative screened out or distorted	Positive and negative accepted Search for more information
FEEDBACK RELATIONSHIPS WITH OTHERS	Frenetic talk or complete silence Loss of connection Alienation and suspicion Hopelessness and despair Utter selfishness or selflessness Capricious Reliance only upon self for self Threats and pleading	Fear of rebellion Generally critical reaction to other's ideas Talks rather than listens High defense level Insecure and cynical Partial responsibility Dependent or counterdependent Fear and guilt	Interested in sharing ideas Listens and talks Meaningful exchange of feelings Low defense level Secure and calm Responsible Interdependent

FIGURE 38

A GROWTH MODEL
SEVEN

As has been pointed out earlier, growth in all of life's manifestations is transdeterminational. If we supply positive and nutritive feedback as growth progresses in those around us they will achieve higher levels of growth. In constructing a model of growth behavior, therefore, two fundamental properties of the environment must be considered. One is the amount and variety of nutrition that is available in the environment, and the other is the form of feedback received from the environment when growth attempts are made.

We can use many possible categories for nutritive materials in the environment. For purposes of simplification, we could categorize them in the following broad groups: people, information, and objects. These can be further subdivided under people as individuals, homogeneous groups, and heterogeneous groups; under information as writing, symbols, and speech; and under objects as objects, sets, and systems. One way of assessing the nutritional mix that a growing individual receives is to measure the quantity and quality of each of these.

We can, as illustrated in the graph, set relative measures on the kind of exposure that an individual receives in each type of nutrition. This would give us a preliminary idea of the elements that can be manipulated in experiments with growth. If an imbalance of materials existed, it would be relatively easy to detect and remedy it. For example, a child who is exposed to a wide variety of objects and is allowed to manipulate them, but who does not have the opportunity to come into contact with heterogeneous

Environment

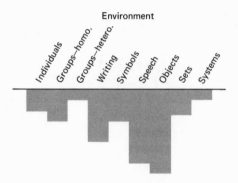

Level of Availability of Materials

FIGURE 39

groups, will tend later to be more interested in using physical materials as his growth medium, but might not develop broad and new relationships with people.

On the other side of the coin, the quality of feedback determines whether or not the use of any of these nutritive materials will be achieved through accretive, replicative, or mutual growth. As we have seen, the pattern of behavior encountered by the growing infant tends to re-express itself in his adult behavior.[1] Today, in the highly developed western civilizations, children are exposed to an extremely broad nutritional environment.* The widespread availability of inexpensive books, games, and so forth, and almost universal use of television provide abundant nutritional enrichment. Yet this can produce its own paradox, one never before encountered in such magnitude by Mankind. Parents who in their youth did not have the opportunity to absorb the vast materials now available often do not provide the breadth of feedback needed by the child. By practicing more replicative behavior and attempting to produce "a chip off the old block" or a child "cast in the same mold," they attempt to repeat their own patterns. As the child grows and absorbs large amounts of differentiated nourishment from other sources, he may not be able to mutualize the education process. In other words, while parents are willing to educate their children, they may not be willing to join with them and be educated *by* them. This paradox, of course, creates a destructive growth imbalance.

---

*The National Assessment of Educational Progress, sponsored by the Education Commission of the States, in their testing of scientific knowledge in national sample groups of up to 100,000 young people showed that scores of young people are *directly related* to the educational attainments of their parents.

When the maturing and mutualizing child encounters resistance from a replicative parent, larger and larger areas of differences arise between them. These differences can lead to apathy, rejection, and rebellion as both begin to reject each other and to lean toward groups with whom they can have more commonality. The "hippie" retreats from sterile growth of this constructive subculture in order to find commonality elsewhere.[2]

The reverse can also happen, that is, the cultural context applied is too broad. This situation occurs when the parent criticizes a very young child for doing something that might be frowned upon by the neighbors, thus attempting to force a young child into a cultural situation much broader than the real one of the family unit. The child may not have reached the age where his drive has extended to joining with larger cultural units. A similar phenomenon affects adults in mental institutions. The purpose of the institution is to cure the so-called illness of the patient, to provide opportunities for the patient to develop capabilities he has either never developed or lost. In a patient's early attempts to extend himself, the actual cultural area of his growth extends to his relationship with those closest to him, the therapist, his wardmates, and perhaps his family. In this subculture, many forms of experimental behavior are possible and permissible which would not be so in the outside world. Too frequently the broader culture is used for evaluation of the patient's acts and he is denied opportunities for starting incremental growth. Obviously, he must be able to build his cultural framework; but this act, like the development of any new skills, must be done by gradual subculturing until the new capabilities allow him to mutualize with the larger world. In other cases, the narrow nonmutualistic culture imposed by the artificial institutional "caring" process denies the opportunity to subculture with the larger world and creates exaggerated dependence behavior.

Large institutions such as schools often create a similar nonsympathetic environment. They expect the student to grow *on the terms of the faculty*. They want to change but not be changed. Unfortunately, they often relate to a culture either too narrow or too broad for the student population. An example is the condemnation by giant universities of their students for not understanding what administrators perceive as an institutional economic necessity for such activities as participating in governmental defense research. They are not joining *with* the students or growing mutually with them. They expect the student body to accept their own cultural situation without attempting to exchange and to see the other reality of the student's culture. Nonexchange, once demonstrated on one side of a transaction, naturally encourages reciprocal rejection, as by the student bodies of such institutions.

All of these non-empathic relationships deny human beings the opportunity for natural growth. It is a denial that robs both of a great opportunity, for a person must grow as well as help grow. He must grow inwardly through the contributions of others, as well as outwardly by his own contributions. Unfortunately, this fact of natural life has often not been recognized or understood.

The continued process of feedback occurs as an oscillating degeneration or regeneration exchange between any two individuals. To illustrate this, we have diagramed a series of relationships that can exist between two individuals. Their basic forms of growth are expressed as accretive (A), replicative othering $[R(o)]$, replicative selfing $[R(s)]$, and mutuality (M).

In this illustration, we shall not represent both forms of accretive growth, because accretive selfing and othering operate in much the same manner as do replicative behaviors.

Person A   Person B

M   M

R(s)   R(s)

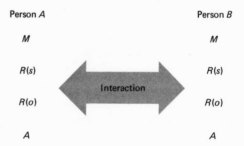

R(o)   R(o)

FIGURE 40   A   A

If, for example, two accretive individuals meet and directly confront one another, each may attempt to enlarge himself by either controlling or diminishing the other. No real growth can occur. In this case, there is no commonality, sympathy, or empathy, because each attempts extensions of his own internal pattern without regard for others.

Person A   Person B

M   M

R(s)   R(s)

R(o)   R(o)

FIGURE 41   A ————————>< ———————— A

A similar relationship exists between two replicative selfing individuals. Once more, the individual is attempting to replicate his own pattern to make the other person more like himself, not by direct control but in thought, deed, dress, and so forth. The relationship becomes one of conformities in conflict. Again, the result is little or no growth because each is unwilling to change his own pattern and wants only to change the other.

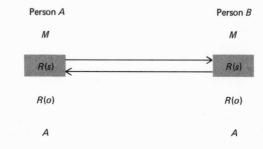

FIGURE 42

Omitting the "psychotic" behavior of accretive growth, if we consider the relationship of a replicative selfing person to one manifesting replicative othering, we see that growth does occur. Each is able to extend himself by either incorporating or emulating the other. This is perhaps the most common form of low-level growth. Since sophisticated cultures have only in recent years begun to emerge from massive replicative movements, many people naturally expect this form of behavior to be the norm. The replicative person, having been denied more mutualistic growth, can often alternate selfing and othering; that is, he may copy others he perceives to represent images of growth, and also sustain this othering as he attempts to replicate his own copied pattern. This can be diagramed:

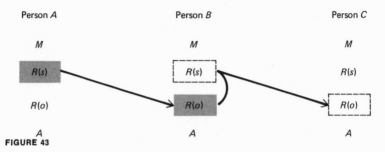

FIGURE 43

A major fallacy in current interpretations of human relationships is the fact that some scholars maintain that only "mature" individuals can grow through each other. Although his highest level of growth is achieved through other mutualistic people, the truly mutual person is capable of mutualizing with people at *any* level of growth behavior. In practicing this type of exchange, the mutual person will, chameleon-like, adopt a variety of behaviors so that information and enrichment can flow. An example is the variety of modes of behavior expressed by an effective supervisor. He might use a direct challenge to motivate a selfing person and, at the same time, use power to influence the othering person. In each of these exchanges, he can attempt ever higher levels of exchange so that more mutual forms of growth can evolve. The broadly mutualistic person will not have to attack "foreignness" in others, because he is able to see himself in them and help them discover and grow through this common base.

In this and other cases, transformation theory takes the position that new growth in repressed areas can often be trans-determined and developed with techniques of incremental and facilitative mutualism.[3]

For positive transformation of behavior, the fundamental conditions of growth are:

I. Identification of potentials that have been realized and those that have been suppressed.
II. Opportunity to experience mutualism in a continuing situation that will not threaten new extension of self, and in which growth is perceived as useful to both the self *and* others.
III. Positive and nutritive feedback accompanying growth attempts.
IV. Gradual broadening of environmental situations so that interface with more of the existing culture is achieved.

Many traditional techniques have actually reversed this process. The therapeutic situation that denies the patient the opportunity to affect his therapist is, to the patient, simply another proof of his inability to grow in mutualistic ways. This frustration can cause reversion to such accretive behavior as extending the self through identification with the therapist or, conversely, a rejection of the absolute "foreignness" of the therapist. False positive feedback also often occurs in these situations. A classic example is the "I'm doing this for your own good" syndrome, which again reinforces nonmutuality by pointing out that "you need me but I don't need you."

New techniques of face-to-face, involved therapy allow the

therapist to admit the commonality he shares with the patient and also allow the patient to affect the therapist. By giving *to* the therapist the patient can accept *from* the therapist. This absolute need and pressure to mutuality can be seen in all organic growth, even in primitive rodents who in experiments prefer to exchange work for food rather than to receive it gratis.[4] In the facilitation of growth, the frequent examples of spontaneous "cures" of mental ills point out how often this call of mutualism will autonomically flourish if even the most fragmentary opportunities exist for it to occur.*

Each of these basic behavioral modes and forms of growth can be related to the series of functions that a person performs in his ever-recurring cycles of psychological growth. To help identify excluded and repressed areas, the following chart represents the relationships of material and feedback as they might occur in a single individual.

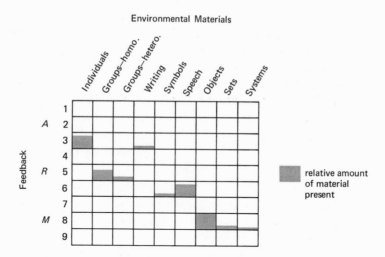

FIGURE 44

The chart is primarily a facilitative instrument to allow any individual to identify more easily which of his or another's growth

---

*Experiments at Hawaii State Hospital with patients such as psychotics, alcoholic drug addicts, and a suicidal male homosexual have shown that putting patients on their own, with practically no therapy, in groups ("family living units") has resulted in significant improvement. These "hospital cases" learned to take care of each other, hold jobs, and solve their own problems.[5]

potentials have been realized. It highlights areas of psychosocial malnutrition as well as how feedback from the environment might be affecting attempts to grow. It is, in effect, a map of ectogenetic nutrition and relational inheritance. It allows us directly to participate in reformulation of the genetic pool and to develop specific means of nourishing human growth, particularly in deprived situations. For instance, in a case of dealing with "retarded" children, some 20 percent of severe retardation is due to genetic organic causes;* the rest is primarily due to ectogenetic deprivation. This statistic is demonstrated by the fact that, although severe organic retardation occurs with the same frequency in all cultural situations, the vast majority of cases of retardation are of "unknown origin" and are almost ten times higher in culturally deprived populations (the poor, black, Spanish-speaking, and so forth). *These cases of retardation occur primarily because of ectogenetic, not genetic, deprivation.*

In a large number of experiments, researchers have well established the fact that not being concerned with the cause of repressed growth, but merely supplying positive feedback and nutrition remedies the problem of repressed growth enormously. Now that many "mystery diseases" of retardation can be traced to the origins of frustrated growth, the opportunity exists to provide more specific treatments and growth encouragement. To amplify the models presented so far requires a more complete picture, however. It must contain both the nutritional elements as well as feedback levels. One way of accomplishing this viewpoint is to relate these in a "system matrix."

The following system model includes the processes (functions) of growth related to the various materials in the environment. The vertical elements represent the functional "inputs" that are used in growth; located horizontally are the materials that represent the things that are affected, the "outputs" of growth. In the middle we shall attempt to evaluate the processes that take place as a function is related to the growth occurring through and with the environment.

---

*Chromosome abnormalities such as mongolism or Down's syndrome, other genetic problems like phenylketonuria (PKU—lack of an essential enzyme), and fetal effects from syphilis and German measles account for serious retardation (IQs of 30 and below).

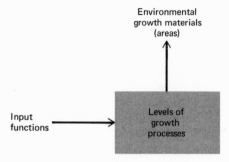

Environmental
growth materials
(areas)

Input
functions

Levels of
growth
processes

FIGURE 45

To determine the level of growth in each part of the above matrix, we could set up a 9-point scale: 1, 2, and 3 represent ascending levels of accretive growth; 4, 5, and 6 of replicative; and 7, 8, and 9 of mutual growth. In assessing the growth system of an individual, for example, an analysis could be made to determine the form of growth behavior dominating the employment of a specific processing function as it applies to each particular type of environmental material. If a person demonstrates that a high level of regulation limits his possible search for connections with other individuals (he does not seek out acquaintances with persons from other ethnic groups, for instance), the relative value for growth in this first cell (search–individuals) might be a 3 or 4. This would indicate that he was essentially self-seeking replicating and restricting his search for individual connections to people very much the same as himself.

As we move down to the next function of screening, we might discover that his selective perception of reality may perhaps be broader than his search; his acceptance of undistorted data about people unlike himself could extend beyond his range of actual acquaintances. In this case, we might enter a value of 5 or 6.

If we return to the search function and go across to other types of materials, we may discover that he has an active and broad interest in painting and is seeking out a much greater range of differentness with this material than he does with individuals. A 7 or 8 might be indicated for this search–symbol cell and, as well, his screening of this visual data admits much heterogeneous data. We can note a 7 or 8 here also.

Thus, at this point, our matrix can be condensed to look something like this:

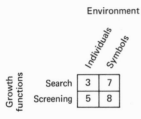

FIGURE 46

We must interrupt our analysis to observe that in a matrix of this type, we are dealing with relative values, not absolutes. As we move from box to box, our evaluations are in relationship to the other values assigned. In this analysis, the actual number used is unimportant; what is vital is the relationship of one number to another. Actually, the very first value entered determines the level of scores in all the rest. This helps avoid what Dr. Karl Menninger calls "the tyranny of words" in dealing with human personality and values. In this type of matrix, we use numbers to *qualify,* not to quantify.

Returning to our foreshortened model, in a growth development situation we might be able to broaden the search for people, for example, by helping the subject discover people through connections with art. This is a process of *growing on growth,* identifying areas of successful extension, and building on them—a process that looks for strength to pry open the closed areas of personality. If in our example we are able to put this person together with someone from another ethnic group by "connecting" them through a common interest in painting, he could begin to grow by assimilating the new differences. This basic technique of hybridization provides the "hook" by which people can use the familiar to discover the strange. Without some considerable amount of common information, neither DNA strands nor humans can join in mutuality.

All of these facts re-emphasize the vital character of the feedback function and the process of *exchange* rather than *change.* When two people come together, whether in friendly socialization or antagonistic negotiation, each party knows what he wants. If each set of desires meets in direct confrontation, it often turns out to be inimical to the other, representing a case of selfing versus selfing. As each tries to gain his own point and replicate himself by changing the other, the process of hybridization can be denied if both interests are not the same. In mutuality, however, the subjects can overcome the differences by "rising above" them to discover interests "in common." Thus, exchange and growth occur.

Let us now consider a somewhat more complex situation and exemplify this process with a present social "pathology"— alienation of the young, or the "generation gap." Let us pick an average, middle-class teenager as a subject. He is an individual with broad availability of ectogenetic information (books, television, good schools), great curiosity about many people and things, acceptance of vast amounts of these data, and assimilation, digestion, and synthesis of ideas related to his wide environment. Following the functional process, we speculate that the synthesis of new data and ideas is tried out in the outside world. We imagine, in specific terms, that he has decided to demonstrate against what he sees as a social injustice, for example, a war. He feels a common bond with all people and wants to end such injustice.

Let us apply a matrix analysis that considers only the subject's relationship to people. We shall let the Individuals column represent "all people," homogeneous groups (his "family"), and heterogeneous groups (the cluster of people that share his ideological views). With the exception of the feedback, every function is scored on a basis of how *he* performs each function. In this case, feedback relates to what he receives from that person or group.

Environment

Growth functions		Individuals	Groups—hetero.	Groups—homo.
	Search	8	8	6
	Screening	8	8	8
	Internal processing	8	8	8
	Use	8	8	4
	Feedback		8	3
	Regulation			

FIGURE 47

Although he is relatively open in his perception and acceptance of data inputs from the various sources, we can see in this simple example that significant conflicts have occurred in the use and feedback functions. (He can receive no feedback from "all people.") As he uses his ideas in confronting the subculture of his parents, the differences between their ideas and his cause his otherwise mutual behavior to regress to the selfing replicative. In other words, he is attempting to pressure them into thinking his way. Rather than starting from a base of common agreement, the high ratio of difference in ideas prevents hybridization. His parents show that they disapprove of his participation in an activity "against his own country" and are also manifesting a replicative selfing attitude. On the other hand, the various people in the demonstration group support and applaud his participation.

What number do we enter in the regulation cell? Is he a success or a failure in his growth? Which way will he go? In observing the matrix, we can see that a complementary relationship is stronger with the outside group—not only in its feedback relationship, but in its other growth process as well. In his growth, through assimilation of new data, he will naturally gravitate to those individuals with whom he can share the highest degree of commonality.[6]

In finding a more ready-made mutualism in outside groups, he directly confronts the integrity and identity of the family. His ideas are too "different" and his values confront the family with an explosive, sometimes catastrophic effect. In his own needs for growth and effect on his environment, the young person who feels he has not been heard by his family and has not experienced mutual growth with them, has used another culture to create an effect. In like manner, he can use this external growth to create an effect inside the family culture. Like the mentally ill, whose negative or aggressive growth behavior is viewed as "irrational," the person in this example actually reinforces his growth *even by a negative effect*. Growth, including the lowest form, serves the organism. Any effect can produce and prove "aliveness" to one's self, even self-mutilation.

Employing the same basic pattern, if we construct a social model that interfaces the growth dynamics of different *groups* in a three-dimensional matrix, we can also see where commonality and conflict occur. The construction of such models and their extension to interacting networks of individuals and groups can aid in the analysis of *what functions* are being used to manipulate *which* materials at *which level of growth*. Commonality between people can be discovered and used as a foundation for differences in growth to be more easily exchanged and assimilated. Internal functions (means) and materials affected (ends) can be formulated in such a model to show the relative value differences in each interface. In other words, the importance (value) of each function in achieving each particular end can be evaluated, and a complete systemic (input–output) system of growth can be derived.

The matrix illustrated in the previous examples shows one way to relate the elements of environment to the function of growth. Many such models can be employed to analyze more clearly the dynamics of living situations. The purpose of all models of this nature is to discover the system of operating interrelationships so that more specific strengths and weaknesses in the growth process can be detected. The discovery of areas of mutuality enormously facilitates developing higher-level behavior; it pinpoints commonality so that new information can be introduced with a higher probability of acceptance and growth for all.

LEARNING AS GROWTH

In all "learning" situations, the goal directiveness of organisms is the pervasive influence and motivation. If information is not perceived as connecting with existing patterns and is not viewed as contributing to effect and growth, learning will simply not occur. If, on the other hand, any information is presented so that it links with existing data and leads to growth effects, learning is autonomic. The vital importance of practical application of learning in formal education often produces misleading short-term results. Because many subjects are considered as means to produce the effect of getting credits, "graduating," or other such goals, once this interim goal is reached the system tends to reject any acquired data not perceived as leading to subsequent growth. Information that can be used for growth, however, is retained. Thus, in all learning situations, from schooling to counseling, information acquisition and behavioral change will result *only* if the individual or group can perceive and experience growth effects—if they can use the information to affect their outside world and to extend themselves.

In transformation terms the models above are envisaged as *growth*- rather than deficiency-oriented. *Growth is first a discovery and sharing of commonality and then an exchange of different-nesses.* In such a situation, any system (for example, therapy, family relations, or organizational and community development) is susceptible to bringing people together in a way that can be greatly growth-facilitating.

In a growth situation, rather than the usual accentuation of differences that results in polarity, the discovery of what is shared in common allows for recombination of new and different data that would not be allowed in ordinary "discussions" of problems. This approach toward building growth connections between people is extraordinarily easy to achieve, even in the most antagonistic groups, because of the extreme pressure in the system tending to mutualism.[7] This can be experimentally observed, for example, in some group process work, when a group of divergent people is simply put together and left "on their own." *Given enough time,* people must ultimately find their commonalities and begin to join in exchanging differences; the use of "tools" such as those described above gets the natural process moving faster and circumvents antigrowth behaviors that can retard or deny joining in brief encounters.

MODELS AND REALITY

When we consider the continuing failure of modeling and simulation techniques as they are generally employed today, we can see that these are overly simplified views of man and psychology. What people "want" and "need" is expressed in the most oversimplified growth definitions; economic and material phenomena dominate the inputs that are used to create instruments for private action and broad policy. The evolving quality of the psychological growth needs of Man is not considered in such present or future projections. Of course, these projective models all predict imminent disaster, as would any view of life based on lower growth forms. In the light of failures to predict the Renaissance or even the Industrial Revolution using the data fed into today's models, we should view these models as sophisticated, but basically as "non-growth"-oriented.

Existing models are simply extrapolations of present and past and do not take into account the discontinuities expressed by all organic growth and multiplied by Man. Systems based on past growth and on analogies of physics, chemistry, and engineering must give way to considerations of growth based on the facts of biological and psychological transformation. This approach will provide a more plausible base for evaluations between choices affecting private and public welfare. The growth model outlined here may provide new insights for projection of the holistic dynamics of human and environmental transformation.

Human psychological growth viewed as a motivation for the complex behavior patterns of Man can provide basic models of behavior that will better relate Man to the networks of interacting growth among people, ideas, animals, and things that make up the total system of life. Perhaps our understanding of behavior will evolve beyond the point of frustration that led to what is called the Harvard Law of Animal Behavior: "Under precisely controlled conditions, an animal does as he damn pleases."[8] What "pleases" is simply growth, manifested in any of its many forms.

To review behavioral functions more comprehensive than those presented here would certainly require much more space. Hopefully this brief outline has demonstrated the integrity of bio-psychological systems and the process of transformation in a broad enough view so that human phenomena can be seen not only to coexist with biological phenomena but also to be derived from them and expressed at every level of human behavior.

ENIGMAS OF MAN
EIGHT

In following the origins, nature, and nurture of human behavior on the path of an evolutionary biology, many previously perplexing acts of Man have become guideposts for our journey, rather than inexplicable examples of the vagaries of our species. Curiosity and creativity, hostility and hate, are all parts of the wide spectrum of growth-motivated behavior. As families became tribes and tribes nations, parallel growth formed the nature of society and social interaction. Why Man once took for granted such organic forms as feudalism and force, and then, just as naturally, pressed for individual freedom as time moved on, is dramatic testimony to the irrepressible momentum of transformation. Natural behavior becomes "unnatural." What is "right" today becomes "wrong" tomorrow as Man ascends the ladder of growth toward mutuality.

In this chapter we shall view the enigmas of Man from the perspective of history to detect evolution and transformation at work. We shall look at behavior that seems to contradict growth and others that seem unrelated to this process. The questions of human values and philosophy—self-sacrifice and sadism, the pleasure of security and the joys of danger, humor and ridicule, beauty and ugliness, liking, love, and hate—have all resisted Mankind's best efforts at understanding. These behaviors have been explained away as motivated "in themselves" or were simply classified as "obvious," "emotional," or "irrational." The average man, when asked why he destroys or ridicules or creates or climbs mountains replies, "I don't know" or "Because." Yet the apparent dualisms of behavior and value, often represented as polar opposites, in truth are simply different manifestations of growth.

SADISM AND SELF-SACRIFICE

Sadism is a form of behavior now understood to be not a sexual perversion or a need to inflict pain. It represents instead the necessity of having absolute control over another human being, of humiliating, belittling, and dominating until the other person becomes a subjugated *extension of the self*. Sadism is accretive growth resulting from the frustration of the more mutualistic growth of affiliation and love. On the other hand, self-sacrifice for one's friends or for a cause is at least replicative and in many cases mutualistic growth. Being a part of a larger organism, a person sacrifices the *exclusive* self to serve the larger whole. We can see this act manifested in other mammalian groups when an animal puts himself in a sacrifical position to fight for and protect the herd.

SECURITY AND DANGER

The need for security is a normal desire not to have one's growth opportunities or extensions threatened. Nonetheless, those who have not realized a self-generated connectedness with and an effect on their environment will exhibit exactly the reverse behavior; they will have exaggerated needs for activities involving excitement and danger. This behavior is one way in which they can produce their own effects on the environment. They are "in control" and can dominate such things as a fast car, a powerful natural phenomenon, or at least can identify vicariously with those effects made by others. Self-extension in *any* form is growth.

HUMOR AND RIDICULE

Perhaps one of the most perplexing expressions of all behavior is humor and laughter. Their mystery can be dispelled, however, when we view them as a form of growth. Laughter can be triggered by the exuberance of a growth effect. Humor, like creativity and invention, is a way of forming new "connections" between previously unconnected ideas. The best humor is the kind that brings the most distantly related things into tentative but meaningful connection. This sudden "fantasy mutuality" of joining things forbidden by accepted stereotypes provokes the explosive, ephemeral pleasure of laughter. In other expressions of humor, we become connected to and identify with the humorist himself. Every speech-maker recognizes that humor is a way of connecting to an audience. We take pleasure from the clown or comic by seeing nongrowth or growth-threatening situations develop in a nonthreatening environment. Minor misfortunes happen, but no one gets hurt. Imagine for a moment the difference in what we feel watching a clown stumble when he juggles, compared to how we feel when we see a professional juggler make the same mistake. Laughter, as well, carries with it an autonomic contagious mutualism. We experience pleasure in seeing another human making connections and we mutualize with him.

Comic humor is quite different from the laughter of ridicule or tragedy. This is not the bringing together of information in symbolic mutualism. Rather it can be either an expression of sheer relief from not having to personally confront a growth threat or it can be a belittling form of comparative growth. It says, on one hand, "I'm glad I'm not in that situation," or, on the other, "I am bigger than you." This lower level of pleasure can be understood when one listens to the veiled insult and "laughter" of someone who deliberately ridicules another. Tragic laughter is the reverse of humor in that the unexpected association is real but in this case growth-threatening. It is the sudden perception of antigrowth in another that provokes such a "laugh-like" reaction, and often the accompanying pang of regret for having reacted in this way.

BEAUTY AND UGLINESS

Beauty is another way we describe the pleasure of mutuality. In contrast to laughter, the effect of this connection is less sudden and more lasting. Beauty is "in the eye of the beholder" and even more so it is the "growth of the beholder." To observe anything—art, nature, friendship—that we identify as beautiful, is an experience of some form of growth. An individual or a society, of course, responds to the form of growth most practiced. A replicative person or group connects well with closed representative art in which they can recognize and project the self. Ascending the growth continuum, the mutualistic "creative" person finds more open symbolic systems more beautiful; he can build connections with them and into them. He is truly mutualistic with art, taking from it and putting the self into it.

Universally, the world of nature evokes feelings of pleasure and beauty in humans. Still, these experiences are limited to those situations in which we can realize an identity and fusion with natural wonders. The frame of mind that prepares us to experience such a connection (and the accompanying pleasure) is one of being open to our deep relationships with all of Nature. We often screen out such perception in the press of narrow growth activities, only lifting the curtain of perception in circumstances of "recreation," perhaps more aptly called re-creation. Eastern religions have long exercised the growth satisfaction of contemplation of Nature to give Man a fusion and integration with his biological heritage.

We, as all of life, live in a dynamic current of mutualizing change. This phenomenon suggests why we respond to both human affiliation and other things that are basically symmetrical and interpenetrated as "good" and those which are greatly out of balance or incomplete, as "bad." (See Figure 48.) The natural symmetry, equivalence, and sharing of atoms, molecular structures, crystals, and organisms lead to increasing homologous ordering in the unique works of Man. We always attempt to attain the dynamism of harmonious, complementary relationship in all things—even, and especially, when the parts are dissimilar.

LIKING, LOVE, AND HATE

The natural tendency of affiliation through likeness is another obvious phenomenon. It is perfectly natural for people to want to associate with people who are like themselves, but why is this so? Humans form bonds *based* on commonality and reciprocal ratification. A number of recent experiments have demonstrated that even in a laboratory situation the creation of artificial likenesses causes automatic affiliation. Interestingly, the word "like" originally meant "to be of the same body." When we say, "I like so-and-so," we are really affirming that "he is like *me*." Biologically this need to initiate growth through common information bonds has been observed at every phylogenetic level, including the immune system and DNA recombinations. Even so, combination of likenesses can be largely an exchange of same-for-same and the result of the output is at best slow accretion of new information. Maintaining an affiliation with someone who is the

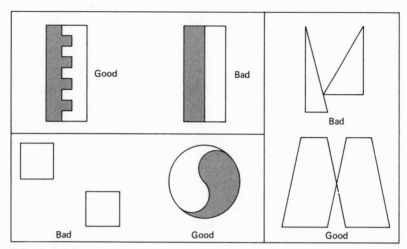

(After Arnheim)
Art students' representation of abstract idea of "good" or "bad" marriage. *Fusion*, rather than simple symmetry, distinguishes good from bad.

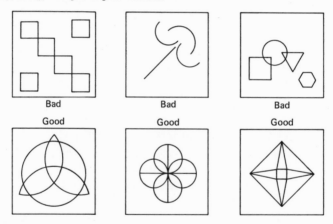

(After Kreitler)
Experiments in choices of "good" and "bad" symbols. Symmetrical *fused* figures were considered good.
FIGURE 48

same as we are does not add much; it does not impart the vigor that comes from *building on sameness with combinations of differentness*—true mutuality.

In biological evolution we have seen the tendency for movement toward methods to build more and more new information into the organism through hybridization and sharing of different attributes. In parallel, we find a tendency in the history of Man for less superficial sameness to be required for people to join together in effective growth.

Thus, the most common and ritualistic human behavior becomes quite understandable and predictable. A fundamental case of this occurs when one meets someone else for the first time. The natural thing to do in achieving likeness is to attempt joining through an assured commonality. "Isn't it a beautiful day?" we might say, autonomically picking a subject that has a high probability of agreement. This is the way that we begin building effective bridges to each other. A first agreement is just as naturally followed by a slightly more intimate bond: "You live in this neighborhood, don't you?" Even the redundant, almost rhetorical "Don't you?" is our natural way of probing for agreement and positive feedback.

When we serve as a catalyst to join others, we employ the same technique. Introducing two friends to each other, we might say: "John, this is Harry, he is also interested in biology." We attempt to unearth whatever likeness can be found before we allow the exchanges of information to reach a potential conflict of different ideas. We try to achieve sufficient bonds to permit interpersonal hybridization.

The process of joining, whether it is in combining ideas, images, things, or people, follows the basic rule of growth—exchanging differences based on commonality. From microbial, virus, and parasitic behavior that attempts to *change* the organisms with whom they relate, relational processes have evolved to that of *exchange.* In human terms, the partnership in which each party demands that the other change is in opposition to the reciprocity that engenders the exchange of growth.

In graphic terms, we can exemplify this process by representing a set of information (a person, idea, or thing) as a circle. In a relationship we can juxtapose several of these to see how growth occurs:

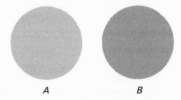

A   B

FIGURE 49

Here between *A* and *B* there is no commonality of information and little or no joining is possible. If a small amount is present:

144

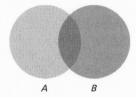

the result is a heightened probability that new information and growth can occur with both parties. If we look at extremely high levels of commonality as:

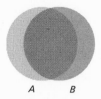

FIGURE 51

we see that although great agreement is probable very little can be shared that is new or different. Growth is extremely limited.

In the case of Figure 51, we can assume liking, but not *love*. The conditions that foster a real and growing love can come about only from both deep involvement and the enlargement of each party. *Discovery of ever deeper commonalities and constant enrichment through exchanging differences provide the quality of relationship defined as "love."* Rather than attempting to force or influence the other to change, each partner finds self-growth by learning from the other. In this case, the differences are perceived as desirable. In Figure 50, there are the possibilities of both love and hate, depending on how the qualities of differentness are perceived.

If we look closely at the difference in differentness, we can portray the love–hate dualism in simple terms:

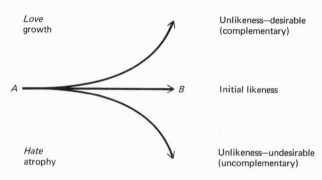

FIGURE 52

This illustration points out the great fallacy in relationships that are based on the idea that one can change the undesirable attributes of a partner. As differences are exposed and pressures grow, the result is anti-affiliation, not growth. It is in those cases in which each partner views the other as having qualities that are both different *and* desirable that great growth is possible.

Love, like an organic relationship, is a function of growth. In this respect, love is a universal phenomenon and explains why we feel impelled to say "I love" about so many things. One can love anything that contributes to growth, that offers new connectiveness with Life. This relationship is obviously very different from that type of agreeable connection as exemplified in Figure 51, where growth is only counterfeit affirmation through relatively exact copies of commonality; it does not create the possibilities to knit new areas of extension. The pleasure of replicative "oneness" is often mistaken for the joy of mutual "twoness." The process of continual growth by enlargement of joining is what Sir Arthur Eddington referred to when he said, "We often think that when we have completed the study of *one* we know all about *two;* that 'two' is 'one' and 'one.' We forget that we still have to make a study of 'and.'"

The study of that "and" is the study of the process of growth. It can be observed when the immunologist experiments with tissue grafting or when each of us works in the laboratory of life in joining people. It is the "and" we create in our mutualizing with others. If, in the case of Figure 49, we have instead:

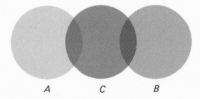

A   C   B

FIGURE 53

we enter the situation as a *human catalyst* and, by perceiving otherwise undiscovered common bonds, we become the "and." Through the third party of catalysis, a human, an enterprise, a goal, or a shared medium on any one of numberless experiences in life continually supplies more of the "ands" that join life in even higher levels of organization and—grows through sharing.

Thus, human love is by far the highest level of the sharing process. It is not a matter of merely exchanging differences but of creating a third entity, something new that is combined of each. Human love creates an entity that is, like physical progeny, a living, united self beyond anything that can be created by a single individual. This is the "and" of you and me and of human growth. The anti-growth environment of many stable marriages—situations in which the wife is secure and "taken care of" and not expected to do more than take care of the house and children—results in the absence of both new information (nutrition) for growth and mutual feedback. This creates a deprivation experience accompanied by the anxiety and dread of non-growth and hate for those who have denied growth. Regressive growth patterns of withdrawal into the internalized accretive/replicative patterns of alcoholism, drugs, and fantasy or the reverse, externalized emphasis on possession, control of environment, and so on. One illustration of this is the manifestation of shoplifting by upper-middle-class housewives. If everything physical is being provided by the husband even acquisition is denied the wife, everything is his—and his growth. To produce her own effect she has little choice but to use her own skills to acquire things that can be really hers. What is often classified as "neurotic" is simply regression to whatever form of growth is possible.

HYPOCRISY

Why do we not always, or even often, act as we feel? The struggles of the unconscious with the conscious leave us wondering at our inability to "be ourselves"; however, not being the exclusive self, we are often opening the door to new growth. Encountering a situation that seems to call for behavior that outwardly does not agree with inner thoughts, we may take the opportunity to test the "not me" of the new act. We may discover, in the process, a "new me," enhanced by learning that such new behaviors are not so foreign after all.

This nonrevelation of the self obviously works against growth as well. It can deny the exchange of differences by agreeing with someone else to ensure positive feedback. At the same time, it can aid the development of someone else by supplying positive feedback. We use the technique of "hypocrisy" not just to deceive others but to facilitate growth if our aim is to reveal ultimately the real differences as soon as contact is established.

In these days of exhortation to behave in "open" and "free" ways, such complete self-projection can be a deterrent to mutual growth. It can even encourage and stimulate a regression to the selfness of replicative or accretive growth—eliminating the sympathy or empathy that brings people together.

The mutualistic person often practices a sort of "regression in joining" by reaching into himself to find lower levels of identification with others. He can thus begin interactions leading to higher levels of behavior, not unlike the way a teacher will empathize with children in order to teach more effectively.

RESISTANCE TO CHANGE

If life is the growth process described above, we must inquire of Nature why organisms and people so resist change and exchange. What is the mechanism that creates rigidity and attempts to preserve the old and outworn? This, too, is part of the process of nature—an intractable resistance to give up achieved growth. But a man does not deny his own growth by destroying those things he has created—those things that are a part of himself—just as biological organisms reject anything sufficiently foreign to the self. In this light, resistance to change is not true resistance to the process of growth; rather it is a protective device to ensure that change is *integrative growth* and will not destroy the very foundations of the existing and evolved organism.

Growth and its inherited need are such an integral process in life and in Man that to lose or to deny them, in any act, is also the precursor of anxiety and guilt. "The moving finger writes," and if, in looking back, we look for our acts of growth negation, we shall feel the universal burden of Man—not the anxiety of unknown threats to growth or the fear of the known, but the ever present knowledge that no man can ever grow enough. Our universal, irremedial, and infinite guilt is interminable growth insufficiency. It is a feeling that can produce atrophy or excitement. Life in memorium of past makes the present untenable; to live and grow in the now creates the challenges of ever new constellations of growth. Growth is never finished; it is only interrupted.

GROWING TOGETHER

The enigmas surrounding human behavior have stemmed from lack of knowledge of the wellsprings of life. It is no enigma that so many incomplete pieces and misunderstandings of the design of growth have led Man into dead ends of explanation. The behaviors that accompany accretive and replicative growth have led us to assume that these are not only Man's past, but also his future. Striving for power, procreation, security, and possession is revealed as shallow demands—the shadows of mutualism—reemerging fully only when the pruning of culture impels their necessary expression.

Spurring the natural process of growth to ever higher forms is the direct responsibility of Mankind, the most effective agent of evolution and natural selection in life's history. Having demonstrated that this is true in plant and animal breeding, knowledge, growth, and the development of improved technologies to serve life, we are now on the threshold of practicing what we have learned *on ourselves,* and growing beyond the accretive–replicative patterns that have permeated our growth-facilitating practices both with individuals and within institutions.

The measure of any growth technique is a balance of effect and affect and the mutualistic facilitation that results. Although the process of increasing mutualism is under way all around us, it is probably helpful to use the theoretical principle that is already being applied in so much empirical practice. Rediscovering the processes that make for growth in such situations as family development, child-rearing, education, and therapy, as well as in institutional policies, can provide a firmer foundation and avoid some of the painful trial and error associated with application of partialistic growth theories.

Culturally, the family presents a broad base for a transformation example. The joining of a man and woman in marriage and the growth or disintegration that subsequently occurs is a vivid demonstration of all of the processes of growth and nongrowth. Originally a couple will be attracted by accretive growth needs, that is, growth by self-enlargement through sex and procreation and commonality of appearance and interests (information). If sufficiently complementary ectogenetic patterns exist, they begin to provide opportunities for exchanges of new information. The original "likeness" can begin to mature into mutual enrichment and "love." As husband and wife continue to enjoy a give-and-take relationship with equality, the phenomenon of love grows. If the marriage is to succeed, the deepening relationship grows by their continual mutual exchange that both broadens their commonality and constantly enriches their extent.

As long as this process of sharing and mutuality exists, love is reinforced and grows. Breakdown occurs and love is diminished and requited if one party "uses up" the vital newness that can be contributed by the other. The ratio of exchange shifts; likeness remains but the authentic joy of love becomes replaced by the pleasures of lower level growth. Growth regresses to the replicative stage or to the malignancy of accretion. When one party is the main contributor, he begins to attempt to change the other rather than to exchange; it is emotional embezzlement. Under these circumstances, pleasure can regress to pain as growth is refuted.

Of course, many family relationships begin and end simply as replicative barters, when each partner is determined to change the other, for his or her "own good." Another common phenomenon is the mixture of a selfing person with an othering one. Here, each person complements the pattern of the other and together they maintain a minimal level of growth throughout the relationship. This pattern passes along to their children. Recognition of the forms of growth practiced in such marriages can help us aid the discovery of new behaviors leading to more mutualistic relationships. Aside from individual application of these principles to personal life, such people as family counselors, attorneys, and therapists may be able to act as catalysts in helping human relationships grow to new heights.

With this simple example of marriage as a foundation, it is appropriate to consider some of the basic policies and practices that are normally applied in present "helping" theories applied to broader relationships. The art of helping others has echoed many ancient growth forms, and often, rather than revitalizing growth, it causes enervating degeneration. This is true because we have long practiced replicative helping; that is, the "let *me* help *you* (become like me)" school. Thus, we have developed the social habit of turning to "experts" to provide transcribed answers to problems. With each act of aid—from welfare payments to therapy, from company employment practices to foreign aid—we consistently point out to the individual or group, "you need me but I don't need you." Forms of worn-out replicative psychological imperialism still permeate many of our policies and practices.

Widespread rejection of such nonmutual practices shows that the age for replicative poaching is socially dead. The result of continuing these practices in this new era is a brutal testament to our errors. "Reformatory" riots, "educational" upheavals, "psychoanalytic" revolutions, "welfare"-spawned sicknesses, and "aid" that makes enemies of old friends, are merely a few of the selective pressures now operating against perpetuation of replicative methods. Man wants and needs mutuality of effect, not just to be affected by someone else. As a young person said recently, "I want to live, not just survive" and, in the words of a rioting prisoner, "I would rather die like a man than live like an animal." Man reaches out for growth. If he cannot get it by transformative evolution, the only answer to the pressure is revolution.

As world cultures evolve, we can detect the shifting of values that represents a broad movement on the continuum of growth. The long replicative phase of development dominated by copying past patterns, functions, and organizations has, with the advent of the "information explosion" in the last two decades, impelled rapid movement into mutualistic patterns. The conventional ethics—work and accumulation of possessions, the need to identify with an omnipotent nation, the replication of class-bound ideas, the sanctity of the family and of belonging to strong institutions (churches, clubs, companies)—all have felt the pressure of more individualized needs. The individual, in this movement, is more than the "I," the isolated self; he has become a representative member of the larger human organism. He has changed, as Paul Tillich put it, from being "apart" to being "a part."

In the current quest for selfhood and identity, what has really happened is a breaking down of old replicative barriers to growth. Structures that maintained insular boundaries have been the first to feel these transformative changes, including traditions such as copying the father's occupation, remaining within static social "classes," maintaining the mores of church dogmas, and segregating oneself as to age, nationality, or race. The strong replicative "ties" that have long kept the ectogenetic inheritance relatively intact were a matter of compartmentalization of information in each system. With today's media penetration and education, the replicative ectogenetic restraints have all but disappeared. In the mutualistic world of the 1970s, people have started to refuse to "keep their place" and "to toe the line." Mutualism has begun, but not without conflict.

As the barriers fall, those who have long maintained the vital integrity of those cultural walls have come face-to-face with emerging pressures of people who demand a share in making the world. When these different growth forms and value systems clash, the ancient and accepted concept of unchanging values has impeded a dialectic exchange between these forces and curtailed growth forms that are not alien to each other, but indeed mutually contributive.

Nonetheless, recognizing the dynamics of the evolution of biopsychocultural processes, we are beginning to see that without the nurturing forces of what are now viewed as "reactionary" or "conservative" processes, the new mutuality could never have come about.

As George Santayana put it:

We must welcome the future
Remembering that soon it will be the past;
We must respect the past
Remembering that once it was all that was humanly possible.

Building on the past with increasingly higher levels of replicative work, the creation of broad, information-rich cultures has become possible. Technological replication created the instruments of growth: the "polluting" transport systems, the "intellectual deserts" of the media, mass literacy, "institutions," "dehumanizing" production machines, and vast, interlocking "artificial" systems that support our biological needs (clothing, shelters, foodstuffs, and medicines). The emotional distance apparently, but fallaciously, existing between the ectogenetic psychospecies of replicative man and mutual man is now, itself, beginning to shorten and to merge as people begin to broaden their range of exchange and as we of the replicative phase learn the new sharing forms of growth. Everywhere the pressure is on. In even the most benign organizations, men want a greater say in their own destiny, even if it means making mistakes. No longer do the simple accretive and replicative rewards work. However, in an intuitively true but simplistic manner, theories of organizational development, from communes to companies, have also proposed that management must change to participative technique. But, as every good manager has discovered, the same degree of mutualism cannot be applied to everyone or even to every culture. Some people respond to threats, some to challenges, and some should simply be left alone. True mutualism allows relationships that meet the particular level of growth of each individual and culture, and in that process, exchange in ever higher levels so that growth continues to evolve.

Mutualistic growth in a group can be achieved with devices of various kinds, although in some cases it may be short-lived, or even dangerous. To accomplish a forced exchange of differentness in biology, for instance, the organism's natural rejection of foreignness in making a transplant is "knocked out" by disabling the immune system. Creating this situation in the biological organism is the same as putting a group of people in an artificial environment, like the psychological "life boat" of some therapy or "encounter" groups. Under these unusual circumstances, the group will naturally tend to join together and to experience new forms of sharing and growth. Of course, in either the biologic or psychologic case, if any one of the parts of the organism or group does not accept this temporary letdown of defense mechanisms, the result can be rejection rather than fusion. However, regardless of what happens in the growth experience itself, the problem in both cases is what will happen when the special growth situation ends and the regular defenses come back into play in a normal environment. Will the growth "take" or not? If circumstances deny the continuing use of new growth behavior, the effect will at least be short-lived as the new growth is rejected, often accompanied by trauma.

In the formation of all relationships, the principle of mutuality exists in so far as both how an individual unit acts as a part of the whole and how the total organism responds to its environment. In every case, what can be observed is a movement toward reciprocity, a dynamic balance of give-and-take that results in growth of both effect and affect. With this principle we can develop a better understanding of the relationships of men to men, organizations to other organizations, and the ecological relationship of Mankind to the environment as a whole. This open, dynamic, growing model of Man allows for the creation of indeterminant but ever evolving futures.

PART THREE
MEANING AND DIRECTION

PHILOSOPHY AND TRANSFORMATION

NINE

The principle of transformation is homologous to so many fundamental philosophical teachings that an opportunity exists to provide a more tenable scientific basis for concepts that have long lingered in the realm of metaphysical speculation. The progressive removal of such "mysteries" by developing concrete and verifiable laws for the behavior of things—for instance, going from alchemy to chemistry—has pointed the way to the ultimate understanding of such unique human traits as love of freedom and the human "creations" of such concepts as morality and ethics. As a basic phenomenon of evolution and growth, it is possible to use the process of transformation as a tool to view more clearly those properties traditionally judged to remain forever obscured by the very unknowable nature of humanness. With it we can unearth the taproots of philosophy that reach down to the deep springs of physical and organic reality. As with the other postulates of transformation theory, the interpretations offered here are intended to meet the basic criterion of scientific knowledge, that is, to conform with observable and reproducible reality. Thus, as philosophic concepts they are not offered as articles of faith, but as tangible realities subject to rigorous research and verification.

The study of values in making human decisions has been a preoccupation and an enigma since the beginning of human history. We cannot attempt to provide even a cursory survey of the many ideas of philosophy. It is worth noting, however, that the concept of an "evolutionary" philosophy was postulated by Spencer even before the promulgation of Darwinian ideas. To

Spencer, life itself was "good," and a natural ethic of promoting life became the basis of his proposed ethical system. The Huxleys and others pointed out later that, in the increasing struggle for existence, such an idea was incompatible with fact. Since then, a number of scholars and naturalist philosophers such as Haldane, Waddington, Romanell, Simpson, and Rensch have attempted to examine the natural ethic of "biological wisdom." Despite the creative and sometimes heroic efforts of these and other thinkers on the subject, the idea of evolutionary ethics has been neither established nor invalidated. Firm clues to such mysteries as the value of the individual versus society, or to the progressive enigma of why we call something "evil" that was once considered "good," have not been found.

Thus, over the span of several centuries, brief even in Man's short span of existence, the study of this problem of human nature has necessitated the compartmentalization of behavior into two distinct systems, the world of *values* and the world of *facts*. Ethics, aesthetics, and morals have been deemed to have no place in such objective sciences as physics, biology, or mathematics even though we have been often told of the aesthetic "beauty" of scientific discovery. Nevertheless, the acts of life do not allow for such an artificial separation between these concepts. The nature of Man's activities always includes what he *desires* as well as what he is. Although the facts of life that permit us to control many of the vast powers of Nature do not tell us how to apply them, we must always make such judgments. The scientist has often pleaded "objectivity" as an abdicator of values to those willing to accept responsibility for the destiny of Man. Yet, as time passes, the demand for a more "factual" wisdom grows urgent. It is this necessary *union of fact and value* that will be considered here.

As to basic fact, Man's motivation to use his imagination constantly to reformulate his world is as empirically real and factual as is his response to food when he is hungry; ours is a world where Man creates, destroys, and evolves. During the broad course of evolution, natural selection decided in favor of this process as a desirable improvement in the basic system of life and evolution. Once more, we shall not depart from the facts of life to speculate on what caused that original mechanism of life to come into being, and whether Life itself "ought to be." What we do know is that life and its processes exist and teach us that there is, in the terms of transformation, a truly *natural philosophy*.

One of the problems in the search for such a philosophy has

been the ancient assumption that there must be "universal and final" answers. With this tautological presumption, we are asked to choose between such value systems as aggressive "will to power" and the ideal of cooperation, love, and individual dignity, without realizing that rather than being polar opposites, these concepts are representative of the manifestations of the continuum of growth—human and otherwise. The evolutionary "rightness" of an idea is a function of matching the form of growth in *general practice* within the system in which an organism lives. In biological terms we can see, for example, that, although replicative growth is necessary to the life of simple protozoa that live a relatively independent existence, this kind of growth within the "social" context of a multicellular organism produces a cancer. By practicing replicative growth, these cells are practicing nonmutualistic "unfitting" growth in a mutualistic society.

EVOLVING MUTUALISM

In the course of human social evolution, we see precisely the same phenomena. There have been eras in man's history where tribal and nationalistic replication were "right" and necessary to the safety and continuance of the fulfillment of the growing human organism. Yet, as society became more complex and interrelated, the need for replicative independence has shifted to a need for mutualistic cultural interdependence.

A brief examination of the growth of the human systems of economics, politics, law, and organizational development shows a natural transformation into mutualistic values. It also demonstrates, in fact, that these progressions have been so intrinsically "right" that, by and large, they have been taken for granted and even now remain substantially unquestioned.

In economic practice it is obvious both from the records of the past as well as from observations of existing primitive tribes that at one time "normal" behavior was to take what one wanted. If territory, things, or slaves were required, they were simply appropriated. This "Genghis Khan" syndrome of extension of authority has gradually been replaced almost completely with the idea of barter and "trading." Why abandon a growth method that allowed things to be acquired by usury or conquest without having to give anything in exchange? Because the natural pressure of mutualism and its *evolutionary consequences* demonstrated that exchange was a far better system. The costs of conquest were high, whereas with trade each could gain something from the other that he did not have. The growth of both was enhanced—and led to more trade and more growth.

So, too, we see that political systems, once based exclusively on the inherited "Divine Right" of monarchs and the absolute power of feudal lords, have also emerged with a "new" concept. Into the mosaic of governmental structures came the Magna Carta and the ideas of "inalienable rights of the individual" and of earned leadership. By now, most of the world has progressed from the heritage of absolute dictatorship to more broadly based systems. As the thrust of this movement continues, it can be no better exemplified than by any newspaper with its reports of exacerbating demands for more local "participation." Everybody wants "a piece of the action" and "to determine his own destiny."

In legal systems as well, no longer does a ruler's fiat suffice for settling disputes. We have naturally evolved to another value system and a new form—justice—the system of *quid pro quo* and decision by a jury of peers. Organic evolution indeed permeates every system. In the development of organizations, Man has progressed from slavery, to child and indentured labor, to labor negotiations, and, today, to the modern concept of participative management.

In all of these cases of developing mutualism, lower growth forms cannot be maintained when the demands of evolution by natural selection always press for the realization of the benefits of mutual facilitation. We simply do what is "right" and "good" and this inevitably turns out to be a higher, more mutualistic form of growth. In the open marketplace, forces such as "consumerism" emerge to insist on new mutualities. The question of what is "right," "good," or "aesthetically pleasing" is a question of relatedness to prevailing growth forms. No expression of Man is immune; even art forms must be "in tune" with evolution. Anything not "with it" is taking from or standing in the way of growth.

Waddington implied this evolution of values and philosophy when he said, "The framework within which one can carry on a rational discussion of different systems of ethics, and make comparisons of their various merits and demerits, is to be found in a consideration of animal and human evolution." Until recently, however, a consideration of evolution could not supply the insight needed to understand "biological wisdom." As Dobzhansky asked, "Do we always know what is and what is not in step with nature?" Waddington had compared the biological ethic with the function of eating—producing healthy rather than unhealthy and abnormal growth. Yet, as has often happened in the sciences, superficial form was to obscure the underlying reality of the function of growth processes. Today, we can find new meaning and value in our understanding of the ever ascending interpenetration of growth process. We can see the evolution of biological "wisdom" and know that "good," like life, matter, and energy, is not only relative and changing, but *definable.*

This is not to say that all mismatches of evolution are regressive. Higher forms of growth that do not fit a system can indeed contribute; they are the "growing tip" of evolution. Often, however, these behaviors generate much natural counterpressure from prevailing forms of growth. We see examples of this resistance to overhybridization on every hand: the persecution of the Christians with their new values, early nonacceptance of impressionist and abstract art, the fate of many innovative scientists, and so forth. The idea whose "time has not yet come" suffers the same fate as any organism trying to manifest a new form of growth within a society in which it does not completely fit.

Human nature is, in fact, Nature. We manifest on every hand the basic facts of natural growth in all of our idealized human activities. The false dualism that has separated Man's ideals and values from the facts of his physical and biological existence can now be rejoined with the same adhesive that we use to join Man and Nature—not as a final quality, but as meaning to be nurtured, like all living things.

There is a fundamental implication in the evolution of behavior and value. Man has long and often been characterized as nothing more than an aggressive brute, a uniquely criminal being, a thief and rapist at least, and a murderer as well. Since the time of Darwin, this age-old belief added its own interpretation to "survival of the fittest" and the idea of a ceaseless "struggle" for existence. The records of human past surely verify this viewpoint of human nature. Man has been all of these things and, in some measure, is today. Unfortunately, until recently we have been unaware of the discontinuous growth process of Nature. It has been easy for us mistakenly to assume that we must still manifest the basic character of our ancestors.

Although it is true that all organisms carry and reflect in their morphology and behavior Darwin's "stamp of lowly origin," he and a multitude of others have illuminated that lowly origin as *precursory functions* continually superseded and supplanted by higher levels of organization. So it is in human behavior. The evolution of intra- and interspecies cooperation is a readily observable fact. The emerging science of ethology has cast an ever brighter light on the fact that, even in the primitive animal world, cooperation became far more prevalent than conflict; it was more successful. Abundant testimony is the immense number of distinct species that live together in harmony. Ancient life in the seas is perhaps the best example of such symbiotic and mutualistic relationships. The rules of natural selection and evolution actually do not permit the ceaseless and bloody struggle that is often seen as evolutionary and behavioral process.

Whereas our ancestors grew in low-level ways at one time, by far the preponderance of human behavior has evolved into inter- and intrasocial cooperation, and on a fantastic scale. Though he carries with him his accretive past, Man rarely solves his problems solely with brute force. Once taken for granted, violent behavior is so unusual today that it preoccupies our media. Who knew then or remembers today the people machine-gunned in the streets of Philadelphia in the draft riots of 1860; yet today, with a Kent State, the horror of a single brutality is magnified and projected to become every man's horror; the bell tolls long and loudly. This pressure of the *new wrong* is only another example of evolution producing a continual transformation of growth in psychosocial systems. The homologous nature of these processes continues to produce the *evolving natural ethic.* It is a process of change aptly described by Dobzhansky's conclusion, "Not only organisms which are the products of evolution, but also the mechanisms of evolution itself evolve."

Any system of growth responds in identical ways to the same pressures: evolution to mutualism. From cellular dynamics to human relations, the system responds favorably to increasing reciprocity of effect. This holds true for the most fundamental environmental relations as well. The farmer, for example, is quick to realize that he must give to the earth to be able to continue taking out, and as he shapes the land it shapes him. The pressures of the ecological movement are just as natural a phenomenon; as Nature's agent we redress unnaturalness. So it is in all organic systems, an emerging natural "ethic"of mutuality. "Do I give as much as I take?" and equally as important "Do I *take* as much as I give?" are the questions evoked by highest levels of life. If a person, organization, or nation gives more than it takes, for example, it reduces the opportunity of the other party to give; it is not "trade," not *quid pro quo* or reciprocity. It is not natural, biologic *or* ethical. In today's evolved world, false altruism does not contribute to evolution and transformational growth.

The ethical answer is the living pragmatic. Whenever a "bad," growth-inhibiting, or degenerating relationship occurs in a mutualistic culture, this "evil" is a consequence of nonmutual exchange. Why schools, prisons, companies, and foreign policies fail is a result of the denial of what has been rightly termed the "need to be needed." In penal "rehabilitation," for example, the archaic answer we have made is simply to exclude these humans in clusters, much as antibodies cluster antigens so they can more easily be destroyed. Exclusion and isolation, in a situation where an organism is not allowed to grow, are the most effective means to select out and destroy the organism. How many of our "corrective" practices allow the subject to affect his environment in any way? In a biological ethic, these practices can only be considered "evil," a holdover remnant of our accretive–replicative past.

The great human love of "freedom" surely illustrates this need to have open alternatives to be able to create effect and grow. The maintenance of interacting systems that produce many alternatives is Nature's freedom. Dynamic instability and constant interdependent change are the natural state. The parallel process of selection prevents total anarchy, just as evaluative judgment naturally balances imagination in humans. Man's great love of freedom is simply yet another biological imperative. We maintain the capability of producing wide varieties of alternatives to allow selection to increase our viability and vitality.

This is totally contrary to the idea of a deterministic world. The Watsonian or Skinnerian model which shows Man to be a function of his environment in a stimuli-response-reinforcement process, omits the search which not only initiates but evolves behavior and modifies environment. A determinist thinker would have us believe that if we study any sequence of events, traveling from one city to another, for instance, at each step our decisions are based on the finite facts of the changing stimuli in the situation, traffic, weather condition, roads, vehicle, and so on. They maintain we will actually be pushed and pulled along the path according to fixed and immutable probabilities. Yet, it is easy to see that if so few alternatives are available to us, the creation of new ideas for better transport systems would never happen.

In fact, given the same situation, as with the "Harvard Animal law," we may decide not to go at all.

To look upon Man as a determined being is to exclude his primary function as an evolutionary agent. He is not limited to the rigid and fixed genetic patterns of animals who will perform their specific growth tasks, whether they want to or not. Man, as a much condensed and amplified evolutionary mechanism, is not satisfied to simply go from A to B, but will continually evolve *new* alternatives to do it better. Rather than being determined, Man is determining. His creativity is the transformative evolutionary function of creating alternatives and naturally selecting among them to bring about new pieces of the growing mosaic of life.

In this light "free will" must be re-examined. "Will" obviously is not "free." While evolutionary forces may be our legacy, if we do not invest in the creation and selection of alternatives, we are indeed not free. If Mankind were to let itself be determined and not invent new alternatives, freedom would disappear. It is the availability of choices that makes up the idea of freedom and is its measure. And it is the interacting responsibility of interdependent judgment that balances the natural creative creature, Man. Freedom is a responsibility of and a medium for growth.

We can see that when the open, dynamic process of growth is denied—when, for instance, a social organization sets up inflexible rules, standards, and controls that prevent the creation of new alternatives and the responsibility for choosing between them in order to avoid mistakes and failures—it is imprisoning the most fundamental forces of life. It is not only contrary to every observable biological and psychological fact, but it creates the conditions for the organism to be selected out and extincted in the larger, more dynamic, environment. The freedom to create and to select among mutations was Nature's way of creating Man. This same freedom and responsibility is the natural way each of us can develop and contribute our own special uniqueness as a part of the growth of the great uniqueness that is Mankind.

As we discover more of Man and Nature, we are put in a position to *use* and to *understand* the intuitive wisdom of many of the world's great philosophers. Without exception, from the Hermetic Magicians to Buddha and from Christ to Luther, we find concurring basic principles about both Man's individual growth and his collective growth. We may find it possible to separate wisdom from dogma as principles and practices reveal their naturalness or artificiality. The idea of "giving of self" becomes not diminution, but growth. St. Thomas Aquinas summed up the wisdom of the natural ethic when he wrote, "Evil is nothing else but the privation of what is conatural and due to anyone . . . therefore, evil is not a real essence." As this "conaturalness" of life evolves in Man and in the social organism, we can identify the pace of Nature and learn how to stay "in step" with biological wisdom.

Philosophy is the natural meeting ground of facts and values. *It is the overriding fact of evolution that requires values of life to emerge.* Within any particular culture, the growth forms manifested autonomically become the cultural value framework. Subcultures as well will evolve other value systems both within and outside of the primary culture, matching their own level of growth behavior—depending on the nutrition–information and feedback available. In this respect, for example, a scientist participating in a mutualistic, international scientific subculture represents values other than those of individuals in his basic culture who do not experience such relationships. This cross-cultural disparity creates the value differences between groups and creates value "facts" that seem equally valid to all participants. The growing hybridization of these disparate cultures and values creates great opportunity for evolvement of broad mutualistic and humanistic values that will become the "facts" of tomorrow.

Each of us lives many lives as we shift our focus of existence from culture to culture. On those many stages of life we are measured as to our worth. In each, we are but a single organism in a biopsychocultural system. How we merge with and grow through each of those cultures is the measure of our ability to respond, our *responsibility,* to growth. If we cannot hybridize with each other, we are like the flower whose pollination mechanism does not fit a new or changed environment. We are subject to a "miniature extinction" as we are excluded from the growth of that culture. As an individual, our social worth is a function of our evolutionary contribution. If an individual cannot contribute to the subcultures that make up the organisms of his environment, he is of little value to the life system. Extinction or exclusion—that is, exile—of the individual results, and the process of "independent" growth replaces cultural mutuality. Philosophy, ethics, and values are indeed relative in the sense that they are *relational.* And they are as factual as breathing.

EVOLUTION RECONSIDERED
TEN

So far in our consideration of behavior we have referred to the process of evolution and natural selection without raising the central problem that clouds the entire idea of evolution. Perhaps it is possible to ignore this question totally without seeming to shake the foundation of the concept of transformation. After all, for over a hundred and fifty years science has successfully evaded a major confrontation with the single question that lies at the very heart of all ideas about Man and Nature—namely, the issue of *directionality* in evolution. We have often assumed such direction on the part of Nature, referring to the observable process of development of "novelty, diversity, and higher levels of organization," but with no mechanism to explain how it could occur. In essence, if natural selection operates on a *random* or chance basis, if Darwinian concepts of repetition hold, why would Nature progress beyond novelty and diversity to higher levels? Why indeed should Man appear?

Prior to Darwin the Lamarckian concept of *cumulative* evolution was popular. That creatures could cause changes and pass them on to their offspring would support the experiential fact that evolution continually adds to the capabilities of organisms. Lamarck thought that evolutionary changes were caused by the organisms themselves. However, the overwhelming weight of the evidence of Darwin and his successors demonstrated that evolution occurred as something done *to* the organism by the environment. Rather than organisms' causing changes, the Darwinian concept was one of *repetition;* that is, the drive of Nature is to preserve the original characteristics of the parents by passing on their genetics unchanged by their experiences. This theory, of course, allowed for *no* change and presented a grave paradox until the initiation of the idea of mutation (random, spontaneous, and induced genetic changes) and the rediscovery of the hybridization work of Mendel (random mixtures of parental genes). These concepts could at least explain why changes of any sort would be introduced. However, if these changes are random it does not help us understand the obvious metamorphosis of species on our planet.

That there is a direction to evolution is clearly true; evidence surrounds us on every hand. That there is some force that makes evolution a cumulative process has been referred to time and time again by the world's greatest scientists, even if it could only be explained as a sort of "vital force" forever to remain an inexplicable mystery. Darwin himself, in later life, admitted that he had to accept some idea of inherited characteristics for, even to him, chance selection was insufficient to explain the behavior of evolution.[1] Jung observed, in 1968, that "the unexpected parallelisms of ideas in psychology and physics suggest . . . a possible ultimate one-ness of both fields of reality that physics and psychology study, i.e., a psychophysical one-ness of all life phenomena." Waddington too has characterized evolutionary theory as something that "in fact merely amounts to the statement that the individuals which leave the most offspring are those which leave the most offspring. It is a tautology."[2] We have been left with another circular explanation, chasing our own evolutionary tail.

Although modern biochemistry, cybernetics, and general systems have shown that blind chance combined with natural selection could not keep evolution going in the direction to which the evidence points, they have only found more critical and sophisticated means once more to express the lack of any acceptable evolutionary theory. The celebrated biologist and general systems theorist Ludwig von Bertalanffy wrote perhaps the most damning epitaph for present evolutionary theories:

> I think the fact that a theory so vague, so insufficiently verifiable and so far from the criteria otherwise applied in "hard" science, has become a dogma, can only be explained on sociological grounds. Society and science have been so steeped in the ideas of mechanism, utilitarianism and the economic concept of free competition, that instead of God, Selection was enthroned as ultimate reality. On the other hand, it seems symptomatic that the present discon-

tent with the state of the world is also felt in evolution theory. I believe this is the explanation why leading evolutionists like J. Huxley and Dobzhansky (1967) discover sympathy with the somewhat muddy mysticism of Teilhard de Chardin. If differential reproduction and selective advantage are the only directive factors of evolution, it is hard to see why evolution has ever progressed beyond the rabbit, the herring, or even the bacterium which are unsurpassed in their reproductive capacities.[3]

While many have openly despaired of a solution to the riddle, the fact is that the very sciences that have nurtured that feeling are the ones to provide us with the new tools to resolve the dilemma. But to proceed we shall have to reformulate a few of the basic ideas in these disciplines. Before postulating the mechanics by which evolution can be "directed ontogenetic change," we shall review for a moment the facts of change and the observable effects using our perspective of three billion years of history.

GROWTH OF INFORMATION ORGANIZATION

- The basic drive of all organisms is to grow: to reproduce and to multiply.

- Growth is accomplished by accumulating capabilities to use energy and to direct its use.

- Use of energy for growth depends on the building up of information in living organisms and the success of this information in guiding the transformation of environmental materials into bodily constituents and special products to aid growth.

- Over time, the method of organically accumulating information has changed through the evolution of information holding and transmission techniques:

  Atomic bonding
  Molecular bonding
  Carbon-based heteropolymeric molecules
  Cell growth (enlargement)
  Cell reproduction (fission mitosis)
  Intercellular information exchange (conjugation and transduction)
  Cell recombination (fusion meiosis)
  Cell colonies
  Multicellular organisms

- Each evolutionary and natural selection step increased the organization of information and the capability of living forms to use energy to reproduce, and to decrease the biological waste of energy through loss of progeny. Less and less energy was required per unit of time to accomplish the same result.

- As complex, integral multicellular organisms evolved, other information-acquisition, storage, and transmission systems emerged to deal with more information—perception systems, nerve and brain systems, and communication systems.

- With improvements in external information handling systems, once more organisms increased their capacity to use energy to reproduce and to transform the environment into more of themselves.

    Multicellular organisms formed colonies
    Intraspecies symbiotic cooperation evolved

- Concomitant with the evolution and selection of species, the capacity to add information increased through learning by experience and imitative and social learning.

- With the advent of a sophisticated stereoscopic, color-perceiving system* and nonreproducing mammalian neurons, the possibility for acquisition and long-term storage of information increased.

- In order to transmit acquired information to progeny through imitative and verbal means, hominoid societies evolved longer infant learning periods and improved their communication techniques.

- To increase substantially the heritability of externally acquired information required the invention of improved information-holding and transmission techniques. With the development of symbolism this goal became possible.

- By the use of culturally spread information, additions of substantially larger amounts of new information to a much broader group became practical.

- As Man continually added to this externalized pool of in-

*Primates are the only animals with stereoscopic color vision.

formation the infantile period was once more expanded so that a child entering adulthood could acquire the ecto-genetic pool of information.

- Parallel with the development of symbolic information systems humans evolved higher levels of multiorganism communication, information exchange, and cooperative effects through:

  Families and tribes
  Villages and cities
  City-states and nations
  International organizations

- Technology and information growth followed the same pattern as a form of ectobiological extension and continually increased the use of energy to form life, life-supporting products, and higher levels of information exchange.

Thus, in psychological and cultural development extending the work of his biologic precursors, Man developed diversity, novelty, and higher levels of organization as a function of the evolving information system. The pressure of information growth continually reconstructs the "genetic" system with nature an unrelenting master of invention in developing better and better methods of carrying information forward.

ADAPTATION

In Darwinian terms, although it is inescapably true that environmental conditions do modify the form and behavior of organisms, the question is whether this phenomenon can truly be characterized by referring to it as an adaptation *to* the environment. A perfect "adaption" to anything would be like the symbiotic relationship of phoresis, where associated organisms are not affected by each other (such as the bacteria carried in the hairs of a fly's leg).[4] However, the *ratio of adaptation* between an organism and its environment is clearly one that demonstrates a far greater effect and adaptation of the environment *by* the organism, rather than an adaption *to* that environment by the organism.

The harmony of a quiescent environment is disturbed greatly when a living being absorbs it, dismembers it, rearranges it, and transforms it into its own living form. The environment changes substantially more than the organism. As with biological systems, this active *adapting of* and *transformation of* the environment is

FIGURE 54

Estimated amounts of DNA (in 10^{-12} gram) information per haploid chromosome complement. (After Mirsky, Ris, Dobzhansky et al.) Evolution and natural selection add genetic information as organisms reach higher levels of organization. The exponential chart below shows examples of large leaps in information – building systems.

Amphibia	3.7	
Man	3.2	Complex multicellular
Cattle	2.8	organism
Green turtle	2.6	
Chicken, duck	1.3	
Sponge	0.11	
Sea urchin	0.90	Simple multicellular
Snail	0.67	organism
Mollusk	0.50	
Yeast	0.07	Complex single-cell
E. coli	0.01	organism
Bacteriophage T2	0.000,2	Simple single-cell
Bacteriophage ϕ X 174	0.000,003,6	organism

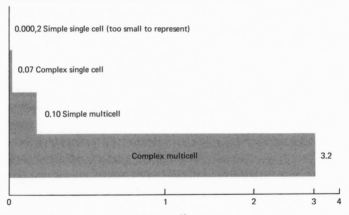

0.000,2 Simple single cell (too small to represent)

0.07 Complex single cell

0.10 Simple multicell

Complex multicell   3.2

0   1   2   3   4

DNA weights (10^{-12} gm)/haploid

actually the most prominent characteristic of both biological and psychological systems.[5]

Darwin's famous finches would never have evolved from their protozoan precursors if "adaptation to" or "equilibrium" had been their goal. Obviously, organisms respond to their environment. They do "adapt." But, like a magician's misdirection, this fact has led many investigators away from seeing the underlying changes on the other side of life's basic transaction: the perpetual enhancement of the capacity of living organisms to *change the environment into themselves*, their progeny, and the special products that serve their life and growth. Those Galapagos finches, like all the living things we have considered, dismantled and totally reorganized parts of their environment as they grew. In its simplest terms, they ate their environment and made it into more finches! By looking closely and at the same time broadening our perspective we can see that evolution and growth are far more an adaptation *of* the environment than solely the reverse. This modification of the environment provides the basic clue to the resolution of the paradox of evolution. It provides the machinery by which evolution can *accumulate.*

DIRECTED SELECTION

In Chapter Three we examined the "second nature" of Man and broadened our examination of genetics to include the idea of ectogenetic information. There we concluded that, "the ectogenetic process amounted to creation of immediate and reversible biopsychologic mutation; in sum *directed and directable evolution.*" Although it is relatively easy to see that culture could become an external genetic mechanism to carry forward and to accumulate the effects of human evolvement, we now can see that ectogenetics existed long before the advent of symbolism. It had been the carrier of genetic data for all time.

Consider for a moment the ectogenetic effect of culture on our species. In recent times, for example, Man decided to make great efforts to reach for outer space. The effect of this thrust was to create an environment conducive to the successful proliferation of certain classes of scientists. Students and institutions were stimulated to follow the course of space-science information and technology. In more recent days, the space effort has been greatly diminished. The viability of scientific professions in the field has substantially lowered. As a result, universities, companies, and government agencies have shifted their priorities and emphasis to other, more viable information. We have created a changed environment that will make other professions grow. We have adapted the environment to new conditions, and the result is not only a changed external world but great changes on the men in it.

In just such a way does the system of Nature provide an *external* means by which to affect the organisms in it. *Organisms create the conditions in their environment that favor the selection of particular kinds of mutations.* In other words, genetic information is not carried solely in the germ cells but is also provided by environment; it is within the *total system* of life.

In the world of the physical sciences, Heisenberg recognized this principle over two and a half decades ago. It is the question of interaction, the act of observing that a phenomenon can affect the phenomenon. Thus, the observer must take this interaction into account. What biological evolutionists have missed is simply that, although random mutations occur, the selection among these

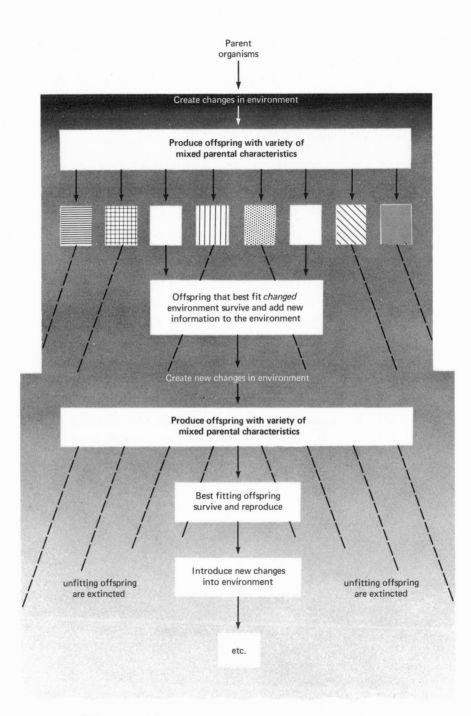

FIGURE 55

174

mutations is far from random. The parental organisms have changed the environment in such a way as to influence the selection process; their *learned behavior causes modifications that are carried forward by the environment;* by the interaction that occurs between their progeny and the environment they have created. (See Figure 55.)

This fact means two basic things: A modified environment can lead either to enhancement of a particular characteristic or to changing it to another direction. If, for example, our Galapagos finches live in a world where there are an infinite quantity of worms to eat—if an environment encounters no great pressure— mutations favoring an improved worm-digging beak will result. On the other hand, if the worm-eating species become so success- ful and plentiful that there are not enough worms for the young developing birds, selection will favor a capacity to extend eating habits to broader ecological niches and other beak structures, etc., will emerge. Because successful progenation is the attribute of surviving species, pressure will inevitably occur for the enhance- ment of broader capabilities of transforming the environment into higher levels of organization, ever more able to transform more of the environment into organized living forms and into the special products to aid them in their own transformations.

This phenomenon occurs not only at every phylogenetic level of "life," but also at every level of matter and energy. Like a "seed" crystal, a molecule creates the conditions of its own succeeding growth. It too, by successful "progenation," creates the condi- tions for exhausting its environment and causing the new en- vironment to effect changes in the molecules to follow. Even in such simple phenomena as magnetism we see the same process: As a magnetic force is applied to a series of randomly oriented atoms in a piece of metal and a small number of these atoms are reoriented in the direction of the force in what are called "do- mains," they begin to influence one another until suddenly all the atoms flip to the new and complementary orientation.

An ancient Chinese saying, "This arises—that becomes," refers to the fact that a thing cannot occur without its opposite; you cannot have dark without light, fullness without emptiness, or right without left. As we can now see it, when anything *becomes,* it automatically begins to create interactions around itself. As noted earlier, our world is one of interrelations. It is just this interaction with the environment—the outside world—that makes up the total information or "genetic" system of all things, atoms, cells, or humans.

Both Darwin and Lamarck were right. In isolation each theory provides a part of the total picture. Darwin was correct in that organisms are changed by their environment; Lamarck, equally so, in the sense that changes are indeed caused by organisms—by *changing their environment.* Evolution is both repetitive and cumulative. Thus it is not totally random. Blind chance alone cannot work in an environment that is being pressured by the organisms in it, just as an "objective" scientific experiment has no meaning if the experimentor continually modifies its environment. The "randomness" of evolution can be compared to the process of "brainstorming" for ideas. Although a large number of random combinations occur, we subject them to the criteria of our ever changing environment to decide which to select.

At the same time, however, the factor of chance does create new and unexpected constellations of possibilities. Just as a random idea may serve to solve a particular problem, its very randomness can also introduce *new* information into the system. Nature's inventions, in this light, are identical in process with Man's. The chance happening—"serendipity," or finding one thing when you are looking for something else—is a common experience in both. Plant and animal breeders have long recognized this phenomenon and it has substantially aided in accidentally "improving the breed," from roses to cattle. This ubiquitous directionality of evolutionary processes and invention also explains why we see so many evolutionary forms and human ideas occurring in parallel: why similar species appeared in different locations in the same period and why so many thinkers and inventors find the same idea occurring to someone else at the same time (Darwin and Wallace, for example).

ENERGY AND LIFE

By enlarging our perspective of information beyond the idea of germ cell genetics, we can begin to comprehend a large body of phenomena. Just as Newton was able to correct Galileo by extending observations from weight on this planet to the moon and planets and as Einstein broadened this view even more, our role here is to seek to coordinate a larger number of facts and phenomena drawn from remoter areas. To do this at levels so far unexpressed here would involve volumes, but we can attempt to grasp a basically new perspective of evolution and behavior by a brief reconsideration of life, energy, and matter. This perspective is necessary because, even though the concept of ectogenetics can explain the basic mechanics of evolutionary direction, behind it is the ever recurring question "why?" whose answer will, of course, provoke new questions.

What is it that causes information to accumulate at higher levels of organization? The bridge to understanding encompasses a single basic principle related to the idea of "information." Since the first chapter we have looked at information as something that "determines the probabilities of an event." Examined closely, this introduces the idea that *information is a form of energy,* for energy causes events or "work." It causes atoms to bond and molecules to form; it provides our food and our thoughts. In each case, however, energy must be in very particular and specific forms or "frequencies" to do its work. It must be expressed in a form that can be "understood" at every level. In this light, energy *is* information (in both kinetic and potential forms).

Growth is a phenomenon that depends on the linking of information, that is, the finding of congruent meaning in its joining. As growth occurs, new phenomena come into being as expressions of higher levels of organization. A photon of light is emitted from the sun and, through photosynthesis, becomes plant life, converting carbon dioxide into oxygen and into the vegetative informational nutrition that sustains animal life. As this level of organized information is absorbed in the animal world, it reaches new heights of organization, joining in larger and larger molecules, becoming cells and the energy to drive them. It can ultimately become the material by which we move, speak, and think. If information is in an inappropriate form—as a chemical, for example—it can become toxic and cause life to cease. Yet it constantly finds the right forms to support life and to support its own transformation to becoming parts of larger organizations.

At the psychological level of growth, the use of information is recapitulated. We learn by communicating with one another using the same mechanics as are used in physical informational processes, through what is called "electromagnetic radiation." Just as an atom "knows" what information it can accept for growth and does this at the level of the photon, the unit of "light energy," so we accept data or not, depending on its frequencies of energy. Vision, for example, is able to absorb particular photons, or spectra, of light. The configuration of the "light energy" gives us information. Just as the light falling on the page is absorbed by dark letters and reflected by the lighter page, the energy enables us to get "data" from these words. Through one form of information energy or another, through all of our senses, we are able to grow.

We are increasingly better able to understand, as another case in point, that information is power or "capital." Far beyond the effect of money or land or machines, the organization or organism that successfully grows is able to do so as a function of the information it possesses. Monolithic organizations have been decimated by much smaller groups who have a new idea. The force of an "idea whose time has come" is irresistible.

It is all very well to call energy "information," but the meaning of this information carries us far beyond the boundaries of "living organisms." It plummets us to the microcosmic universe of atoms and electromagnetic radiation. It impels a postulate to help understand or, at least, explain what is really happening. A basic idea, which is extrapolated here, was first proposed by Paul Kammerer in the early 1900s. Along with his other ideas, which supported Lamarckian evolution, it contributed to the abuse heaped on him by the scientific community and ultimately led to his suicide. In a full exposition of Kammerer's work, Arthur Koestler summarized in *The Case of the Midwife Toad* the new concept put forth by Kammerer:

> The central idea is that, *side by side with the causality of classical physics, there exists a second basic principle in the universe which tends toward unity; a force of attraction comparable to universal gravity.* But while gravity acts on all mass without discrimination, this other universal force acts selectively to bring like and like together both in space and in time; it *correlates by affinity,* regardless whether the likeness is one of substance, form or function, or refers to symbols. The modus operandi of this force, the way it penetrates the trivia of everyday life, Kammerer confesses to be unable to explain because it operates ex hypothesi outside the known laws of causality. But he *points to analogies on various levels, where the same tendency towards unity, symmetry and coherence manifests itself in conventionally causal ways: from gravity and magnetism through chemical affinity, sexual attraction, biological adaptation, symbiosis, protective colouring, imitative behaviour, and so on . . .* [6]

Surely, in 1920 science did not have the advantage of today's knowledge, but it is yet another piece of the evidence for psychospeciation and the unacceptability of differentness of data in the narrowing focus of science that this work and its implications have been overlooked for so long. In an intuitive flash of brilliance

Kammerer originated a concept that we can now see to be true. *Along with the process of entropy there is another process occurring in parallel, that of "syntropy";* information (as energy) constantly produces new combinations, producing diversity and higher levels of organization.

While matter is being disorganized by the forces of entropic breakdown, it is at the same time being organized by syntropy. Entropy runs "downhill" as organized matter continually decays, and syntropy runs "uphill" as matter is continually being put together in more cohesive ways. Syntropy acts very differently from the accepted transactions in the physical universe, just as idea exchange contravenes the basic concepts of economics. The sum *is* becoming greater than the parts.

As a matter of fact, the function of entropy is *complementary* to that of syntropy. Because no organization of information can reach an absolute state, entropy aids our reorganization by helping break down old materials. It is the catabolic function of the physical universe just as syntropy is anabolic. Life cannot exist without death, for life would have nothing to resynthesize into higher organizations if it were in static equilibrium. As the great biologist Haldane put it, "Normal death must apparently be regarded from the biological standpoint as a means by which room is made for further more definite development of life."[7] Death contributes to life in a specific causal chain. Decay is the handmaiden of creation.

As an illustration of the radical difference between the entropy of some manifestations of energy and the syntropy of information, consider the Second Law of Thermodynamics as it applies to two bodies of unequal temperatures that are brought together. In time, heat energy will distribute itself evenly between the two bodies, and in contact with a wider environment as well, will continually equalize and redistribute their heat. The order of heat runs "downhill," from organization to chaos. Yet, if we consider *information as a function of energy,* we see the reverse phenomenon. The two bodies, rather than diffusing their data, can actually *increase their order and organization.* Two atoms, molecules, cells, or humans can exchange and share information, and will, in time, through evolution, continually organize it to higher levels.

Yet the foundation of physics assumes the verity of the law of Entropy: that the universe is progressing into disorder. Time and time again experiments have demonstrated the facts of the Second Law of Thermodynamics. And the facts are true—as far as they go. Unfortunately a great deal of scientific thinking is based on investigation of what we can only characterize as *closed systems,* systems isolated from their normal environment. A classical statement is that when a phenomenon is "left to itself," this or that will happen. A researcher will do his best to isolate his experiment so that it will not be affected by outside influences or "perturbations." In doing so he in fact creates an *isolated system,* one which has *no* choice but to behave in an entropic manner as it is removed from interactive growth with the larger system. Even in our age of sophisticated science this artificial methodology continues—violating the advice given by Max Planck over four decades ago when he said, "The assumption that the orderly course of a process can be represented by an analysis of it into temporal and spacial processes must be dropped. The conception of wholeness must therefore be introduced in physics as in biology."

The results of such experiments provide a distorted picture of reality—from the behavior of atoms to that of men. What we really learn from such data is the type of behavior to expect from a *deprived* sub-system.* Animals, men, and molecules when subjected to "test-tube" isolation naturally fall back on lower forms of growth. Referring recently to the misleading results of such studies in animal learning the noted animal behaviorist Eckhard Hess said, "I have had to conclude that the usual laboratory imprinting has only a limited resemblance to natural imprinting."[8] Imprinting, the early and rapid learning of animals, has been a cornerstone concept of behavioral theory ever since Konrad Lorenz observed in the 1930s that goslings would follow him rather than their mother if they saw him before her; yet studies *in vivo* show these *in vitro* studies to be, as Dr. Eckhard put it, "deprivation experiments" which " . . . do not produce the maximum effect."

Attempts to provide more holistic environments for experiments invariably lead to unexpected results, that is, unexpected in the light of entropic laws. A case in point is the now classical

---

*The experimentor is usually not considered to be part of the experiment, and thus, the energy "lost" in the experiment is not observed as being translated into new *information.* Looked at as a more holistic system, the experimentor must be treated as a part of the experiment. Brillouin postulated this with his concept of "negentropy" although he believed that the information obtained was always less than the energy lost and in this way, held fast the idea of entropy. If we look at the relationship of the physical system to the experimentor's mental system we derive a very different picture from that of Brillouin's negentropy; we see instead a demonstration of syntropy—higher not lower order.

"origin of life" experiment. Less than a decade ago a young graduate student, Stanley Miller, at the University of Chicago tested the possibility of organic compounds arising "spontaneously" in the simplified environment of the primeval earth. Creating a considerably more realistic—holistic—laboratory copy of this environment, methane, ammonia, hydrogen, and water, he subjected it to another common environmental agent, an electric spark much like lightning. The result was the formation of several amino acids and formaldehyde—complex building blocks of life. Following these astonishing results laboratory upon laboratory has duplicated this experiment with the same results. Melvin Calvin's work and other investigations have shown that such simple environments when subjected to *any* form of natural energy input, heat, ultraviolet rays, etc., will form not only simple amino acids but complex compounds including adenine, quanine, uracil, and various sugars.[9] We can see that "chance" alone cannot explain such consistent results. There is an inevitability to such phenomena.

From the standpoint of classical ideas of entropy, the laws of universal decay have been likened to such things as the behavior of masses of different billiard balls. All matter, we have been told, would behave like an orderly arrangement of billiard balls which, in the presence of an outside force, will become progressively disarranged until no order exists. This seems reasonable; billiard balls do not rearrange themselves into orderly patterns. Yet in the Miller experiment above, what we are really seeing is an initial situation of mass disorder in which order occurs spontaneously. Imagine a billiard table with a thousand numbered balls in random disarray, which upon being struck by an outside force—a player shooting a high-energy ball into their midst—would suddenly arrange themselves into orderly rows and columns by their numbers! This is exactly like what Miller and many others experienced with atoms and molecules in their laboratories. Nature, instead of further disordering things, was *ordering* them.

We can see why such results were unexpected. When we are asked to think of billiard balls we are not invited to include the *players*. If we were to observe a billiard room instead, we would expect to see people disarranging and rearranging the balls—a very different phenomenon. It is a more holistic environment. One could have objected at this point by saying that humans are involved in the billiard room and are thus using their *intelligence* to provide order from disorder; however, since this is what we can now see is happening in all natural processes, we can only assume that even the most simple things contain intelligence. It is an intelligence dedicated to providing ever higher levels of organized, mutualized interrelationships; they are syntropic rather than entropic.

The human syntropic machine is indeed something special, particularly if we look at the accumulation of energy potentials. One way to do this is to measure the energy reserve of animals versus Man. It was shown, shortly after the turn of the century, by the physiologist Rubner [10] that while mammals are characterized by energy reserves which average 16,000 kilocalories, Man's average energy exceeds 700,000 kilocalories! This and other of his studies demonstrated that high levels of activity actually *increase* the working potential of organisms. Once more, the facts are in sharp disagreement with classical laws. Intensive work is supposed to contribute to the wear and destruction of a system. Yet we can see that work, in truth, enhances the capabilities of an organism to do *more* work. As has been pointed out in recent research by Arshavsky, this "stands the test from the point of view of so important and basic a criterion as the life-span." Energy begets energy.*[11]

In engineering practices there is also a tendency to see things in isolation. An engineer would say, "The harder you work this machine, the more wear will occur—it will run downhill." Yet, we must recognize that a machine, any machine, does not exist in isolation, it is an indivisible part of a system. What must be considered is *why* we have the machine. If it is to manufacture something, its working is dependent on the demand for the product and the economic potential of the manufacturing company. If the company is in order, the more the machine works, the more earnings it achieves, the more need there is to improve it (as competition emerges in a successful market), and finally it replaces itself by having translated its work into another form. Considered within the *system,* it contributes to subsequent reordering at higher levels. It is a part not apart and is mechanically

---

*Human life-span and intensive work may be as directly related as the life-span of cattle and horses; that is, while horses will expend far more active energy than cattle they live twice as long or longer. As Arshavsky notes, active approaches to stimuli prove to be a positive factor and avoidance (or self-sparing for comfort) is negative. The Soviet Institute of Gerontology states that "Man could live longer if he were allowed to work longer," a fact which is frequently and tragically verified by the deterioration that so often accompanies idle retirement.

syntropic. A badly designed machine would not perform the same syntropic function and, being "unfit," would be extincted in short order. Even an inanimate bit of matter such as this is still subject to the basic laws of nature—grow or die.

By removing the artificial constraints of "solitary confinement" in the laboratory and taking an interrelational, growth, or "systems" perspective of the "laws of Nature," we are left with the irrefutable facts of a physical* and mental universe that violate some of the most ancient and basic principles of science. It is from this point of view that transformation theory postulates the "*directed* ontogenetic change" of evolution.

SAMENESS OR DIFFERENTNESS

The idea of evolution toward organized systems can lead to concepts that predict an ultimate humdrum sameness. Both to Man and Nation this is an intolerable idea. The continuing interaction between living organisms and their relationship with the broad environment involve, as well, organizational-changes that are characterized by an upward swing of both integration *and* differentiation. We allow larger amounts of distinct information to be expressed and then synchronously mesh these multitudes of differentness into high-order interdependent interactions. As anything becomes more organized it can actually tolerate more distinctiveness. A molecule is more complex, yet it is simpler to describe than its component atoms. In human terms the "liberation" of races, women, youth, music, clothes, and so forth, has created the possibilities, and the fact, of creating more complementary and mutually enriching relationships. For instance, the European Anglo-Saxon once practiced genocide, physically and culturally, with the American Indian. The level of growth of the early American colonies did not permit the absorption of these differences. Today, we see the reverse; efforts are being made to rediscover the heritage of these cultures and to absorb them. We accept more differentness from each other and at the same time grow more closely together.

Although attempts are made to explain these many ordering phenomena as "progress" or "humanization" or in other equally vague terms, it is possible to see them in the light of irreversible and basic laws of the known universe. Our recent efforts to stop

---

*Physical phenomena are reviewed in Appendix II.

non-decay in the ecological movement, to encourage "biodegradable" materials, illustrate our need to maintain the dynamics of universal growth. We do not now and probably never will realize a balanced or equilibrium state, for this would be a denial of the most fundamental laws of being. Those who maintain that we must stop or slow our "growth" simply do not understand that there are various forms of growth and that growth cannot be arrested. What they unknowingly espouse is a surpassing of older and lower growth forms and the movement of our species to a higher level of organization and growth, that is, to mutuality.

The freedom to form new alternative combinations and mutualisms increases at every new level of evolution from the atomic level to the molecular level to the organic. Each step makes it possible to form more new and different juxtapositions; as a consequence, we naturally find more compounds than there are elements, more words than there are letters, and so forth. At the human social-psychological level, the possibilities of new combinations are, for all practical purposes, infinite. In such an evolving "deterministic" universe, as more organized mutualized growth occurs, the *less* individually deterministic it becomes. The freedom to grow is only mediated by the need to grow *with* the system of life. As long as an idea or behavior can be made to contribute in some way, any way, it survives, just as does an atom or molecule as part of a compound.

In all of these phenomena we are observing the phenomenon of "as below—so above" *and* vice versa. This universality of process makes it possible to begin to explain any or all of the universe by starting at practically any point and adding the new behaviors that occur with changes in scale and complexity. In the case of this exposition of transformation theory we have attempted to forge links between the biological, psychological, and cultural as a starting place. We could just as well have chosen the physical and chemical, or musical and mathematical. The basic phenomena of growth are isomorphic at all levels. Perhaps we can more easily see and realize transformation at the biopsychocultural level because this is Nature's highest level of organization and it is within the experience of each of us. In this light it is unfortunate that creative thinkers have often been criticized for having classified their ideas as "anthropocentric," as if to build outward from humanness were a fallacious concept. Indeed, we can conclude that this accusation is not true, not if we can see Man as *a part* of the total system of being.

ACHIEVING GROWTH
ELEVEN

In 1959, gathered at the University of Chicago for the 100th anniversary of Darwin's *Origin of Species,* scientists summed up their position on evolutionary theory: "Evolution is definable in general terms as a one-way irreversible process in time, which during its course generates novelty, diversity and higher levels of organization. It operates in all sectors of the phenomenal universe but has been most fully described and analysed in the biological sector." As an extension of the Darwinian revolution that replaced a score of basic beliefs and theories about our biological origins, transformation has offered in this introductory volume a union of evolutionary theory with psychosocial phenomena and with basic physical theory. It is well to recall, however, that any theory is but a small piece of reality, an incomplete description of our universe, one to which we will add information as we go in a never-ending process. All that we can do here is to show that transformation theory is consistent, orderly, logically structured, and in agreement with broad experimental evidence. Inevitably old facts will be discarded, new facts will be found, and new theories will be written. New "laws of nature" will be discovered in the ever-unfinished business of searching for the truth of being.

Most of all, this treatment of transformation has tried to meet the need to understand the profound demands of the human system that go far beyond such visceral needs as sex, hunger, and thirst and those that often defy the pressures of the physical environment. To do this, it views Man as a part of all of Nature, grown from the basic character of all being and motivated by the same growth drives that move the rest of life. Transformation theory sees the functions of evolution and natural selection as a real and viable foundation for a unitary and dynamic basis of psychosocial life, one that provides an understanding of human growth that joins with the underlying growth forms of physical and biological activity.

Man's thought and acts, from this vantage point, become part of the panorama of historical unity of life that fuses our most distinctive and unique human characteristics with those existing everywhere. These natural principles of psychosocial growth have long been intuitively practiced without recognition of this principle or even that a principle was involved. By showing why a person selects or discriminates between various forms and values of behavior—*why* we act and think rather than how or what—on a basis of modern science, transformation becomes the mucilage by which to integrate the disparate sciences of Man and to join these with the independent conceptual fields of the aesthetics and the philosophies of Life.

AGENTS OF TRANSFORMATION

When we consider human "nature" in the context of today's mounting conflicts, we can employ transformation to reconcile the "greening" of our culture with its traumatic "shock." The outcries against horror, violence, and absurdity; the accusation of an establishment-created depersonalized and robotized life; the anxiety of helplessness, boredom, and cynicism—all demonstrate with unsettling verity that Man is changing and that decay accompanies development. He will no longer accept with equanimity what has gone before. At the same time that Mankind has lengthened life and increased the probability of survival, he has created exacerbating conflict and potential world holocaust— the conditions necessary for new growth forms to emerge.

The dynamism of the open system of transformation manifests itself in many phenomena. Individually we grow by learning and forgetting, by expanding ourselves and enriching the lives of others. As a society we eagerly invade the promise of the future while we grudgingly abandon our cherished beliefs of the past. We constantly take our physical world apart so we can reformulate it into new levels of organized material. Local cultures dissolve as they bring their differences into new cultural organizations. In all of this we see the process of transformation as we disorganize in order to reorganize at higher levels. Nowhere is this more evident than in the process of thinking and memory, as we take old facts and dismember them to fit into new organization of thought; the freedom of creating new ideas balanced by the responsibility of joining them with what has gone before.

Experiencing the process of creative mutual growth does not preclude us from the manifestations of accretive and replicative growth. Each man, each society in its infinite acts of behavior is an ever-changing supportive mixture of all forms of growth, working through and with each other. Just so, each of us emphasizes one form of growth more than others as our progression through the evolution of a single life climbs the many ladders of growth. Full growth is a relational process, one which calls on us to play the full repertory of growth. The vital question is one of recognizing what kinds of growth are occurring so that all growth can be facilitated to serve mankind, and in so doing serve the self.

Each of us is a transformational agent as we go about our daily lives—taking and giving, giving and taking. As we transform ourselves, we transform our environment and as we remold our world we create the growing ectogenetic system of Man. By mutualizing with those around us, with others, and with our environment we bring new disorder and order into being, an order which will inexorably be carried forward and built upon for our children and our children's children. This is our great legacy. Not all the wealth in the world can create meaning, and yet to live meaningfully is the most important thing in life. Transformation theory incorporates the idea of "meaning" or value as a basic fact of existence, and a *changing* fact.

Yet evolution carries with it the message of extinction. If we isolate ourselves from the "system" of life; if we do not make new friends of old enemies; if we do not find a balance of trade with our environment, we face a future known in all of its frightening dimensions. We, as a culture, as a species even, will join with the other unfit systems of our world. The message is abundantly clear: Grow or die, evolution or extinction. It is in our hands, not just as governments or even cultures, but as humans.

Just like the nature of a cell, the manifestations of Man's nature are forever in the process of becoming. As mutuality becomes the norm, we can expect to discover more of the richness of "human nature." Rather than viewing a Man as a creature born perhaps good or evil or simply subject to environment, we shall be able to see human character as a result of the interwoven effects of the pruning or flowering of innate evolutionary growth urges. Man can become the transdetermining agent of his own nature.

There are a host of practical possibilities as to how individuals and societies can apply the evolutionary leverage of transformation. In general, all depend on two vital functions:

Providing a greater abundance of psychosocial nutrition to more people and cultures.

Increasing opportunities to experiment with and use this material for growth in mutual interaction.

In specific terms, we can transdetermine and enhance life and living in many ways. Some have already been noted in preceding chapters and the reader has surely added many more. A few examples here will suffice:

For parents and teachers, providing the freedom for safe, exploratory play with the environment and incrementally granting responsibility to the growing child; providing a belief in dignity, respect, and self-affirmation by being willing not only to educate but to learn *from* and mutualize with our children and allow the expression of their growth through affecting their environment.

For our institutions of rehabilitation, awareness of the deformative functions of non-effect and exclusion, a recognition of the latent developmental values existing in all men, and formulation of *subculturing* techniques to facilitate the learning of new growth forms and the pride of reciprocal worth.

For our institutions of influence, policies and practices that provide opportunities for all to make *contributions to mutual growth* by abandonment of the "let us solve *your* problems" approach.

For counselors, therapists, and ministers, a relationship with clients that admits the potential of mutual, rather than one-way, growth; a *willingness to be changed as well as make change.*

As we look into the future and consider the problem of technological, social, and cultural analysis and attempt to set our goals, and to allocate our limited resources for the achievement of those goals, we must recognize that many of our present mechanisms of development and control are inadequate to the tasks of facilitating and catalyzing growth.

For example, even in relatively small groups like government and managerial bodies, information is often generated, disseminated, and used slowly, inaccurately, and nonreciprocally. Decisions, goals, and priorities are too frequently merely responses to the limited and narrow pressures of closed information systems that exclude inputs from the very people and environments to which policy-makers should respond. We must give more due to real, timely, and objective relationships and information that can tell us more of the authentic human processes of change.

ECOLOGY AND TECHNOLOGY

Already priorities important to our species are being decided on the basis of prejudicial data—the question of conservation and ecology, for instance. In this, as in many other cases, the systemic relationships of natural ecology have been distorted by lack of a human growth perspective. Because Man himself is frequently not included as an integral part of the preservation of "Nature," many so-called ecological movements call for a "return to (nonhuman) Nature." Policies and practices are adopted to attempt regression to *past* systems; technology is seen as a sort of "enemy" to be defeated, without the realization that it too is a naturally evolved process, one that creates the very special products that are mandatory to support evolving humanity. Technology, in a very real sense, is a large part of the "balance of Nature."

Man constantly *redistributes the balance of natural systems,* always in a dynamically unstable way that presses for new forms of growth. If we suddenly diminish human products, it can have effects on human systems far more detrimental than the loss of small parcels of Nature that some are attempting to conserve.

One example of this misunderstanding is the employment of resources that could be used for human needs for the overprotection and preservation of endangered animal species. Today, although less than 2 percent of all the species known are still in existence, overprotection of animal forms is hardly "in tune" with Nature. It is worth imagining what might have happened if today's ideas had been implemented in past times. Progress toward a better future is never a matter of redressing the future with past forms, but of discovering how to create the ever new possibilities of tomorrow.

As part of our growth toward mutualism, the technologies and ideas of Man not only are the present means to support our progress toward new goals, but are themselves in a state of rapid evolvement, life-support systems in transition to mutualism. The idea of technological "dehumanization" is not withstanding once we realize that only by extending our biologic nature through the *ectosomatics* of such functions as protection, manufacturing, transportation, and communication have we been able to create the *freedom* necessary to be the agents of accelerating evolution. Like all biologic advances, the "degradation" of machinery has released more energy for transformation. Without them, the time and energy necessary to learn about our world and act on it would simply not be available, nor would we live long enough to see the fruition of our efforts. Technology is the self-extension that liberates Man to use his energy and information to transform our world.

The mutualistic biotechnology of our future world will surely amaze even our most far-seeing futurists. Although we have amplified many of our natural systems, in many cases we have done so in the crudest terms possible. As a vital example of this, consider the problem of our present "energy crisis." The history of energy development demonstrates again the discontinuous processes of growth. For tens of thousands of years, fire was Man's primary source of extrabiologic energy. The use of wind as a supplement and replacement for fire was to last only several thousand years before Man harnessed water power. The industrial mills' use of water was to give way in several *hundred* years to the force of steam, and before a hundred years had passed, steam power surrendered to the internal combustion engine. Less than half a hundred years later, we entered the age of atomic power. Like all growth processes, each new advance in form has occurred in a much compressed time frame.

We are provoked to ask "What next?" With the advantage of applying a biologic perspective, we can see that the energy system of nature can provide clues to potential alternatives. Organic systems have always utilized the atomic power of the sun. By photosynthetic and biosynthetic processes, the primary energy of this gigantic reactor has been used to support life for billions of years. What then of *controlled biologic systems?* In comparison to our crude use of catalyzed chemical energy, biological enzymatic processes can be a great many times more efficient.[1] Our incessantly rising demands for energy may very well come from Man's

190

re-creation of living systems. With a form of efficient biochemical energy production, more of the almost 99 percent of solar energy now wasted might be captured for human use. Plant-like photo-synthetic electric transducers may indeed be the new "greening" of our world.

CULTURAL TRANSFORMATION

As we move into that unknown future, we can try to appraise the trends of evolution as it affects the quality of our lives and culture—our internal and external peace and progress. We are today surrounded by a proliferation of new expressions of growth; like all of the peaks of evolution, it is characterized by a wide variety of alternatives on which selection can operate. What we see today is an incessant and spreading psychosocial hybridization manifested in both new conflicts and new freedoms. The clothes we wear, our hairstyles, the music we listen to, the professions we choose, the causes we support, and the ideas we create are only a few of the new pressures of growth, ones no longer dominated by the replicative and redundant growth forms that have created "tradition." The success of those past forms has caused us to become dominated by the pressures of the new age of mutualism.

The idea of overcoming the *status quo* and reformulating our society is growing. As this re-evolution progresses and grows, it too is changing its own evolutionary form, as the less fit mechan-isms of social change are extincted and new methods emerge. Accretive–replicative protest and activism are mutating into the mutualization of ideas. This is not to say that all manifestations of change are progressive. Through a variety of types of cultural and "cultist" isolation, some subcultures invariably develop regressive and antagonistic forms of growth. Some of this evolutionary "backsliding" is only to be expected as our growing social organism develops new communication and metabolism methods. Isolated though these efforts may be, in an era when the information and technology necessary to extinct our species are widely disseminated, our mandate is to move quickly in order to broaden our culturization to embrace and to mutualize with *all* cultures, creating the *status ascensium.*

As we look backward into our future, the instruction of Nature shows the tragic results of evolutionary change that was resisted too long. The muted remains of the earliest accretive cultures culminate in the testimony of massive disintegration and reconstruction. The great accretive cultures of Egypt, China, Greece, and Rome show the inevitable result of enlargement beyond the capability of the system to communicate and to metabolize.

In our own time, the less obvious but more real ruins of the replicative empires that followed the accretive age are strewn about our planet. The demise of British, French, Portuguese, and our own American colonial empires represents only a few examples of how evolution from accretive boundary expansion, absolute ownership, and control, to that of replicative influence (to think, act, and value like us) is pressuring us to transcend yet another form of cultural growth very near extinction.

Inability to find new ideas and resources to meet the pressures of change gives the forces of natural selection the opportunity to select less fit forms of growth at every phylogenetic level. If our ectogenetic cultural reconstruction of the future is not to suffer this fate, we must prepare innovative ways to meet the coming discontinuity of today's rapid evolvement.

It is a sad but easily observable fact that concepts of fixed replicative mores, value systems, and political and ideological systems attempt to stand in the way of the capacity of mutuality to be realized in many advanced cultures and subcultures. Examples abound of our own inability to accept the idea of exchange with less "advanced" Third World cultures: perceptual screening that excludes the subtleties of creative cultural adaptations far beyond the limited changes we propose and often impose. Anything, however—beliefs, language, appearance, history, or geography—that presents barriers to the call to mutualism, that is, the pressure to create a whole organism of Mankind, will ultimately crumble under its irresistible force. If we cannot mutually evolutionize the parochialism and "lofty ideals" of narrow culturalism, Man's very deepest nature will be compelled to revolutionize them.

Unfortunately, the new freedom is seen by many as "revolution" rather than the accelerated evolution that it really represents. Thus, in our institutions there has been retarded development of strategy or plans to cope with the rapid changes of this epoch. However, as we plunge into the future, we must evolve new political structures to accommodate the reality of this new expression of life and to join *with* it in breaking down many of the artificially imposed barriers that stand between now and the evolved tomorrow. By acknowledging that cultural hybridization will lead to vitality rather than degeneration of national character, we can initiate new exchange processes with other cultures. This action may alleviate the fear that we may be "giving up too much" or "losing face," ideas that now serve as cultural isolation mechanisms. As agents of transformative evolution we can create new transformations rather than respond to the advocates of limitation. The historical continuity of these evolutionary forces cannot be denied—nor will they be, even if it means self-extinction. Our mistakes and failures are our way—Nature's way—of keeping the pressure on; to help us learn how to be transformed by Nature's newest evolutionary form, the organism of a united Mankind.

CONCLUSIONS

The homologous principle of transformation, evolution growth, leads to broad and fundamental conclusions about Nature, its processes, Man as he is today, and as he may be tomorrow. Some of these are:

The evolution of life is a discontinuous and accelerating growth process represented by a series of "inventions" of Nature which elevate the level of organization and behavior of organisms through major reconstructions of information programs and growth systems. We can expect to see other and more rapid discontinuities in our own human megaorganic systems. Therefore, in analyzing and assessing the shape of the future of our social systems, our evaluations of alternative courses must be made with the awareness of the possibility of emergence of unique forms of growth expression, not merely repetitions or extrapolations of the past and present.

The human uniqueness that causes this process is an extension of ubiquitous biological processes, obeying the same basic laws, rather than an unknown, mysterious process that "divorces" Man somehow from the rest of Nature or produces a meaning beyond logic. Thus, not only is Man a fit student of himself, but he can continually discover more about his own individual and cultural nature and how to improve it.

In this sense we must drastically revise our studies and ideas about human "nature," since we can now verify that the *nature* of Man and culture is not a static phenomenon but is evolved and evolving. Human nature can be defined only by response to the pressures of evolution and natural selection and the continuing transformation of behavioral patterns. *The only permanence of human nature is the direction and continuity of this transformational change.*

As the evolved mechanism for evolution, Man is therefore the *sole responsible agent* to and for his species and environment. As an emerging megamutualistic species, we can thus continue to transform our environment through new growth processes and products and select out nonmutual expressions of technology and society at ever increasing rates. We can safely assume that in our evolution there is no finite or visualizable end to growth or to transformations to *unique* levels of growth on the part of each individual and of a total culture.

As participants in the thrust of transformation to mutualism, we can envision the mandate of the task at hand. We must re-examine many of the basic and accepted concepts about Man and Nature that have traditionally guided us—old ideas and processes carried forward from an extinct past, ones that could propel us to an extinct future. We must not only avoid repeating the mistakes of the past but refrain from limiting growth by repeating our successes—successes that, at best, are less than perfect to fit in the changed world of today and tomorrow. Thus, our institutions, our relationships with others, and our attitudes about Man and his future are the imperative subjects of invigorated scientific inquiry and enlightened public action.

As we have seen in the records of fossils, artifacts, and history, evolution does not wait. Its message has been repeated over and over; yet in each era of Man some have insisted on the lessons of catastrophe, believing that because a particular form of growth was successful it revealed enduring and unchanging truths. Each of those "eternal" values calls out from a restless grave to heed the fact of changing growth. We can only hope that our era has discovered the means by which to listen, and to act. If not, we shall continue to create and to face enemies because of calcified beliefs that ours is the *only* way, that we cannot learn from them or, in mutuality, teach them. In the process of mutual growth we can both expect to effect and be affected, to change and be changed.

Through a new *humanological revolution,* our aims, processes, and activities can and must be adjusted to meet the evolving opportunities of rediscovering and improving Man and Mankind. By mutualizing our resources, we can realize the latent growth of our species. To bring this about, however, will require a rapid and radical integration of the *quality* of human growth into the processes of planning, forecasting, and creating a future still and always largely unknown; but we can do so with the knowledge that by and through Nature's processes, we can determine the quality and form, if not the content, of things to come.

Finally, because the postulates set forth in transformation theory are not offered in the spirit of intuitive or "revealed" truth, but as verifiable propositions, we hope they will stimulate others to test them and discover deeper harmonies in Nature, Life, and Man—such is Nature's irresistible imperative: grow or die.

TRANSFORMATION PRINCIPLES
APPENDIX I

1. Physical, biological, psychological, and social systems are *growth motivated;* that is, their behavior acts in the direction of development of higher levels of and more widespread interrelationships. Thus, all systems tend to evolve more organized behavior, becoming integrated through the incorporation of diversity. In the aggregate systems of Nature this is a ubiquitous and irreversible process.

2. These interrelationships grow through a progression of *different forms of linking behavior* which, having been successful in a particular sub-system, are repeated at the next highest level. Each form of growth is necessary to support the next highest level. These forms are:

    a. Accretive-Inclusion through sameness (identicality and complementarity)
    b. Replicative-Influential affiliation through similarity
    c. Mutual-Attraction through differentness

    Each of these phenomena depends on commonality to initiate the linking action and progresses to inclusion of higher levels of distinctiveness.

3. All growth is a *function of information* (energy) and an evolution of coding methodology. As information handling—acquisition, communication, storage, and retrieval—evolves, each higher level of growth can contain (bind) more data, and less energy is lost in growth transactions.

These three principles apparently operate in all behavior and may be considered to make up a basis for a *unified general systems theory* that is applicable in the seemingly disparate behaviors of science, art, and philosophy.

TRANSFORMATION AND PHYSICS
APPENDIX II

When working with a new theory it is an irresistible temptation to extend it to the farthest possible limits; such is the case in this hypothesis relating transformation to physical processes. As mentioned in the body of this work, the tendency to isolate phenomena in order to observe them has led to conclusions which do not conform to the facts. Just as certain theories in psychology offer concepts (such as survival drives) as the definitive motivations for human behavior, most physical theorists see the universe driven toward *the* "final state"—decay and death. This view of physics assumes a regressive rather than a progressive future (and present). In the light of the principle of transformation, this view deserves serious reconsideration.

ENERGY AND GROWTH

The taproot of our concern for the physical properties of life lies within the idea of "energy." Energy has been variously described as the ability to do work or that which diminishes when work is done (by an amount equal to the work done). Many subtleties of energy transformations were unexplained until the nineteenth century, and today new concepts of energy have been so useful that they are the primary concern of physics. The manifestations of energy include mechanical, electrical, chemical, nuclear, and heat. It exists in the potential and kinetic forms and is "conserved" in that it can neither be created nor destroyed; as it is used, it is transformed from one form into another with no loss.

The new idea of matter and energy equivalence was introduced by Einstein in the twentieth century and this idea seemed to resolve the most basic questions of energy form and function.

All forms of energy are not equivalent, however, for different types of energy act on one another and either add or subtract to the efficiency and directionality of physical transformations. This interaction of different kinds of energy contributes to the ordering or disordering of our universe. All forms of energy, however, can be reduced to heat, so we can see why the "heat death" of the universe is the generally accepted prediction of the ultimate fate of all life, matter, and energy. Yet the observable facts show that if energy is *organized* in some manner it will serve to organize other energies in its environment to ever higher levels, becoming more and more ordered and efficient at each new level of organization. Rather than simply being conserved it is transformed.*

---

*Entropy S
Information (Negentropy, syntropy) I
First, entropy is a property of the physical system only. Information is a property of the mind of man. What is the relation of these in an experiment?

Step one:
    Ideation, imagination, experimental design—
non-entropic—extremely small entropy changes in system but large information
        changes in man's mind.

$$S' = S \quad \text{but} \quad I' > I \quad \text{or} \quad \Delta S' = 0 \; \Delta I' = I' - I > 0$$

Step two:
    Experiment is performed. According to Brillouin the entropy of the physical system is increased more than the information received:

$$S^2 > S^1 \quad \Delta S^2 = S^2 - S^1 > 0$$
$$I^2 > I^1 > I \quad \text{and} \quad \Delta I^2 = I^2 - I^1 > 0$$
$$\text{but} \quad \Delta S^2 > \Delta I^2$$

Step three:
    Analysis of results, again in man's mind—non-entropic.

$$S^3 = S^2 \quad \Delta S^3 = 0$$
$$I^3 > I^2 \quad \Delta I^3 > 0$$

Total Interaction:

$$\Delta S = \Delta S^3 + \Delta S^2 + \Delta S^1 = \Delta S^2$$
$$\Delta I = \Delta I^3 + \Delta I^2 + \Delta I^1 \neq \Delta I^2$$
$$\text{in fact} \quad \Delta I^3 + \Delta I^2 + \Delta I^1 > \Delta I^2$$

So we *cannot* say that

$$\Delta S > \Delta I$$

This "ordering" and "efficiency" phenomenon is most easily observed in living systems. The reduction of biological waste through reduction in the death rate of offspring is one example. Another is how energy is consumed by differing levels of animal organization. As Arshavsky has demonstrated, the more evolved the organism the more work it can do and the longer it lives and maintains its organization.[1] On a more subtle level, given an equal environment of energy, more organized molecules will *use more of the available energy for further organization,* as exemplified by the Miller and Calvin experiments.[2] Thus, a complex molecule will accept and employ more ambient energy than the sum of its atomic parts. There is in terms of traditional concepts an energy paradox inherent in this phenomenon.

A crucial example of this is the formation of the diatomic hydrogen molecule. For two hydrogen atoms to join and form the molecule H_2 requires that they go to a lower energy state, resulting in their "least energy" state. They appear to represent less energy. Yet as H_2 their capability to *use* more energy for further organization is greatly enhanced. They have achieved what we may call a higher "transformational" energy level. The word "energy" is used here, for the molecule is indeed capable of doing more work than its separate atomic parts. It is synergistic in that the whole is greater than the sum of its parts.*

Transformation thus views this and other physical transactions

---

simply because of the non-entropic use of mind. Intelligence itself is the mind of man.

In fact it may well be that the experiment itself and the data received from it have no meaning outside of the idea-fabric weaved by the mind to begin with, in a non-entropic process.

*The original separated hydrogen atoms have in their structure the inherent ability to combine with environmental energy and evolve a more complex, energy-order structure. The separate atom's structure, reflected in the energy it will receive and transmit, has been well known since Bohr's theory. The hydrogen molecule has a far more complex structure, including not only electronic energy structure but rotational and vibrational structure. This makes it a far more intricate "interactor" with its energy environment.

Electromagnetic energy which could have gone totally unnoticed by the separated atoms is now absorbed by the molecular system, resulting in its internal excitation, thereby preparing it for more complex bonds, or is perhaps retransmitted at later times and other points, resulting in the appropriate available energy for the building of other complex structures in totally different atoms. An example of the latter phenomena is the laser.

as ordering phenomena: self-catalyzing processes, order leading to more order. Thus transformation projects the ultimate fate of the universe as a super-orderly system incorporating all the infinite differentness contained therein. This ultimate state results from the progression of successive levels of growth (interrelationships) reflected in the accretive, replicative, and mutual states. To observe more closely how these forms of growth naturally occur and achieve new and higher levels we can follow the pattern of their successive appearance.

PHASES OF GROWTH

In Figure 56 the opposing directions of interrelational ordering and random disordering are represented on the vertical axis, while time flow is indicated on the horizontal axis. At first glance we can see that the overall aspect of the process curve assumes the classic S or sigmoid shape. We have all seen this curve many times in measurements of diverse phenomena in all the sciences—and with good reason. It represents some of the most fundamental

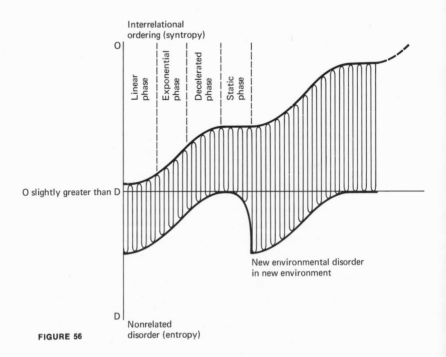

FIGURE 56

phenomena in the universe, from the transitional states of atoms,* to the state changes from solid to liquid to gas, to individual and population growth.

There is in natural phenomena a progression of stages from linear growth to exponential growth to decelerated growth and finally to an apparently static or "steady" state. When we observe the total envelope of movement in the accretive phase we see an initial point of slow building of interrelationships until a unit capable of replication is established. In other words, a largely disorderly system gradually assumes a degree of individualized order. At this point, individual units become capable of catalyzing their replicas, and exponential spreading of this basic ordered unit occurs. As the supply of disordered material begins to become exhausted a phase of slowed growth occurs until all available material of the type involved is organized and a period of stasis occurs.

TRADITION VS. CHANGE

During this progression we can see a system moving from high rates of randomness to high rates of order; the ratios of changing material to self-conserved order diminish as more bonds are made. The process of transformation demands that as high rates of order are achieved resistance to change also increases. Yet in any system where *a high level of energy* (information) *input occurs, static order cannot be maintained*—old bonds will be broken and new ones must be formed. The ordering system must establish bonds with more and *different* kinds of environmental materials. As a new growth form emerges into relationships with new environments—*into a new level of disorder*—once more growth is slow and linear. A new accretive phase begins. Thus is a discontinuity born, always maintaining the lower orders as a foundation for growth in new areas.

In this case we are discussing a case of environmental conditions in which constantly high levels of energy input occur. The resulting order-to-disorder ratio is somewhat greater than 1; $O/D>1$. In other cases, as we see in Figure 57, where insufficient energy exists to break old bonds the results are the achievement of

---

*See Appendix IIA.

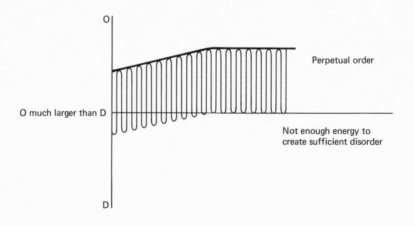

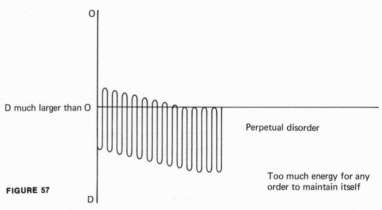

FIGURE 57

low-level relatively static accretion order. The reverse, as in Figure 57, occurs when D>>O; too much disorder is in progress for any order to maintain itself. In a simplistic manner environments from local to cosmological can be described as a continuum:

$$O>>D \quad O>D \quad O\cong D \quad D>O \quad D>>O$$

In another light, this continuum relates directly to the accretive, replicative, and mutual continuum of transformation.

Accretion (selfing)	Replication (selfing)	Mutualization	Replication (othering)	Accretion (othering)

EXCLUSION AND INCLUSION

An accretive selfing type of growth is self-maintaining order, which can be referred to as "exclusiveness." Any phenomenon of this type will form bonds very slowly and accept for growth only those environmental materials that are practically indistinguishable from the existing self. On the other end of the continuum we find accretive othering, an "inclusive" phenomenon. It is in a high-level state of disorder and will bond itself to an ordering structure. In this situation it gives up its own identity as it is included within the other system. As we move toward the center we see that both inclusion and exclusion ratios change, and there is an acceptance of or attachment to similar but not identical order. Finally at the center we find a dynamic balance of order/disorder in mutualized growth. In other words, the "exclusive" individuality of the unit is maintained at approximately the same level as its ability to "include" other materials and include itself as part of others.

GROWTH OF MOLECULES

Considering a specific physical-chemical example we can observe how the accretive, replicative, and mutual continuum occurs in the atomic-molecular bonding system. As we go across a row of the periodic table of elements, we find the shell and subshell structure of the atoms results in varying degrees of tendencies to accrete, replicate, and mutualize with each other in forming molecules.

Col.	1	2	3	4	5	6	7	8
Row 1	$_3\text{Li}^7$	$_4\text{Be}^9$	$_5\text{B}^{11}$	$_6\text{C}^{12}$	$_7\text{N}^{14}$	$_8\text{O}^{16}$	$_9\text{F}^{19}$	$_{10}\text{Ne}^{20}$
Row 2	$_{11}\text{Na}^{23}$	$_{12}\text{Mg}^{24}$	$_{13}\text{Al}^{27}$	$_{14}\text{Si}^{28}$	$_{15}\text{P}^{31}$	$_{16}\text{S}^{32}$	$_{17}\text{Cl}^{35}$	$_{18}\text{A}^{40}$
	Accretive	Replicative		Mutual		Replicative		Accretive

FIGURE 58

Atoms in column 1 of the table have their outer electrons in a shell fairly well removed from the attraction of the nucleus, as well as being shielded from it by the inner electrons, so they are removed from the atom easily—a case of accretive othering and high inclusion. Atoms such as those in column 7, on the other hand, need only one electron to completely fill their subshell structure. They represent the accretive selfing order, with high exclusion. Usually an electron is *completely transferred,* taken from one and given to the other, and two charged ions are formed. These are attracted to each other simply by electric attraction and

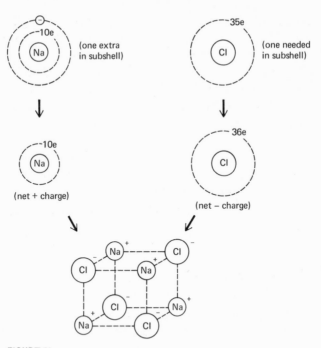

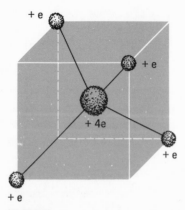

FIGURE 59

FIGURE 60
The geometry of the methane molecule. The hydrogen nuclei are at the corners of a regular tetrahedron, or at 4 of the 8 corners of a cube. The electrons are concentrated along the carbon-hydrogen lines.

remain closely bound. This is not a true sharing of electrons. As they continue their growth the atoms usually form a crystalline structure which is insulating, i.e., does not conduct energy readily. An example is salt, NaCl. These crystals are also in themselves accretive structures, simply adding identical units. They follow the growth pattern of their sub-units.

Atoms in columns 2 and 3 of the periodic table have electrons that can be given away because they are far enough away from the nucleus and shielded enough from it; but these electrons may be completing or partially completing a subshell within the atom itself, so it is "reluctant" to do so. These atoms form crystallized metals in which electrons are set "semi-free" in conduction bands. They are not associated with any particular nucleus and are free to roam throughout the solid, but remain in it. Here we have an accretive structure which will transmit energy. This system in a sense will interact more with its surroundings; for example, different metals, if just put next to each other, will start infusing into each other.

REPLICATIVE NON-POLAR COVALENT BONDS

The elements of column 3 in the table, such as boron, are not as likely to form metallic solids. They have partially filled higher subshells and are capable of forming the more replicative, non-polar covalent "sharing bond." These bonds take the forms of replicative-similar-growth in the sense that the units that join together are so similar that they appear, for all practical purposes, to have a *common* spatial center of positive and negative charge. The joined units must have great similarity for this to occur. This commonly occurs as replica atoms join in diatomic molecules, as with oxygen. Non-polar covalent bonds do not necessarily have to be formed between identical atoms. In methane, the aggregate

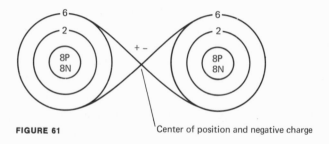

FIGURE 61 Center of position and negative charge

spatial symmetry of the four hydrogen bonds about the carbon nucleus also results in a net non-polar molecule. The centers of positive and negative charge are the same because of a symmetry of all four bonds.

It should be mentioned that as we cross the periodic table the growth abilities of various atoms become *cumulative.* For example, beryllium does form non-metallic salts as well as metallic crystals. Boron will form non-metallic salts, metallic crystals, and has the ability to complete its electron structure by sharing electrons with other atoms in symmetrical arrangements, forming non-polar covalent bonds.

We skip for a moment to columns 5 and 6 of the periodic table to observe other cases of the replicative bond. The atom nitrogen, for example, needs three electrons to complete its subshell structure, for it already has three and the total subshell contains six. By bonding with itself in such a way that the six appropriate electrons are sometimes found "around" one nitrogen atom and sometimes "around" the other, the fulfillment of this demand for symmetry in the electron structure can be partially met. Thus a replicative sharing of electrons takes place between two nitrogen atoms. By a replicative action, then, a molecule which is quite useful is achieved, N_2, nitrogen gas. Of course, such a covalent bond is formed between nitrogen and many atoms, and it is just this type of bond that was beginning to appear in boron.

POLAR COVALENT BONDING

True mutualism is achieved in the dynamic balance of inclusiveness/exclusiveness represented by polar bonds. These bonds allow each atom not only to join with atoms quite different from itself but to maintain its own individuality and exclusiveness. This joining of differentness results in a separation of charge and a very interactive molecule. Water is an example. The polar bond is particularly useful in forming more ordered structures. Its mutualistic character allows for and insists on the joining of great differences. The epitome of atomic mutualism is, of course, carbon. Its bonds are always covalent and because of its rather unique subshell structure, it can share (give or take) electrons in more ways with other atoms than any atomic element. As a result it forms more chemical compounds than all other elements combined, some 2,000,000, versus about 60,000 for all the other

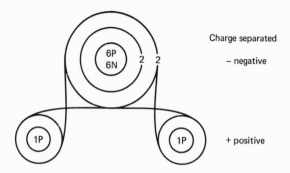

Charge separated

− negative

+ positive

FIGURE 62

elements combined. It has a subshell structure which allows the formation of covalent or sharing bonds in many spatial directions, and as a result it can form many unusual and vital structures, such as organic ring compounds. It also forms replicative bonds such as a covalent non-conducting crystal with itself—the diamond. So the transformation process truly culminates on the atomic level with the atom carbon. It is that atomic mutuality which allows for the building of large macromolecules and the structures of life.

The stability or self-maintaining ability of the carbon nucleus is also of importance here, since we need such an atom not only to be inclusive but to stay around long enough to allow complex bonds to develop. It has six protons and six neutrons, which is only a slight redundancy of the ultra-stable helium nucleus. The *even* number of protons and neutrons results in the nucleus having no net magnetic "handle" and the *equal* number of protons and neutrons means there is also no electric "handle." This means the nucleus is not susceptible to disturbance by exterior electric or magnetic fields. Truly the inclusive-exclusive process in nuclear and electronic growth has evolved a stable, very mutualistic species in carbon.

On the periodic table we see located directly below carbon another highly mutualistic atom, silicon. Although, like carbon, silicon can link up in many ways, its chains are neither as long nor as stable as with carbon. Silicon thus plays an extremely important role in the growth of more simple orders. It is the keystone of the mineral world just as carbon is in the world of plants and animals. It combines so readily that in a variety of compounds it makes up a quarter of the surface of the earth. Clay, sand, quartz, granite, cement, and glass are a few of its important mutualisms.

CHEMICAL GROWTH

It is clear that the basis of all chemical reactions is the phenomenon of growth. Transformation occurs through interrelative joining, loss, gain, or sharing of electrons. As with all other transformative phenomena there are three principle growth forms:

1. Accretive—giving up electrons and attachment to another atom (othering), or obtaining electrons from another (selfing). These are essentially ionic and metallic bonds.
2. Replicative—joining by sharing electrons with similar atoms or groups. These are mainly non-polar covalent bonds.
3. Mutual—linking with dissimilar atoms by sharing electrons. Polar covalent bonds.

Just as in other systems, the transformation of atoms is directly related to nutrition in and feedback from the environment. In the presence of appropriate information (energy and material) and a positive feedback environment, primeval molecules become monomers, the monomers can then become polymerized, and self-catalytic as well as reproducing systems can then occur.[3] Once more what we find is a directed system, creating order from a less-ordered environment.

PROBABILITY OR INEVITABILITY

What we actually observe in physical, chemical, biological, psychological, sociological, etc., behavior is a series of steps going from one level of growth to another. Each step leads to the creation of new growth behavior so distributed that as long as energy continues to enter the system, the emergence of high-level growth phenomena is sure. The curve is the S curve.

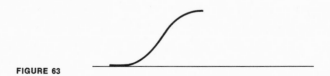

FIGURE 63

This is essentially the inevitability of real systems—growth to a higher, more capable state. When we realize that this can occur through two basic paths in terms of the transformation process, either selfing or othering, we see that the goal of a mutualistic system can be achieved through a growth pattern which looks probabilistic. A normal probability curve, or something very much like it, is obtained by reflecting the S curve about a vertical axis.

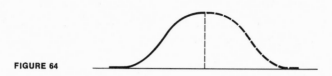

FIGURE 64

This is more than a simple illustrative device, for indeed, accretive selfing and othering, and replicative selfing and othering are simultaneous and complementary bonding processes in any system. Thus we obtain a broadly based accretive-replicative phenomenon culminating in the mutualistic or highly capable entity.

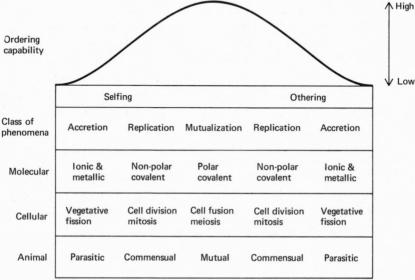

Class of phenomena	Selfing		Mutualization	Othering	
	Accretion	Replication	Mutualization	Replication	Accretion
Molecular	Ionic & metallic	Non-polar covalent	Polar covalent	Non-polar covalent	Ionic & metallic
Cellular	Vegetative fission	Cell division mitosis	Cell fusion meiosis	Cell division mitosis	Vegetative fission
Animal	Parasitic	Commensual	Mutual	Commensual	Parasitic

Ordering capability — High / Low

FIGURE 65

Thus the probability of the evolution of a viable, capable structure is maximized as the three stages of growth are approached from the selfing-othering (inclusion-exclusion) paths. The dynamic balance of mutualism is the most probable state of all inclusion/exclusion balance—it is inevitable. The function of "probability" is in reality a *law of inevitability*. The behavior of such a total system is actually more predictable than the distribution of millions of throws of dice. The emergence of new states of higher orders of accretive, replicative, and mutual behavior is certain. The global "noosphere" postulated by Teilhard de Chardin[4] is within the system of orderly and *ordering* laws of the universe. Far from an entropic heat death, the probability distribution of the cosmos can mean only one thing—evolvement* of a syntropic living universe.

THE MICROCOSMOS

While it is hypothetical, it seems probable that all we are seeing in the phenomena of growth is a reflection of an order that was *already present in its component parts*. The unique properties of the atom and its subatomic make-up may fit the pattern of accretive, replicative, and mutual interrelationships. At the atomic level the elemental unit is the hydrogen atom. As the extension of subatomic growth it represents both lower-level mutualism and the beginnings of higher-level accretion. It has already incorporated a good deal of mutualistic differentness in its polar electromagnetic arrangement. This is the subatomic version of dynamic inclusion/exclusion balance. We refer to hydrogen as subatomic in the sense that in an energy-rich interactive environment it is impossible for free (independent) hydrogen to exist. If we take into account the fact that the "atom" of hydrogen is the most abundant substance in the universe (relative abundance ratios: H = 10,000, Helium = 1,600, Oxygen = 10) yet in complex planetary environments only occurs independently as H_2,* it may well be that H_2 is the elementary "atom" and that H is truly a *subatomic unit*. H_2 approaches the make-up of all other atoms in that, in effect, it is a proton-neutron-electron combination. By using hydrogen in its singular state we can very probably provide a foundation for a hypothetical subatomic growth model.

---

*The gas H_2 only comprises 0.00005% of the earth's atmosphere, yet in combination it is the ninth most abundant element and occurs as a variety of isotopes.

At the accretive level hydrogen grows by excitation to meta-stable states and thereby increases its electron boundaries. This is short-lived, however, and true accretion or growth through identi-cality occurs in the formation of the hydrogen molecule H_2. While this form of atomic growth is very successful, helping to form molecules such as water, it is limited in the possible arrangements of its bonds. As well, as an accretive othering structure it always has the possibility of losing its sole electron and being reduced to an ion, $H+$, essentially merely a proton.

The replicative stage of atomic growth begins with the forma-tion of "true" nuclei: atoms with both protons and neutrons. In essence, the elemental atom replicates itself by now including both proton and electron in a new way, combined in a neutron. It thus has grown not by identicality but similarity.

In this growth step the identity, exclusiveness, of the original structure is well maintained both in the nuclear and electron "shells"; that is, as Wolfgang Pauli pointed out in his exclusion principle, atomic growth demands increasing amounts of differ-entness, or distinguishability. No two identical nuclei or electron states will be tolerated. So as the atom replicates, higher levels of differentness will be incorporated.

Mutualistic behavior begins to occur in atoms as they grow to achieve very high levels of differentness in their shell structure. This can be easily observed in a simplistic representation of the three types of atoms:

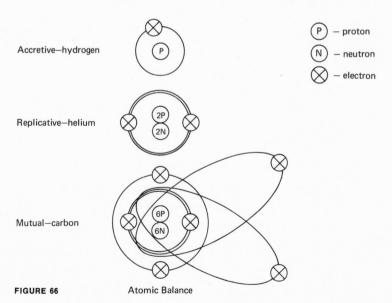

Accretive—hydrogen

P — proton

N — neutron

$\otimes$ — electron

Replicative—helium

Mutual—carbon

FIGURE 66   Atomic Balance

While all these atoms are balanced electrically between the positive proton charge and the negative electron charge, the critical distinction is that they are *not balanced in their inclusiveness/exclusiveness ratios,* with rare exceptions. As we observed, earlier exclusiveness is a self-conserving, self-maintaining function. It is, as Pauli demonstrated, the mechanism by which a particle retains its individual identity. On the other side is the need to be *included:* to become part of a similar structure. In atomic growth the ratios of inclusion/exclusion are determined by the completeness of shell structures. Chlorine has a very high exclusiveness ratio. It grows by "selfing," by completing its own outer electron shell at the expense of the atom from which it is taken. Sodium is inclusive; with one extra electron in its outer shell it wants to include itself as part of another structure, "othering," by giving up its electron. When these atoms join they both increase their individual growth potential and stability. The *half-filled* outer shell of the carbon atom gives it a *dynamic balance of inclusion and exclusion* and permits it a great variety of bonding behaviors.

SUBATOMIC GROWTH

If we assume the hydrogen "atom" to be the mutualistic phase of subatomic growth, then it becomes possible to reach down to an even deeper level in our speculations. It seems evident that the *polarity* of the proton-electron structure indicates a high degree of mutuality. If this is true, its appearance must have been preceded by replicative and accretive sub-structures. Representing our imaginary subatomic particles as □(positive), 0(negative), and △(neutral), we can construct such a system. (Obviously these symbols are illustrative only, for charge is only one of many particle attributes.)

Accretive growth (identicality)	— (□□) and (□) — a "subon"* A　　　　B
Replicative (similarity)	— (□□) (□) and (□□) (△) — the proton A　B　　　A　C
Mutual (difference)	— (□□) (□) (□□) (△) and (0) — H atom A　B　A　C　　　D

*Coined by the author to indicate a sub-proton particle.

In this model the neutron would take on the combined hydrogen, proton plus electron form:

(□□)　(□)　(□□)　(△)　(0) — the neutron
　A　　　B　　　A　　　C　　D

Of course, in our imaginary structure it is impossible to guess the number of original accretive particles. It could be quite large, especially if the accretive-replicative-mutual series were to occur several times within the structure. This model, as speculative as it is, does indicate one very interesting phenomenon, that is, we should expect to find within atoms *forces that are not polar.* Attractive forces or bonds internally should be based on similarity and with an accretive force; a fundamental identicality force common to all matter—perhaps "bound gravitons." As well, it should be no surprise to us if, in the course of attempting to break these forces, the massive energies we use create extinct "fossil" particles which were "selected out" of Nature's system long ago. We may create new and short-lived realities that have little or no bearing on the facts of today's atomic structures.

THE TRANSDYNAMIC UNIVERSE

On reconsidering energy, structure, and thermodynamics there is yet another point to ponder; that is, how do we actually define what we have been referring to as "disorder." A basic example of this question is the phenomenon of gas distribution. If a container is filled with gas so that its initial state is distributed unevenly

FIGURE 67

it will soon redistribute itself to an "equilibrium" state with relatively even distribution.

FIGURE 68

Considering these two states, while conventional definitions indicate a progression from order into disorder, the actuality may be quite the reverse. Perhaps the "tendency to maximize entropy" is really an attempt to distribute energy in such a way as to maximize the probability that a growth step will occur. If we were in a position to purposefully design a system which could take advantage of random energy inputs, we would end up with just such an "open net" random distribution. Its probabilities of capturing stray energy are far greater than the *disorder* of uneven distribution. Even for the very fundamental role of a simple gas, the capture function of order may be its most vital contribution to growth and universal transformation. Suppose we consider the activity of the universe to be continuous interaction between unformed energy and structured matter (really ordered energy). If it is an energy-structure interaction in varying states of order, then there should be regions of self-interaction which demonstrate the entire order/disorder continuum, from O>>D to D>>O. And so we find "black holes" of gravitational collapse, where O>>D, the extreme example of accretive selfing, and exploding stars, where D>>O, where we have extreme accretive othering.

Somewhere between these two extremes, which may be considered, hydrodynamically speaking, "sinks" and "sources" of the structured universe, there should be the continuum of the order/disorder process, in particular the regions of the life zone where O is slightly greater than D. The tendency to order in our life region just slightly exceeds the disorder tendency and actually the interaction of the two is the dynamic interaction which is at the basis of growth. Unusable structures must be broken down to reorganize at higher levels. The regions of O>>D, such as the black holes, provide the universe system with tremendous amounts of energy from the literal collapse of structured energy. The D>>O regions, or the novas, are energy giving itself up to form and distribute structured energy (particles). The ultimate state of structured order breaks down to give unstructured energy and the ultimate state of unstructured order (pure energy) expands until structures capable of interaction are formed. Of course, this is idealizing since there is still some entropy in the black holes and some syntropy in the exploding stars. The cyclic attribute of the universe system becomes clear when we see structured and unstructured energy interacting upon itself in a continuum of degrees to form zones where complex intelligent structures can evolve and broaden their ordering capabilities to zones not conducive to initiating or maintaining their own order. The "life zone" is expanding.

If we believe, with Einstein, in the equivalence of matter and energy, then we see there is only one thing, pure energy, organizing and reorganizing itself to higher and higher degrees of order. The centers, or zones, of distinct order/disorder ratios mutualize with each other over the billions of light years of interstellar space to form the life zones. In some four dimensional time-space region, precisely the right energy interacts with precisely the right structures to evolve a more complex structure, say an atom, which is also in the right environment to grow and so forth. Far from being a random process, however, the existence of such life zones is guaranteed by the extremes of $O>>D$ and $D>>O$ and the necessary continuum which must exist between them. What is often observed to be random, even chaotic, when seen in the broad perspective of a whole evolutionary process of a universe is actually a part of the inevitable generation of order.

In this example, as well as others cited in this probe into the physical universe, what is intended is primarily to knock on some neglected doors of investigation. If we can begin to understand the true nature of order and disorder, inclusion/exclusion, and growth of our physical universe, many new and exciting opportunities lie in wait. Among these are such things as biophysical energy production, disease transformations, economical material transmutation, and endless others. All in all it seems to be a matter of better learning how to live with life, even that long considered to be lifeless.

Appendix IIA
THE EXCITATION LEVELS OF THE DIATOMIC MOLECULE

Assume that a diatomic molecular system has now been achieved, and further assume the molecule is at a very low energy state. The question arises in thermodynamics as to just what behavior this system exhibits as temperature (and thus energy) is increased.

Basically it becomes easier to consider the molecule in what is termed the center of mass system of coordinates, which is simply the system in which the mass acts as a single point in space. That such a simplified way of looking at a molecule of two distinct particles is a valid procedure takes a bit of mathematical juggling, but it is intuited from the realization that we are not really treating two separate particles, but rather a more or less rigidly connected combination of particles, similar in some aspects to a dumbbell. One might suspect that at least some of its properties might be handled in this way.

The basic motions of the diatomic system then break down into three types which we will examine in some detail. First, vibrational energy through the center of mass. Second, rotational energy about the center of mass. And finally, translational energy of the center of mass. The three types of motion are indicated below:

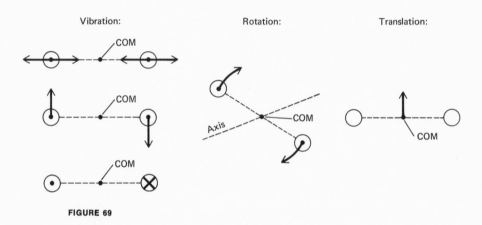

Vibration: Rotation: Translation:

FIGURE 69

THE VIBRATIONAL MOTION

No matter what the form of the vibrational motion, whether the nuclei are vibrating toward and away from the center of mass along a line joining the two, or vibrating toward and away from the center of mass perpendicular to the line joining the nuclei, we observe the motion to be a form where both participants are performing the same motion *at the same time* (or perhaps mirror reflections of each other's motion, still at the same time). If we think in terms of the motion of the molecule system, we label this accretive motion, because of the exact duplication of motion in simultaneity.

THE ROTATIONAL MOTION

This involves motion of the nuclei about some axis perpendicular to the plane of the motion. The nuclei are now performing the same motion, but not simultaneously. In other words, we call this a replicative form of motion. Each nucleus is replicating and influencing the action of the other.

THE TRANSLATIONAL MOTION

This involves the simultaneous motion of both nuclei in such a way that the center of mass moves in some direction (as opposed to the vibrational motion where the center of mass remains stationary). This truly involves the *cooperation* of both nuclei and can only be termed mutual motion.

A quantity often used in thermodynamics to discuss the properties of a particular gaseous system is the Specific Heat at constant volume, which is a measure of how much the energy of the system (in this case the diatomic molecule) changes with changes in temperature. For our diatomic system a typical diagram looks like that pictured below:

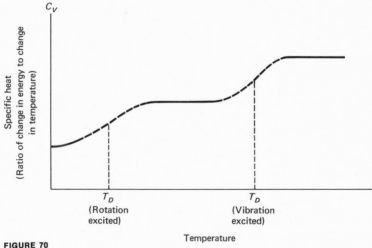

FIGURE 70

The flat places on the graph indicate that the energy of the system is changing at a constant rate as temperature is changing. The transition portions of the graph indicate that the *energy is not increasing at a constant rate as temperature is increased, but rather that a new mode of motion is being excited by the incoming heat radiation.* The temperatures where these transition parts occur are called "degeneracy" temperatures which denote the region where one must be concerned with using a quantum mechanical treatment of the analysis of the indicated types of motion. This gets into a rather mathematical discussion of the specific entropy function of the diatomic system, but suffice it to say the temperatures are characteristic of the various forms of molecular motion. This very graphically illustrates the growth of molecular motion from translational to rotational to vibrational.

As we add energy to this system, we see that the mutual mode (translational motion) reveals a structure of replication (rotational motion) and finally the accretive mode (vibrational motion). So this stage of growth displays the stages which preceded it.

It should be noted that the specific heat is a macroscopic measurement; i.e., a measurement on a large sample of gas. Thus the gas as an aggregate has become a more complex structure region, which will interact with its environment in a different way from the simple nonatomic constituents.

A BIOPSYCHOLOGICAL APPROACH TO CANCEROUS GROWTH
APPENDIX III

Although it is not the purpose of this book to examine all the possible applications of this theory, a pertinent example of reverse homology will show how we can work backward from social to biological systems. The phenomenon we shall examine is uncontrolled cell growth, in particular, cancer. Although causes such as viruses have been suspect, there is still no theory which explains why this type of growth occurs. Let us see how a social behavior homology might apply.

The closest transformational homologue we can use is that of a large, well-developed "multicellular" social organism, a city, for instance. We encounter the phenomenon of uncontrolled and destructive growth in this environment most often in the case of subcultures whose deprivation has repressed them to almost pure biological growth alternatives. An old saying goes, "the rich get richer and the poor have children," and birth-rate statistics verify the truism. The group we are considering can be characterized most broadly as uneducated, unskilled, resourceless, and unable to fit into and contribute to the larger social unit. The evidence shows that, as this population becomes educated, skilled, and able to perform productive work, they contribute to the community and, concomitantly, their birth rates decline.

Here we see a classic case of movement on the growth continuum. Referring to the model proposed earlier, we can see that this group, unable to mutualize successfully with the other social units, automatically regresses to replicative and accretive forms of behavior. The needs exemplified are those of parasitic self-growth—regardless of the effect on the rest of the environment. The highest expression of this form of growth drive is to have power to extend the self. This is manifested in maintaining insularity, counterdependence, threats, use of force, and so forth. In other words, if they can't grow *with* the rest of society, they will grow *against* it, making it more like them rather than becoming like it.

Adjusting to our biological homologue view, we can compare this situation to the behavior of a developing organism. In the fetal stage, because they do not have the larger organism with which to mutualize, the as yet undifferentiated, unspecialized cells are intent on self-replication. We can see that as the organism grows and each cell or group of cells begins to specialize and to contribute in particular ways to the organism, the need simply to grow by replication is reduced sharply. We can speculate that if a group of these cells were put in a position in their environment where they were deprived of either proper nutrition or feedback, they would regress to earlier and lower forms of behavior. Thus, we could expect these cells to demonstrate characteristics of replicative growth cells. In this light any and all cells are potentially cancer-producing. Recent research shows that cancer cells do in fact have many of the attributes of embryonic or fetal cells. Also, major changes detected in their outer membranes could be indicators that the perception/screening mechanism has severely limited the type of feedback they will permit from neighboring cells.

In many ways, this homology also applies to fanatical, cult-like groups in our society. They are driven to grow by making everyone else like themselves; their own perception/screening apparatus limits incoming psychological nutrition to that which is like themselves. They do not, and cannot, mutualize with other segments of society because that would weaken their attempt to control self-extension.

What can be done to "cure" this growth behavior that is destructive to the larger social or biological organism? One method is exorcism or killing, although in social terms, to a great extent, this has been superseded by less drastic measures. It is possible to provide heavy doses of nutrition and feedback so that the members of the deprived group can make a mutual contribution to their society. This method has been successful in reacculturating social groups. In cancer treatment, we can hypothesize that, rather than killing or removing these groups, if they are detected at an early stage, it may be possible to *nurture* them instead. If, by providing the right nourishment and feedback, these cells can be recultured, they could once more begin to contribute to their cell society.

Of course, this treatment provokes the question, both in society and in organisms, of what conditions in the environment caused the original deprivation and what materials should be provided in new nourishment? A sub-hypothesis, in this case, is that of *how* to provide the proper nourishment and feedback. If we can use the body's resources to supply the body's proper needs, it is conceivable that creating a sort of "fire in Watts" could signal the sources of supply. Thus, rather than attempting to build up the health of a patient, we might *create* a means by which the bodily system would be called upon to use its resources and to feed the deprived, as well as to rid the system of the totally hopeless. Another approach is to create a total situation of common need, depriving the entire system of nourishment. The "outcast" cells might find opportunities in this cataclysmic situation for new and unexpected contributions to make to the system. In war-torn areas, the most deprived and undesirable elements of society often find they have a place in society because their primitive skills can be very useful when all are deprived.

To delve deeper than a biosocial homology requires a set of hypotheses regarding how cancerous growth is triggered in normal cells:

1. Redundancy of nuclear DNA information is primarily related to initial growth functions of multicellular organisms. This assures that the embryonic organism can react efficiently to growth conditions requiring a large load of metabolic functions in the absence of support from well-developed organs. They (embryonic cells) are thus more complete, albeit primitive, organisms.

2. As the total organism grows and differentiates, a complex system of interdependent relationships evolves. Each cell begins to *repress* the functions of replicative growth as new materials—proteins, alosterics, charge changes, and so forth—enter the system and old (simpler) nutrients and communication media are reduced. At this point embryonic functional DNA becomes relatively quiescent, only maintaining the cell.

3. As the normal life cycle of a cell is approached, permeability

changes and a broader mix of represser and inducer compounds are allowed to enter the system while other compounds are screened out. In this way, the cell can limit its mytotic growth.

4. If detrimental materials enter the system, or if nutritive materials are denied entry into the system and intercellular communication breaks down, the potential exists for a reduction of complex inducers and for re-expression of mytotic growth. In cancer, however, since a *colony* of cells is involved, whereas single offspring cells would ordinarily return to accepting specialized nutrients and feedback, in this case they do not. Permeation would become modified and a broader range of simple material would be absorbed for growth.

5. As mytotic growth proceeds, the community of mytotic cells serves as a self-regenerating feedback mechanism, growing and reinforcing each other in self-duplicative growth. Because the material that makes up this colony is of the body itself, autoimmune reactions do not come into play and growth continues unchecked.

In order to check the uncontrolled (somatic) growth patterns thus produced, a transformative method might be attempted:

1. Foremost in this approach is not to attempt remission by excision or death of the growing cells. Although this type of treatment can reduce the growth spiral it does not get to the root of the growth problem, for the conditions for mutual growth repression still prevail in any remaining cells and the cycle can continue to re-enact itself.

2. Positive transdetermination of the total colony may occur through "re-acculturation" of the outlaw cell group by:
   a. Providing nourishment for normal growth, possibly by supplying an artificial signal (a controllable infection) to trigger the somatic system to supply extra nutrients to the affected area (*not* in order that antibodies be generated).
   b. Depressing *all* somatic cells so that the community of cells will be more interactive and mutually facilitative with the cancer.
   c. Using a combination of these; for example, providing the nourishment indicated in 2a by localized signals and, at the same time, providing a controllable threat to the entire system.

This approach emphasizes providing the environment (nutrition and feedback) that will autonomically bring about normal socialized interdependence on the part of repressed cell members. The speculation is that the "virus" activity indicated in past research simply has identified some of the informational (DNA, RNA) components of early growth patterns. This may be "floating" nuclear data that, in primitive forms of growth, are shared or recombined by means of conjugation, temperate induction, and so forth. (These types of "viruses" may actually be a means of intercellular communication as in reverse transcriptese.)

Of course, the initial site of cell repression must still be identified and dealt with. This brief outline does not touch the problem of reforming the original environment, which, if left untreated, will probably set up the conditions for subsequent recapitulations of repressed growth.

Clearly the foregoing is a highly speculative example, but it points out one of the possibilities of finding new viewpoints in applying transformation theory to both psychological and biological situations.

It is hoped that the hypothesis presented here can provide fodder for "experiments and thought," alternative steps on a seemingly infinite ladder of life. It is in this spirit that these speculations are offered. They are but a few of the new questions evoked by transformation theory, a theory that like all others asks more than it answers.

NOTES

CHAPTER ONE

[1]HOLDEN, C.: "Psychologists Beset by Feelings of Futility, Self-Doubt," Science, 1971, Sept. 17:1111

For other contributors see Bibliography.

CHAPTER TWO

[1]DOBZHANSKY, T.: Genetics of the Evolutionary Process; Columbia University Press, 1970, p. 30

[2]SIMPSON, G. G.: The Meaning of Evolution, Rev. Ed.; Yale University Press, 1949, 1967

[3]CHAMBERS, K. L.: "Biochemical Coevolution," Proceedings of the 29th Annual Biology Colloquium, April 26–27, 1968, p. 117; Oregon State University; Corvallis, December, 1970

[4]WERZ, G.: "Determination and Realization of Morphogenesis in Acetabularia" in Brookhaven Symposia in Biology No. 18; Brookhaven National Laboratory, 1965

[5]JEON, K. W.: "Development of Cellular Dependence on Infective Organisms—Micrurgical Studies in Amoebas," Science, Vol. 176, June 9, 1972, pp. 1122–1123

[6]MONOD, J.: Chance & Necessity; Translated by Austryn Wainhouse; Alfred A. Knopf, N.Y. 1971

[7]DOBZHANSKY, op. cit., p. 396

[8]Ibid., p. 399

[9]CRUMPACKER, D. W.: "Genetic Loads in Maize (Zea Mays L.) and other crossfertilized Plants and Animals" in Evolutionary Biology I (T. Dobzhansky, M. K. Hecht, and W. C. Steere, eds.) Appleton-Century-Crofts, 1967, pp. 306–424

[10]DOBZHANSKY, op. cit., p. 326

[11]BATTAGLIA, B., SMITH, H.: "The Darwinian Fitness of Polymorphic and Monomorphic Populations of Drosophila pseudoobscura at 16° C.," Heredity 16, 1961, pp. 475–484

BEARDMORE, J. A., DOBZHANSKY, T., PAVLOSKY, O.: "An Attempt to Compare the Fitness of Polymorphic and Monomorphic Experimental Populations of Drosophila pseudoobscura," Heredity 14, 1960, pp. 19–33

BODMER, W. F.: "The Evolutionary Significance of Recombination in Prokaryotes," 20th Symposium of the Society for General Microbiology, 1970

GUSTAFSSON, A.: "Induction of changes in genes and chromosomes. II. Mutations, environment and evolution," Cold Spring Harbor Symposia on Quantitative Biology 16, 1951, pp. 263–281

—— "Mutations and the concept of viability," E. Akenberg, A. Hagberg, et al., eds.; Recent plant breeding research; John Wiley, 1963b, New York

—— "Productive mutations induced in barley by ionizing radiation and chemical mutogens," Hereditas 50, 1963A, pp. 211–263

—— "The Cooperation of genotypes in barley," Hereditas 39, 1953, pp. 1–18

—— "The effect of heterozygosity on viability and vigour," Hereditas 32, 1946, pp. 263–286

JENSEN, N.: "Multiple Superiority in Cereals," Crop. Sci., Vol. 5, 1965, pp. 566–568

LEWONTIN, R. C.: "The Effects of Population Density and Composition on Viability in Drosophila melanogaster," Evolution 9, 1955, pp. 27–41

—— "Interaction of Genetypes Determining Viability in Drosophila busckii," Proceedings of the National Academy of Sciences 49, 1963, pp. 270–278

ROY, S. K.: "Interaction Between Rice Varieties," Genetics Vol. 57, 1960, pp. 137–152

[12]WILLMER, E. N.: Cytology & Evolution; Academic Press, 1960, New York and London

[13]MCBRIDE, G.: A General Theory of Social Organization & Behavior; Faculty of Veterinary Sciences Publication, Vol. 1, St. Lucia, Brisbane Australia: University of Queensland Press 1964, W.D.

[14]CHENG, T. C.: Symbiosis (Organisms Living Together); Pegasus, 1970

[15]MONTAGU, A.: The Direction of Human Development; Hawthorne Books, N.Y. 1970, rev. ed., pp. 33–58

[16]SMITH, C. U. M.: The Brain: Towards an Understanding; G. P. Putnam's Sons, 1970

[17]SINGER, M.: "The Regeneration of Body Parts," Scientific American, October, 1958, p. 79

[18]VAN LAWICK-GOODALL, J.: In the Shadow of Man; Houghton Mifflin Co., 1971

[19]LENNEBERG, E. H.: Biological Foundations of Language; John Wiley & Sons, N.Y., 1967, p. 374

[20]MCBRIDE, G.: "On the Evolution of Human Language," Social Science Information, Vol. 7 (5), 1968, pp. 81–85

CHAPTER THREE

[1]EISENBERG, J. F., DILLON, W. S.: "Man and Beast: Comparative Social Behavior," Smithsonian Annual III, Smithsonian Institution Press, 1971

[2]WADDINGTON, C. H.: "Epigenetics and Evolution," Symposium for the Society of Experimental Biology, London, No. 7, 186, 1953

[3]MARSCHACK, A.: The Roots of Civilization; McGraw-Hill, 1972

[4]EISENBERG, L.: "The *Human* Nature of Human Nature," Science, Vol. 176, No. 4031, April 14, 1972, pp. 123–128

[5]DOBZHANSKY, T.: Genetics of the Evolutionary Process; Columbia University Press, 1970, p. 391

[6]Ibid.

[7]KROEBER, A. L.: Anthropology; Harcourt, Brace & World, 1948, rev. ed.

[8]MEAD, M.: New Lives for Old: Morrow, 1966

[9]LAND, G. T.: "Psychological Imperialism vs. Humanization in National Policies," Human Forum, L.A., August, 1970

[10]MCBRIDE, G.: "Society Evolution," Proceedings of the Ecological Society of Australia, 1:1–13, 1966

[11]WYATT, H. V.: "When Does Information Become Knowledge?" Nature, Vol. 235, January 14, 1972, pp. 86–89

[12]DOBZHANSKY, T.: Genetics and the Origin of Species; Columbia University Press, 1st, 2nd, and 3rd eds., 1937, 1941, 1951

GRANT, V.: The Origin of Adaptations; Columbia University Press, 1963

MAYR, E. C.: Animal Species and Evolution; Belknap, Cambridge, 1963

——— Systematics and the Origin of species; Columbia University Press, 1942

RILEY, H. P.: "Ecological Barriers," American Naturalist 86, 1952, pp. 23–32

STEBBINS, G. L.: Variation & Evolution in Plants; Columbia University Press, 1950

CHAPTER FOUR

[1]FISCHER, H.: "Des Triumpschrei der Graugans (anser anser)," Zeitschrift fur Tierpsychologie 22:247–304, 1965

[2]SUCHMAN, E. A., et al.: "Desegregation: Some Propositions and Research Suggestions," Anti-Defamation League of B'nai B'rith, 1958

[3]DOBZHANSKY, T.: Genetics of the Evolutionary Process; Columbia University Press, 1970, p. 407

[4]HALDANE, J. B. S.: "The Cost of Natural Selection," J. Genetics 55, 1957, pp. 511–524

[5]GURDON, J. B.: "Transplanted nuclei and cell differentiation," Scientific American, Dec. 1968, p. 24

[6]BEER, S.: Cybernetics and Management; Science Editions, John Wiley & Sons, N.Y., 1964

[7]MOHOLY-NAGY, L: The New Vision, from Material to Architecture, translated by Daphne M. Hoffman; W. W. Norton & Co., N.Y., 2nd ed., 1938

[8]TEILHARD DE CHARDIN: The Phenomenon of Man; William Collins & Sons, Co., 1959, London

[9]DOBZHANSKY, op. cit., p. 106

[10]CHASE, A.: The Biological Imperatives—Health, Politics, and Human Survival; Holt, Rinehart and Winston, N.Y., 1971

CHAPTER FIVE

[1]DOBZHANSKY, T.: Genetics of the Evolutionary Process; Columbia University Press, 1970

[2]WEISS, P.: Analysis of Development, B. H. Miller, P. Weiss, and V. Hamburger, eds.; Saunders Company, Philadelphia, 1955, p. 346

[3]VOGEL, H. J.: "Control by Repression in Control Mechanisms" in Cellular Processes, edited by David Bonner; Ronald Press, 1961, pp. 23–65

[4]THOMPSON, D'ARCY: On Growth & Form; Cambridge University Press, 2nd ed., 2 vols., 1942

[5]BERELSON, B. & GARY, STEINER: Human Behavior—An Inventory of Scientific Findings; Harcourt, Brace & World, 1964, p. 663

[6]PIAGET, J.: Six Psychological Studies; Random House, 1967

[7]RIESEN, A. H.: "Stimulation as a Requirement for Growth & Function in Behavioral Development" in Functions of Varied Experience; The Dorsey Press, Inc. 111, 1961, pp. 57–80

[8]HALL, E. T.: The Hidden Dimension; Doubleday, 1966

——— The Silent Language, Doubleday, 1959

[9]RENSCH, B.: Biophilosophy; Columbia U. Press, New York and London, 1971, p. 35

[10]FISKE, D. W. & SAL, MADDI: Functions of Varied Experience; Dorsey Press, Inc., 1961

EISENBERG, J. F. & WILSON S. DILLON: Man & Beast, Smithsonian Institution Press, 1971

KRECHEVSKY, I.: "The Genesis of 'Hypotheses' in Rats," University of California Publications in Psychology, 6, 1932, pp. 45–64

[11]HERON, W.: "Cognitive and Physiological Effects of Perceptual Isolation" in Philip Solomon et al., eds., Sensory Deprivation, a symposium at Harvard Medical School; Harvard University Press, 1961, pp. 6–33

[12]HARLOW, H. F., M. K. HARLOW, D. R. MEVER: "Learning Motivated by a Manipulation Drive," J. Exper. Psychol. 40, 1950, pp. 228–234

PAVLOV, I. P.: Conditioned Reflexes; Trans. and ed. by G. V. Anrep; Oxford U. Press, 1927

WARDEN, C. J.: Animal Motivation Studies: The Albino Rat; Columbia U. Press, 1931

[13]PAVLOV, I. P.: Selected Works; Foreign Languages Publishing House, Moscow, 1955, p. 184

[14]THORPE, W. H.: Learning & Instinct in Animals; Methuen, London, 1956

[15]PRICE, D.: "Dynamics of Proliferating Tissues." Report of the Conference on Dynamics of Proliferating Tissues held at Upton, N.Y., 1956; University of Chicago Press, 1958

[16]HESS, E. H. & JAMES POLT: "Pupil Size as Related to Interest Value of Visual Stimuli," Science, 132, 1960, pp. 349–350

[17]ABERCROMBIE, M. L.: The Anatomy of Judgement; Hutchinson, London, 1960, p. 54

[18]BLUM, G.: "An Experimental Reunion of Psychoanalytic Theory with Perceptual Vigilance and Defence," J. Abnorm. Soc. Psychol., 48, 1954, pp. 94–98

FESTINGER, L.: A Theory of Cognitive Dissonance; Harper & Row, 1957

HOVLAND, C. I., O. J. HARVEY, M. SHERIF: "Assimiliation and Contrast Effects in Reactions to Communication and Attitude Change," J. Abnorm. Soc. Psychol., 55, 1957, pp. 244–252

[19]CABANAC, M.: "Physiological Role of Pleasure," Science Vol. 173, September 1971, pp. 1103–1107

[20]LACK, D.: "Of Birds and Men," New Scientists 41, 1969, pp. 121–122

WILLIAMS, G. C.: Adaptation & Natural Selection—A Critique of Some Current Evolutionary Thought; Princeton University Press, N.J., 1966

[21]MCCLELLAND, D. C., J. W. ATKINSON: "The Projective Expression of Needs: I. The effect of different intensities of the hunger drive on perception," J. Psychol., 25, 1948, pp. 205–222

[22]ADAMSON, R. E.: "Functional Fixedness as Related to Problem-Solving—A Repetition of Three Experiments," J. Exper. Psychol., 44, 1952, pp. 288–291

[23]BERELSON & STEINER, op. cit., p. 161

[24]IRVIN, R.: "The Role of Repetition in Associative Learning," Amer. J. Psychol., 70, 1957, pp. 186–193

[25]DEMERIC, M. & U. FANO: "Bacteriophage Resistant Mutants in Escherichia Coli," Genetics 30, 1945, pp. 119–136

LURIA, S. E. & M. DELBRUCK: "Mutations of Bacteria from Virus Sensitivity to Virus Resistance," Genetics 28, 1943, pp. 491–511

[26]LEVY-BRUHL: How Natives Think; Alfred A. Knopf, N.Y., 1925

[27]FISKE & MADDI: op. cit.

[28]HILGARD, E. R.: Introduction to Psychology; Harcourt, Brace & World, 1962, 3rd ed.

[29]MAX, L. W.: "An Experimental Study of the Motor Theory of Consciousness: III. Action-Current Responses in Deaf-Mutes During Sleep, Sensory Stimulation, and Dreams," J. Comp. Psychol., 19, 1935, pp. 469–486

[30]JANIS, I. L. & B. T. KING: "The Influence of Role Playing on Opinion Change," J. Abnorm. Soc. Psychol., 49, 1954, pp. 211–218

[31]JONES, E. E. & J. ANESHANSEL: "The Learning and Utilization of Contravaluant Material," J. Abnorm. Soc. Psychol., 53, 1956, pp. 27–33

[32]MENNINGER, K.: The Vital Balance; The Viking Press, N.Y. 1963

[33]MONOD, J.: Chance & Necessity; Translated by Austryn Wainhouse; Alfred A. Knopf, N.Y., 1971

[34]SPIEGELMAN, S.: "Physiological Competition as a Regulatory Mechanism in Morphogenesis," Quarterly Review of Biology, XX, 1945, pp. 121–146

[35]ANDERSON, N.: "Cell Division. Part One: A Theoretical Approach to the Primeval Mechanism, the Initiation of Cell Division, and Chromosomal Condensation," The Quarterly Review of Biology, XXXI, 1956, p. 169

ROSE, S. M.: "Feedback in the Differentiation of Cells," Scientific American, December, 1958, p. 36

[36]CHILD, I. L.: "Socialization" in Gardner Lindzey, ed., Handbook of Social Psychology, Vol. 2; Addison, Wesley, 1954, pp. 655–692

[37]MONTAGU, A.: The Direction of Human Development, rev. ed., 1970, Hawthorne Books

WYNNE, E. V. C.: Animal Dispersion in Relation to Social Behavior; Hafner, N.Y., 1962

[38]DAVIS, K.: Human Society; Macmillan, 1949, pp. 204–205

[39]SEARS, R. R., E. E. MACCOBY & H. LEVIN: Patterns of Child Rearing; Harper & Row, 1957, p. 525

[40]WOLPE, J.: Psychotherapy by Reciprocal Inhibition; Stanford U. Press, 1958

[41]FOA, U. G.: "Interpersonal & Economic Resources," Science, Vol. 171, January, 1971, pp. 345–351

HAYWOOD, C. H.: Social-Cultural Aspects of Mental Retardation; Meredith Corp., 1970

[42]BERELSON & STEINER, op. cit., p. 664

DOOB, A. N.: "Deviance," Psychology Today, October, 1971

[43]BAUER, R. A. & A. H. BAUER: "America Mass Society and Mass Media," J. Soc. Issues, 16, 1960, pp. 3–66

[44]HAMMOND, K. R.: "Computer Graphics as an Aid to Learning," Science, May, 1971, pp. 903–907

[45]GRAY, P. H.: "Theory and Evidence of Imprinting in Human Infants," J. Psychology, 46, 1958, pp. 155–166

BOWLBY, J.: "Maternal Care and Mental Health," World Health Organization, Monograph Series, #2, 1952

[46]HERON, op. cit.

[47]ASPY, D. N.: "A study of three facilitative conditions and their relationships to the achievement of third grade students," Unpublished doctoral dissertation; University of Kentucky, 1965

———— "The effect of teacher-offered conditions of empathy, positive regard and congruence upon student achievement," Florida Journal of Educational Research, II (1), 1969, pp. 39–48

———— & W. HADLOCK: "The effects of empathy, warmth and genuineness on elementary students' reading achievement," Reviewed in C. B. Truax & R. R. Carkhuff, Toward Effective Counseling and Psychotherapy; Aldine Publishing Co., Chicago, 1967

FERSTER, C. B.: "Arbitrary & Natural Reinforcement," The Psychological Record, Vol. 17, #3, 1967, pp. 341–347

———— Operant Reinforcement of Infantile Autism. An Evaluation of the Results of the Psychotherapics (S. Lasse, ed.); Charles C Thomas, 1968

ROSENTHAL, R. & L. F. JACOBSON: Pygmalion in the Classroom; Holt, Rinehart & Winston, 1968

[48]HEBER, R. & H. GARBER: "An experiment in the prevention of cultural familial Mental Retardation" in Proceedings of the

Second Congress of the International Association for the Scientific Study of Mental Deficiency, August 25–September 2, 1970 (in press)

[49]LAND, G. T.: Innovation Technique Manual; Transolve, 1966, St. Petersburg

[50]JOHN, E. R.: "Switchboard vs. Statistical Theories of Learning & Memory," Science, Vol. 177, 1972, pp. 850–864

VOLKMAR, F. R. & W. T. GREENOUGH: "Rearing complexity affects branching of dendrites in the visual contex of the rat," Science, Vol. 176, 1972, pp. 1445–1447

[51]RIEGE, W. H.: "Environmental Influence on Brain and Behavior of Year-old Rats," Developmental Psychobiology, Vol. 4, #2, 1971, pp. 157–167

ROSENZWEIG, M. R.: "Effects of Environment on Development of Brain & Behavior" in Biopsychology of Development, edited by Ethel Tobach; Academic Press, 1971

[52]BROSS, I. D. J., P. A. SHAPIRO & B. B. ANDERSON: "How Information is carried in Scientific Sub-Languages," Science, Vol. 176, 1972

CHAPTER SIX

[1]CABANAC, M.: "Physiological Role of Pleasure," Science, September 17, 1971, p. 1103

[2]DUNN, H. L.: High-Level Wellness; R. W. Beatty, Ltd., Va. 1961

[3]BARKER, R. T., T. DEMBO & K. LEWIN: "Frustration and Regression—An Experiment with Young Children," University of Iowa Studies in Child Welfare, 18, 1941, No. 386

LANTZ, B.: "Some Dynamic Aspects of Success and Failure," Psychol. Monogr., 59, No. 1, 1945

CHAPTER SEVEN

[1]"Education Commission of the States—The National Assessment of Educational Progress," AAAS Bulletin, Vol. 17, No.1, 1972

[2]NEWCOMB, T.M.: "The Study of Consensus," Robert K. Merton et al., eds., Sociology Today—Problems and Prospects; Basic Books, 1959, pp. 277–292

[3]BARRETT-LENNARD, G.T.: "Dimensions of therapist response as causal factors in therapeutic change," Psychological Monographs, 1962, 76 (whole No. 562); Brown & Tedeschi Graduate Education in psychology; A comment on Rogers' passionate statement. Journal of Humanistic Psychology, 1972, 12 (1)

HALKIDES, G.: "An experimental study of four conditions necessary for therapeutic change." Unpublished doctoral dissertation, University of Chicago, 1958

KOBLER, R. & R. WEBER: The Crisis in Human Under-Development; Responsive Environment Corp., March, 1967, pp. 19–20

PIERCE, R.: "An investigation of grade-point average and therapeutic process variables." Unpublished dissertation, University of Mass., 1966. Reviewed in R.R. Carkhuff & G.B. Berelson, Beyond Counseling and Therapy, N.Y.; Holt, Rinehart and Winston, Inc., 1967

ROSENTHAL, R. & L.F. JACOBSEN: Pygmalion in the Classroom; Holt, Rinehart & Winston, 1968

[4]SINGH, D.: "Animals Respond for Food in The Presence of Free Food," Science, Vol. 166, Oct. 17, 1969, pp. 399–401

KAVANAV, J.L.: "Behavior of Captive White-Footed Mice," Science, Vol. 155, 1967, pp. 1632–1639

[5]DELEON, P.: Reported at American Psychological Association Convention; Honolulu, September, 1972

[6]DOOB, A.N.: "Society Side Show," Psychology Today, October, 1971, pp. 48–51

FREEDMAN, R., A.H. HAWLEY, L.S. WERNER, G.E. LENSKI & H.M. MINER: Principles of Sociology; Holt, Rinehart & Winston, 1956, rev. ed.

[7]BERZON, B. & L.N. SOLOMON: "The self-directed therapeutic group: An exploratory study," Int. J. Group Psychother., 1964, 14, pp. 366–369

BLAKE, R.R. & J.S. MOUTON: "The instrumented training laboratory." In I. Weschler and E. Schein (eds.), Issues in Human Relations Training. Selected Reading Series No. 5, Washington, D.C.: National Training Laboratories, National Education Association, 1962

SOLOMON, L.N., B. BERZON & D.P. DAVIS: "A personal growth program for self-directed groups," J. appl. behav. sci., 1970, 6 (4), pp. 427–451

[8]WALD, G.: "Determinancy, Individuality and the Problem of Free Will" in John R. Platt (ed.), New Views of the Nature of Man; University of Chicago Press, 1965

CHAPTER TEN

[1]DARWIN, C.: Origin of Species; Macmillan, 1962

[2]WADDINGTON, C.H.: The Listener; London, Feb. 13, 1952

[3]VON BERTALANFFY, L.: "General System Theory and Psychology," In J.R. Royce, ed., Toward Unification of Psychology; Toronto University Press

[4]CHENG, T.C.: Symbiosis (Organisms Living Together); Pegasus, N.Y., 1970, p.11

[5]SIMPSON, G.G.: The Major Features of Evolution; Columbia University Press, 1953

[6]KAMMERER, P.: Das Gesetz den Serie; Stuttgart, 1919 (2. AuF1. 1921)

[7]HALDANE, J.S.: The Philosophy of a Biologist; Clarendon Press, Oxford 1935

[8]HESS, E. H.: "Natural History of Imprinting in Integrative Events in Life Processes," Annals of the New York Academy of Sciences, Vol. 193, in press

[9]CALVIN, M.: Chemical Evolution; Oxford University Press, New York and Oxford, 1969

[10]RUBNER, M.: Das problem der Lebensdauer und Seihe Beziehunger zu Wachstum und Ernahrung; Munchen, Berlin, 1908

[11]ARSHAVSKY, A.: Musculoskeletal Activity and Rate of Entropy in Mammals from Advances in Psychobiology, edited by Grant Newton & Austin H. Riesen; Wiley-Interscience, a division of John Wiley & Sons, Inc., 1972

CHAPTER ELEVEN

[1]LOCKE, DAVID M.: Enzymes—The Agents of Life, Crown Publisher, N.Y., 1969

FARAGO, PETER and J. LAGNADO: Life in Action, Alfred A. Knopf, N.Y., 1972, p. 102

APPENDIX II

For the work in this section the author wishes to thank in particular Dr. William Little and acknowledge the contribution made by the books *The Single Reality,* by Preston Harold (Dodd, Mead & Co., New York, 1971), and *Scientific Uncertainty, and Information,* by Leon Brillouin (Academic Press, New York and London, 1964).

[1]ARSHAVSKY, A.: "Musculoskeletal Activity and Rate of Entropy in Mammals," in Advances in Psychobiology, edited by Grant Newton and Austin H. Riesen; Wiley-Interscience, a division of John Wiley & Sons, Inc., 1972

[2]CALVIN, M.: Chemical Evolution; Oxford University Press, N.Y. and Oxford, 1969

[3]Ibid., p. 243

[4]TEILHARD DE CHARDIN, P.: The Future of Man; Harper Torchbooks, Harper & Row, New York and Evanston, 1969

GLOSSARY

*ACCRETIVE GROWTH

Growth by addition or accumulation of the environment into the self. Biologically represented by cell enlargement and vegetative growth. Psychologically all possession or control of any parts of the external environment manifested in both selfing and othering through counterdependent and dependent behavior.

ADRENALIN

A hormone produced by the adrenal glands. A drug, CoH18NO3, with this hormone in it, made from the adrenal glands of animals or synthetically, and used to raise blood pressure, stop bleeding, etc. Also called *epinephrine.*

ALLELE

n. an allelomorph; in genetics, either of a pair of contrasting characteristics inherited alternatively according to Mendelian law.

AMINO ACIDS

A group of nitrogenous organic compounds that serve as units of structure of the proteins and are essential to human metabolism.

ANALOGICAL

adj. of, using, or based upon analogy.

---

*Asterisks refer to terms defined in a special sense in this text.

ANALOGY

n. (pl. analogies) 1. Similarity in some respects between things otherwise unlike; partial resemblance. 2. An explaining of something by comparing it point by point with something else. 3. In biology, similarity in function between parts dissimilar in origin and structure; distinguished from homology.

ANTHROPOCENTRIC

adj. considering man as the central fact, or final aim of the universe.

ANTHROPOGENY

n. anthropogenesis. (*anthropogenesis:* The study of man's origin and development.)

ANTHROPONOMICS

n. pl. (construed as sing.), anthroponomy. (*anthroponomy:* The science dealing with the laws of human development in relation to environment and to other organisms.)

ANTIGEN

A substance, usually a protein, carbohydrate, or fat-carbohydrate complex, which causes the production of an antibody when introduced directly into the body, as into the blood stream.

ASEXUAL

Having no sex; sexless. In biology, designating or of reproduction without the union of male and female germ cells.

AUTISTIC

adj. of or having autism. (*autism:* In psychology, a state of mind characterized by daydreaming, hallucinations, and disregard of external reality.)

AUTONOMIC

Autonomous. Of or pertaining to the autonomic nervous system. In botany, resulting from internal causes. (*autonomous:* Of an autonomy. Having self-government. In biology, functioning independently of other parts.)

BACTERIOLOGICAL

adj. of or connected with bacteriology. (*bacteriology:* Science that deals with bacteria.)

BEHAVIORISM

(social) (human) A theory of conduct which regards normal and abnormal behavior as the result of conditioned reflexes quite apart from the concept of will. It does not apply to conditions resulting from structural disease.

BIOCHEMISTRY
n. the branch of chemistry that deals with plants and animals and their life processes; biological chemistry.

BIOPHYSICS
Application of physical laws to life processes and functions.

*BIOPSYCHOLOGICAL
Of or pertaining to the combined disciplines of biology and psychology.

BUDDING
A method of asexual reproduction in which a budlike process grows from the side or end of the parent and develops into a new organism which in some cases remains attached, and in other cases separates and lives an independent existence. It is common in lower animals (sponges, coelenterates) and plants (yeasts, molds).

CHROMOSOME
A microscopic rod-shaped (J- or V-shaped) body which develops from the nuclear material of a cell and is especially conspicuous during mitosis. Chromosomes stain deeply with basic dyes. They contain the genes or hereditary determiners.

COGNITIVE
Having to do with cognition. (*cognition:* The process of knowing or perceiving; perception. Anything that is known or perceived.)

COMMENSALISM
The symbiotic relationship of two organisms of different species in which neither is harmful to the other and one gains some benefit such as protection or nourishment. Example: nonpathogenic bacteria in human intestine.

CONJUGATION
A coupling together. In biology, the union of two unicellular organisms accompanied by an interchange of nuclear material, as in paramecia.

CONTINUUM
A continuous whole, quantity, or series; thing whose parts cannot be separated or separately discerned.

COVALENCE

The number of pairs of electrons that an atom can share with its neighboring atoms. The bond formed by shared pairs of electrons between two atoms.

CROSS FERTILIZED

past part. (*cross fertilization:* The combining of gametes of two different individuals of the same species.)

CYBERNETICS

A science dealing with the comparative study of complex electronic calculating machines and the human nervous system in an attempt to explain the nature of the brain.

CYTOPLASM

The protoplasm of a cell which envelops the nucleus. Cell plasm not including the nucleus. syn: cytosome.

*DISCONTINUUM

In transformation theory, a break or gap between two phenomenological levels. This occurs when successful accretive, replicative, and mutual growth create the conditions by which a higher level of organization is required to continue broadening of informational transformation, as from heteropolymeric molecules to cells or from social hominoids to Homo sapiens.

DNA

Abbreviation for deoxyribonucleic acid, endogenetic coding of information for the perpetuation of species characteristics.

ECOSPHERE

The total ecology of the planet.

ECTOBIOLOGICAL

Of or pertaining to biological functions that have externalized, i.e., that are outside the organic biological system, primarily through technology.

*ECTOGENETIC

Information transmitted from generation to generation carried outside the individual physiological genetic (endogenetic) system.

ELECTRON

An extremely minute corpuscle or charge of negative electricity which revolves about the central core or nucleus of an atom. It is the smallest known particle that exists, its mass being 1/1845 that of a hydrogen atom. When emitted from radioactive substances, electrons are known as beta particles or rays.

ENDOCRINE
An internal secretion. (*endocrinous,* adj: Pertaining to a gland that produces an internal secretion.)

*ENDOGENETIC
Commonly used as "genetic" and used to describe information carried in the physiological-biological information system.

ENVIRONMENT
The surroundings, conditions, or influences which affect an organism or the cells within an organism.

ENZYME
An organic catalyst produced by living cells but capable of acting independently of the cells producing it. Enzymes are complex colloidal substances which are capable of inducing chemical changes in other substances without themselves being changed in the process.

ETHNOLOGY
The branch of anthropology that deals with the comparative cultures of various peoples, including their distribution, characteristics, folkways, etc.

ETHOLOGY
The science of character. Study of manners, customs, and mores, their formation, growth, decay, and effectiveness.

FISSION
In biology, a form of asexual reproduction, found in various simple plants and animals, in which the parent organism divides into two or more parts, each becoming an independent individual.

FUSION
Meeting and joining together; the process of fusing or uniting.

GENETICS
The branch of biology which deals with heredity and variation among related organisms largely in their evolutionary aspects. In its study of inheritance it includes the physiology of reproduction.

HETEROGENEOUS
Of unlike natures composed of unlike substances. In contrast to homogeneous.

HETEROZYGOTE
An individual in which the members of one or more pairs of genes are unlike.

HOMEO
Prefix: Likeness or resemblance.

HOMEOSTASIS
The state of equilibrium or the state of relative constancy.

HOMOLOGOUS
Similar in fundamental structure and in origin.

HOMOLOGUE
An organ or part common to a number of species. One that corresponds to a part or organ in another structure.

HOMOLOGY
Similarity in structure and in origin.

HOMO SAPIENS
The species to which all races of modern man belong.

HOMOZYGOTE
A homozygous individual: an individual developing from like gametes and thus possessing like pairs of genes for any hereditary characteristics.

HORMONE
A chemical substance originating in an organ, gland, or part, which is conveyed through the blood to another part of the body, stimulating it to increased functional activity and increased secretion. Contains amino acids which may be the precursors of hormones. The secretion of the ductless glands, such as insulin by the pancreas.

*HYBRIDIZATION
In biology, the mating of individuals differing in genetic make-up, i.e., cross-breeding. In psychology, the linking of informational units or ectogenetic material with differences of content.

HYDROCARBON
A compound made up only of hydrogen and carbon. Hydrocarbons may exist as aliphatic chain compounds in which the carbon atoms are arranged in the form of a chain, or as aromatic or cyclic compounds in which the carbon atoms form one or more rings.

*INFRASTRUCTURES
Organizations lying far below observable patterns.

INORGANIC
In chemistry, occurring in nature independently of living things, substances not containing carbon. Not pertaining to living organisms.

ISOMORPHISM
Condition marked by possession of the same form.

MACRO
A combining word form meaning long (in extent or duration), large, enlarged, or elongated (in a specified part), as in macrocosm. Also, before a vowel, macr-. Opposed to "micro."

MEIOSIS
Method of cell division which allows each daughter nucleus to receive half the number of chromosomes present in the somatic cells.

METABOLISM
The sum of all physical and chemical changes which take place within an organism; all energy and material transformations which occur within living cells. It includes material changes, i.e., changes undergone by substances during all periods of life (growth, maturity, senescence) and energy changes, i.e., all transformations of chemical energy.

METABOLITES
Any products of metabolism.

METAPHYSICS
n. pl. (construed as sing.) The branch of philosophy that deals with first principles and seeks to explain the nature of being or reality (ontology) and the origin and structure of the world (cosmology); it is closely associated with a theory of knowledge (epistemology).

MICROCOSM
n. a little world; miniature universe, specifically, (a) man regarded as a miniature or epitome of the world, (b) a community, village, etc., regarded as a miniature or epitome of the world. Opposed to macrocosm.

MITOSIS
(pl. mitoses) Indirect cell division involving indirect nuclear division (karyokinesis) and division of the cell body (cytokinesis);

the process by which all somatic cells of multicellular organisms multiply.

MONOMER
A single molecule of a compound formed by uniting several such molecules.

MONOMORPHIC
Unchangable in form.

MORPHOLOGY
Science of structure and form without regard to function.

MUTANT
In heredity, a sport or variation which breeds true.

MUTATION
1. Change; transformation; instance of such change. 2. Sudden, permanent variation, with offspring differing from parents in a marked characteristic, as differentiated from gradual variation through many generations.

Also person showing such change. Change in a gene potentially capable of being transmitted to offspring.

*MUTUAL GROWTH
Growth through relatively equal exchanges of materials, information, influences, etc.; reciprocal behavior that leads to the growth of both individuals or groups concerned. In symbiosis, mutualism.

NEURONAL
Pertaining to one or more neurons.

NUCLEOTIDE
syn: mononucleotide. A compound formed of phosphoric acid, a sugar, and a base (purine or pyrimidine), all of which constitute the structural unit of nucleic acid.

NUCLEUS
A central point about which matter is gathered as in a calculus. The vital body in the protoplasm of a cell; the essential agent in growth, metabolism, reproduction, and transmission of characteristics of a cell. See: cell structure. A group of nerve cells or mass of gray matter in the central nervous system, esp. the brain.

ONTOGENETIC
adj. of ontogeny. (*ontogeny:* The life cycle of a single organism;

biological development of the individual; distinguished from phylogeny.)

ONTOLOGICAL
adj. of ontology. (*ontology:* The branch of metaphysics dealing with the nature of being or reality; cf. phenomenology.)

OPERON
The site of operator or regulator mechanisms in the genetic code.

ORGANELLE
A specialized part of a cell which performs a definite function. Exmitochondria, Golgi apparatus, endoplasmic reticuluum, lysosomes, and cell centriole.

*OTHERING
In accretive and replicative growth, refers to growth by attachment to a large organism, person, social or cultural unit. In symbiosis, referred to as "parasitism" or "commensalism."

PARAMETER
In mathematics, a quantity or constant whose value varies with the circumstances of its application.

PERMEABLE
Capable of or allowing the passage of fluids or substances in solution.

PHENOMENOLOGY
The science dealing with phenomena as distinct from the science of being (ontology). The branch of a science that classifies and describes its phenomena without any attempt at explanation.

PHYLOGENETIC
Concerning the development of a race or group.

POLYMERIC
Of a complex chemical combination, a molecule which is a multiple of the original but whose physical properties are different.

POLYMORPHIC
Occurring in more than one form.

PRECURSORY
adj. serving as a precursor, or harbinger; indicating something to follow. Introductory; preliminary.

PROSTHETICS
The making and application of an artificial part to remedy a want or defect of the body, such as an artificial arm or leg.

PROTOPLASM
A thick viscous colloidal substance which constitutes the physical basis of all living activities, exhibiting the properties of assimilation, growth, motility, secretion, irritability, and reproduction.

PROTOPLASMIC
Pertaining to protoplasm or composed of it.

PROTOZOA
The phylum of the animal kingdom which includes the simplest animals. Most are unicellular, although some are colonial. Reproduction usually asexual by fission, although conjugation and sexual reproduction occur.

RECESSIVE
Tending to recede or go back; lacking control.

REGENERATION
Repair, regrowth, or restoration of a part, as tissues. Opposite of degeneration, q.v.

*REPLICATIVE GROWTH
In selfing behavior, growth that occurs through either direct or influential transformation of parts of the environment into replicas of the self. In othering, growth by imitation or emulation of outside growth phenomena; becoming a replica.

RNA
Abbreviation for ribonucleic acid, q.v.

ROTE
A fixed, mechanical way of doing something; routine.

*SCREENING
A selective mechanism operating as a filter for either physiological or biological growth materials. In biology, selective permeability. In psychology, selective perception.

*SEARCH
The active physiological or psychological seeking of growth material (nutrition) in the form of physical, chemical, or psychological materials.

SELECTION

Process by which individuals possessing characteristics which adapt them to their environment survive, whereas those lacking these characteristics die or fail to leave progeny. Darwin's theory of evolution or origin of species.

*SELFING

Referring to growth by self-enlargement through the attachment of smaller organisms to the self or to growth by pure self-enlargement, i.e., conversion of the environment into self-extensions.

SOMATIC

Of the body, as distinguished from the soul, mind, or psyche; corporeal; physical. In biology, of the soma. In anatomy and zoology, of the framework of outer walls of the body, as distinguished from the viscera; parietal.

SPECTROSCOPE

An instrument for separating radiant energy into its component frequencies or wave lengths by means of a prism or grating to form a correct spectrum for inspection.

*STASIS

Stagnation or stoppage of growth. Also referred to as homeostasis.

SYMBIONT

An organism which lives with another in a state of symbiosis.

SYMBIOSIS

The living together in close association of two organisms of different species. "Phoresis" refers to casual contact where neither organism is affected. If neither organism is harmed, such contact is referred to as commensalism; if the association is beneficial to both, it is mutualism; if one is harmed and the other benefited, it constitutes parasitism.

SYNAPTIC

Pertaining to a synapse or synapsis, a field in cerebral cortex, cerebellar cortex, and retina where large numbers of contacts between neurons can take place.

SYNDROME

A complexus of symptoms.

SYNTHESIS

The putting together of parts or elements so as to form a whole; opposed to analysis. A whole made up of parts or elements put together. The formation of a complex chemical compound by the combining of two or more simpler compounds, elements, or radicals. In philosophy, deductive reasoning, from the simple elements of thought into the complex whole, from cause to effect, from a principle to its application, etc.

TECHNO

Art, science, skill, as in technocracy, technical; technological, as in technolochemistry.

*TRANSDETERMINATION

The phenomenon of a specialized or semi-specialized organism changing its course of behavior and growth.

*TRANSFORMATION

The theory of recapitulation of accretive, replicative, and mutual growth leading to the manifestations of higher levels of organization and distinct phylogenetic evolution, as from atoms to molecules, molecules to cells, cells to multicellular organisms, multicellular organisms to societies, and societies to cultures. A continuing ability to transform or change the environment into life-supporting organizations.

BIBLIOGRAPHY

Aside from direct references in the body of this book, the following represent only a few of the major contributors and works that make up the foundation of Transformation theory.

ANGYAL, A. L.: Foundations for a Science of Personality; Commonwealth Fund, N.Y. 1941

BERGSON, H.: Creative Evolution; The Modern Library, N.Y., Random House, Inc., 1944

BERNSHTEIN, N. A.: Biological Aspects of Cybernetics; Moscow, 1962

DOBZHANSKY, T.: "Human Nature as a Product of Evolution" in New Knowledge in Human Values, A.H. Maslow, ed., Harper, N.Y. 1959, pp. 75–85

FROMM, E. & R. XIRAU: The Nature of Man; The Macmillan Co., 1968

GEORGE, F. H.: Cybernetics; English Universities Press, 1970

GLASSER, W.: Reality Therapy; Harper & Row Pub., 1965

GOLDSTEIN, K.: Human Nature in the Light of Psychopathology; Cambridge, Harvard University, 1940

GUTMAN, H.: The Biological Roots of Creativity; Genetic Psychology Monographs, 1961, pp.419–458

HACKER, F.J.: "Symbole und Psychoanalyse." Psyche 11, 1958, pp. 641–671

HAROLD, P.: The Single Reality; Dodd, Mead & Co., 1971

HUXLEY, J.S.: Evolution, The Modern Synthesis; Rev. Ed., Harper 1942, 1963

LANGER, S.K.: Mind–An Essay on Human Feeling; Johns Hopkins Press, 1967

——— Philosophy in a New Key, 3rd ed.; Cambridge, Harvard University, 1957

LEWIN, K.: A Dynamic Theory of Personality; McGraw-Hill, N.Y., 1935

MCHALE, JOHN: World Facts and Trends; Collier Books, N.Y., 1972

MASLOW, H.A.: "Cognition of Being in Peak Experience," J. Genetic Psychol. In Press.

——— Motivation and Personality; Harper & Row Pub., 1954

MEAD, M.: Culture & Commitment; Natural History Press, 1970

MENNINGER, K. with ELLENBERGER, HENRI, PRUYSER, PAUL AND MAYMAN MARTIN: "The Unitary Concept of Mental Illness," Bull. Menninger Clinic 22, 1958, pp. 4–12

MUMFORD, L.: The Myth of the Machine Technics & Human Development; Harcourt, Brace Jovanovich, Inc., 1966

MURPHY, G.: Human Potentialities; Basic Books, N.Y., 1958

PIAGET, J.: Structuralism; Basic Books, Inc., 1970

RASHEVSKY, N.: Mathematical Biology of Behavior; University of Chicago Press, 1959

REISER, O.L.: Cosmic Humanism; Schenkman Publishing Co., Cambridge, Mass., 1966

RENSCH, B.: Biophilosophy; Columbia University Press, 1971

RIBOT, T.: Essai sur l'imagination creatice, 1st ed., 6th ed., 1921 Paris, Alcan, 1900

STERN, W.: Person Und Sache; Bd. I: Ableitung und Grundlehe, 1906 Bd. II: Die Menschliche Persoenliehkeit, 1918

TRONCALE, L.R. and D. RANSEY-KLEE: "Information and Control Processes in Living Systems," Science 166:132–139, 1969

VON BERTALANFFY, L.: "A Biologist Looks at Human Nature," Science Monthly 82: 1956, pp. 33–41

——— "General System Theory and Psychology," R. J. Royce, ed., Toward Unification of Psychology; Toronto University Press, pp. 220–230

——— "Some Biological Considerations on the Problem of Mental Illness," Bulletin of the Menninger Clinic, Vol. 23, No. 2 March, 1959

WEISS, P.: "Knowledge—A Growth Process," Proceedings of the American Philosophical Society, 104, No. 2, 1960

WHITE, R.W.: "Motivation Reconsidered: The Concept of Competence," American Psychological Association—Psychological Review, 1957 #66, pp. 297–333

WHYTE, W.J., JR.: Organization Man; Simon & Schuster, N.Y., 1956

WIENER, N.: Cybernetics: Or Control & Communication in the Animal and the Machine; John Wiley & Hermann, N.Y. & Paris, 1948

WOODWORTH, R.S.: Dynamics of Behavior; Henry Holt, N.Y., 1958

Organizations for whom research has been performed:

American Can Co.	General Foods Corp.
Association of Mfg. Jewelers & Silversmiths	J. P. Stevens & Co.
	Monsanto Corp.
Atlantic-Richfield Sinclair	New England Nuclear
Block Drug Co.	Proctor & Gamble Co.
Bristol-Myers Co.	R. J. Reynolds Foods
Carter-Wallace Inc.	Roman Company
Child Development Group of Mississippi	S. C. Johnson & Son
	Squibb Beech-Nut
Citizens & Southern Bank	Sweetheart Cup Co.
Coca-Cola Co.	Sweetheart Plastic Co.
E. I. DuPont de Nemours & Co.	Time Inc.
	United Presbyterian Church
Edison Electric Institute	Urban Directions, Inc.

Educational institutions supporting research and seminars:

State University of New York
Massachusetts Institute of Technology
Harvard University
University of South Florida
Southern Illinois University
Macalester College
Mary Holmes Junior College
Eckerd College
St. John's University

INDEX

A

abstract art, 65, 161
accretive growth:
  feedback, 101
  growth model, 126
  meaning of, 11
  origins of
    animal forms, 28
    discontinuum of, 26–27
    individual, 45–46
    pre-life, 18–19
    social forms, 42–43
  psychological, 113–114,
    117–118
    characteristics of, 117–118
acellular organism, 21
Acetabularia (green alga),
  21
acetylcholine, 69
activity, meaning of, 15–16
Adams, Henry, 70–71
adaptation, evolution and,
  171–172
adaptive immunity, evolutionary
  origin of, 87
adenine, 180
Adler, Alfred, 84

adrenalin, 33–34
affective emotions, 119
African art, 65
Agape, 114
agents of transformation,
  186–189
alcoholism, 118, 129, 147
algae, 21, 22, 30
allosteric interactions, 85
altruism, false, 118
American Psychological Association, 4
animal growth forms, 27–34
  accretive, 28
  evolution to human forms,
    30–34
  mutual, 28–30
  replicative, 28
anticipatory arousal, 81
antigens, cultural, 115
Aquinas, St. Thomas, 165
architectural systems, 59
Arshavsky, A., 182, 201
art, 65, 161
  stylized, 36–37
  and transformation, 64–67
asexual replication, 23
  rate of, 78
autoimmune systems, 47

automatic temperature control, 89–90

B

Babylonian civilization, 36
Bacon, Francis, 66
bacteria, 21, 22
Bauhaus School, 64
beauty and ugliness, 141–142
Beer, Stafford, 63
behavior, 111–153
  biopsychological, 6
  concepts of, 4–5
  instinctivists, 4
  origins of, 17–34
    animal growth forms, 27–34
    cell-growth forms, 20–26
    discontinuum, 26–27
    pre-life-growth forms, 18–20
  patterns of human growth and motivation, 111–122
  growth motivation, 111–113
  psychological forms of growth, 113–122
belittling, technique of, 119
Bertalanffy, Ludwig von, 7, 168–169
biological growth systems, 75–78
biological wisdom, ethic of, 158
biopsychological behavior, 6
blue-green algae, 21, 22, 30
Bohr, Niels, 7
Brillouin, L., 180
Buddha, 164

C

Calvin, Melvin, 180, 201
cancerous growth, biopsychological approach, 221–225

carbon atom, mutuality function of, 18
Casals, Pablo, 66
Case of the Midwife Toad, The (Koestler), 178
cave paintings, information-preserving capability of, 36
cells:
  allosteric interactions, 85
  biological growth system, 75–78
  development of, 9–10
  embryonic, replication of, 20
  nature of, 9
  origins of growth forms, 20–26
change, resistance to, 148
chemicals, lifeless amalgamations of, 19
childhood, idea of, 44
China (ancient), 43, 192
city nucleus, 47
Civil War, 72
coacervates, 20
cocaine, 72
cocktail party syndrome, 82
Coghill, Robert D., 8
collective unconscious, theory of, 115
colonial empires, demise of, 192
Columbus, Christopher, 43
comic humor, 141
commensalism, 28
community growth, 47–49
conditioned reflexes, 5
conjugation, replicative growth by, 23
consumerism, 160
control and evolution, natural methods of, 63–64
cross-culturing, 44–45
cross-pollination, 29
crystals, 18–19
  duplicating, 19

formation and growth of, 13, 18–19
isomorphic replacement, 18
cultural hybridization, problem of, 49
cultural transformation, 191–193
cutting down to size, technique of, 119

D

Da Vinci, Leonardo, 59, 64
Dart, Raymond A., 7
Darwin, Charles, 6, 58, 68, 161–162, 167–168, 172, 175, 176, 185
desoxyribonucleic acid (DNA), 6, 7, 22, 23, 38, 40, 49, 50, 54, 56, 70, 104, 113, 142, 225
  in insects, 105
  molecules of, 13
  viruses and, 22
destructive growth, 118, 119
diatomic molecule, excitation levels of, 217–220
  rotational motion, 218
  translational motion, 219–220
  vibrational motion, 218
dictatorships, 55, 160
Dictyostelium (amoeba), 30
digestion and assimilation, system functions, 82–83
directed selection, evolution and, 172–176
discontinuum of growth, 26–27
Divine Right, theory of, 160
Dobzhansky, T., 23, 41, 69, 160–161, 162, 169
Down's syndrome, 130
drug-taking, 118, 129, 147
Dunn, Dr. Halbert, 113

E

ecology and technology, 189–191
ectogenetics, 36–41
  psychospeciation, 41–42
  system of writing, 37–38
Eddington, Sir Arthur, 146
education, as a replicative act, 57
Education Commission of the States, 124
Egypt (ancient), 36, 43, 192
Einstein, Albert, 176, 216
embryonic cell, replication of, 20
energy, Man's, 181–182
energy and life, evolution and, 176–182
enigmas of Man, 139–153
  beauty and ugliness, 141–142
  growing together, 148–153
  humor and ridicule, 140–141
  hypocrisy, 147–148
  liking, love, and hate, 142–147
  resistance to change, 148
  sadism and self-sacrifice, 140
  security and danger, 140
environment:
  adaptation to, 171–172
  transformation, 58–67
    art and, 64–67
    form vs. function, 67
  variations in, 25–26
Eros, 114
essence, Man's, 4
evolution, 15, 167–184
  from animal to human growth forms, 30–34
  Darwin's concept of, 167–168
  directionality in, 167

evolution (*continued*)

of information-coding systems, 33–34
meaning and direction, 167–184
adaptation, 171–172
direction selection, 172–176
energy and life, 176–182
growth of information organization, 169–171
sameness or differentness, 183–184
of Social Man, 42–45
transformative, 67–73
evolutionary change, paradox of, 55–58
evolution of man and environment, 53–73
environmental transformation, 58–67
art and, 64–67
form vs. function, 67
paradox of change, 55–58
and symbolism, 53
transformative, 67–73
growth and future, 70–73
evolving mutualism, 159–164
exchanges of information, development of, 47

F

Feedback, 111–112, 115, 119, 124, 126, 144, 147
accretive growth, 101
assimilation and regulation, 85–101
cumulative effect of, 98–99
from the environment, 9
in a growing system, 91–101
mutual growth, 101
negative, 86

replicative growth, 101
transformative growth and, 72
fitness, demonstrating, 54, 69
form vs. function, 67
Freud, Sigmund, 5, 84, 115–116
Fromm, Erich, 5

G

Galapagos finches, 172, 173
Galileo, 176
genetic information, substitution of, 55–56
genetic shift, 35–42
ectogenetics, 36–41
psychospeciation, 41–42
German measles, 130
Goethe, Johann Wolfgang von, 66
Goodall, Jane, 33
Greece (ancient), 192
green alga (*Acetabularia*), 21
group dynamics, 85–86
group therapy, 120
growth:
achieving, 185–195
agents of transformation, 186–189
conclusions, 193–195
cultural transformation, 191–193
ecology and technology, 189–191
atomic and molecular levels, 19
forms of, 11–12
activity, 15–16
animal reproduction, 27–34
cell division, 20–26
discontinuum in, 26–27

evolution from animal to
human, 30–34
pre-life, 18–20
and the future, 70–73
of information organiza-
tion, 169–171
interactive joining of, 11
meaning of, 10–12, 84
model, 123–137
accretive, 126
fundamental conditions
of, 128
learning situations, 135–
136
mutual, 127–128
processes (functions),
130–135
and reality, 136–137
replicative, 127
motivation, 111–113
process of, 8, 10–12
sharing of information,
12–14
usefulness for, 55
See also accretive growth;
mutual growth; replicative
growth

H

habitat isolation in social sys-
tems, 49–50
Haldane, J. B. S., 56, 158,
179
Harvard Law of Animal Behav-
ior, 137
Harvey, William, 59
Hawaii State Hospital, 129
Heisenberg, Werner, 173
Hess, Eckhard, 180
Hippocrates, 5
Hobbs, Thomas, 5
humor and ridicule, 140–141
Huxley, J., 7, 158, 169

hybridization:
inbreeding and, 23–24
isolation and, 49–51
hypocrisy, 147–148

I

ideas, formation of, 104
impressionist art, 65, 161
inbreeding, hybridization and,
23–24
individual growth forms,
45–46
Industrial Revolution, 44, 59,
136
information, meaning of,
12–14
information organization,
growth of, 169–171
inherited cultural information,
38–39
insects, DNA in, 105
internal systems, function of,
101–107
non-thinking, 105–107
thinking, 101–105
isolation, hybridization and,
49–51
isomorphic replacement, 18
isomorphism, biological, 8, 76,
184

J

Jung, Carl, 67, 84, 115, 168

K

Kammerer, Paul, 177–178
Kent State University, 162
Koestler, Arthur, 178

L

Lamarck, Jean Baptiste, 175
Langer, S. K., 7
laudanum, 72
learning as growth, 135–136
Levy-Bruhl, 84
like-mindedness, maintenance
of, 36
liking, love, and hate, 142–
147
Locke, John, 5
Lorenz, Konrad, 180
Luther, Martin, 164

M

magic, 35
Magna Carta, 160
Maslow, Abraham, 3–4, 5,
116
Mead, Margaret, 7
meaning and direction, 157–
195
achieving growth, 185–195
agents of transformation,
186–189
conclusions, 193–195
cultural transformation,
191–193
ecology and technology,
189–191
evolution, 167–184
adaptation, 171–172
directed selection, 172–
176
energy and life, 176–182
growth of information or-
ganization, 169–171
sameness or different-
ness, 183–184
philosophy and transformation, 157–165

evolving mutualism, 159–
164
mechanical isolation, 59
meiosis, process of, 24–26
Mendel, Gregor Johann, 6, 41
Menninger, Karl, 85, 132
mental disease, 118–120
mental health, 111
mental illness, 111
Miller, Stanley, 180, 181, 201
mimicry of nature, 32–33
Moholy-Nagy, Laszlo, 64
mongolism, 130
Mrs. Winslow's Soothing
Syrup, 72
multicellular relationship, 9
mutations:
in offspring, 22–23
phenomenon of writing and,
39
mutual gene recombination,
24–26
mutual growth:
feedback, 101
growth model, 127–128
meaning of, 11
origins of
animal forms, 28–30
cell development, 24–26
discontinuum of, 26–27
individual, 45–46
pre-life, 19–20
social forms, 44–45
psychological, 114, 116
characteristics of, 116
mutualism, evolving, 159–164

N

National Assessment of Educational Progress, 124
nature, continuum of, 6
negentropy, concept of, 180
neurotics, 118

Newton, Sir Isaac, 176
noradrenaline, 69
nucleation, process of, 18

O

operant conditioning, 5
opium, 72
organisms, primitive, 21–22
Origin of Species (Darwin),
 185
origins, 3–107
 of behavior, 17–34
  animal growth forms,
   27–34
  cell-growth forms, 20–26
  discontinuum, 26–27
  pre-life growth forms,
   18–20
 evolution of man and en-
  vironment, 53–73
 environmental transfor-
  mation, 58–67
 paradox of change, 55–58
 transformative, 67–73
 overview of, 3–16
  growth, 10–12
  information, 12–14
  principles, 14–16
  transformation theory,
   8–10
 psychology from biology,
  75–107
  biological growth sys-
   tems, 75–78
  psychological growth systems, 78–79
  system functions, 80–107
 second nature, 35–51
  community growth,
   47–49
  genetic shift, 35–42
  individual growth forms,
   45–46

isolation and hybridiza-
 tion, 49–51
social growth forms,
 42–45

P

para-azo-oxycinnamic acid
 ethyl ester, 19
parasites:
 bacteriological, 22
 genetic hybridization, 23
participation mystique, concept of, 84
patterns of human growth and
 motivation, 111–122
 growth motivation, 111–
  113
 psychological forms of
  growth, 113–122
  accretive, 113–114, 117–
   118
  functional description of,
   120
  mental disease, 118–120
  mutual, 114, 116
  replicative, 114, 116–117
Pavlov, I., 80
phenylketonuria (PKU), 130
Philadelphia draft riots of 1860,
 162
Philia, 114
physics and transformation,
 199–200
 chemical growth, 210
 energy and growth, 199–
  202
 excitation levels of diatomic
  molecule, 217–220
  rotational motion, 218
  translational motion,
   219–220
  vibrational motion, 218
 growth of molecules, 205–
  207

physics and transformation (*continued*)

microcosmos, 212–217
  subatomic growth, 214–217
phases of growth, 202–203
polar covalent bonding, 208–209
probability or inevitability, 210–212
replicative non-polar covalent bonds, 207–208
tradition vs. change, 203–205
  exclusion and inclusion, 204–205
Picasso, Pablo, 66
Planck, Max, 179
postzygotal, the, 49
pre-life growth forms, 18–20
  accretive, 18–19
  mutual, 19–20
  replicative, 19
prezygotal, the, 49
psychological growth, symbolic language and, 35
psychological growth systems, 78–79
psychology from biology, 75–107
  biological growth systems, 75–78
  psychological growth systems, 78–79
  system functions, 80–107
    digestion and assimilation, 82–83
    feedback—assimilation and regulation, 85–101
    internal systems, 101–107
    screening, 81–82
    search, 80–81
    use, 83–85
psychospeciation, 41–42

psychotics, 118, 129
punitive emotion, 119–120

Q

quanine, 180

R

reality, growth models and, 136–137
Reiser, O. L., 7
religion, 35, 36
Renaissance, 136
Rensch, B., 158
replicative growth:
  feedback, 101
  growth model, 127
  meaning of, 11
  origins of
    animal forms, 28
    cell growth, 22–24
    discontinuum of, 26–27
    individual, 45–46
    pre-life, 19
    social forms, 43–44
  psychological growth, 114, 116–117
    characteristics of, 116–117
reproductive isolation, biological homologue of, 49
resistance to change, 148
retardation, chromosome abnormalities and, 130
Rh incompatibility, 41
ribonucleic acid (RNA), 23, 225
  molecules of, 13
Rignano, Eugenio, 65
ritualistic techniques, 35
Rogers, Carl, 5
Romanell, Patrick, 158
Rome (ancient), 43, 192
Rubner, M., 181

S

sacredness of information, 36
sadism and self-sacrifice, 140
sameness or differentness,
    evolution and, 183–184
Santayana, George, 152
schizophrenia, 118
Schoenberg, Arnold, 66
Schrödinger, Erwin, 22
Science (publication), 4
scientific language, evolve-
    ment of 42
screening, system functions,
    81–82
search, system functions,
    80–81
Second Law of Thermodynam-
    ics, 179
second nature, 35–51
    community growth, 47–49
    genetic shift, 35–42
        ectogenetics, 36–41
        psychospeciation, 41–42
    individual growth forms,
        45–46
    isolation and hybridization,
        49–51
    social growth forms, 42–45
        accretive, 42–43
        mutual, 44–45
        replicative, 43–44
security and danger, 140
self-hate, 119
self-love, 119
self-pollination, 29
Simpson, George G., 158
Skinner, B. F., 5
social growth forms, 42–45
    accretive, 42–43
    mutual, 44–45
    replicative, 43–44
social mutualism 44–45
Soviet Institute of Gerontolo-
    gy, 182

specialization, development of,
    47
species, ectogenetic differ-
    ences, 41–42
Spencer, Herbert, 5, 157–158
Spinoza, Baruch, 84
status ascensium, 191
status quo, idea of overcoming,
    191
stereochemical sympathy,
    13
stereoscopic color vision, 170
Stone Age civilization, 42
    technologies, 32–33
subculturing, 44–45
suburbs, use of, 47–48
Sumerian civilization, 36
surface phenomena, exten-
    sions of, 59
symbolic representation, de-
    velopment of, 33–34
symbolism, ectogenetic evolu-
    tion and, 53
syntropy, concept of, 178–
    179
syphilis, 130
system functions, 80–107
    digestion and assimilation,
        82–83
    feedback—assimilation and
        regulation, 85–101
    internal, 101–107
        non-thinking, 105–107
        thinking, 101–105
    screening, 81–82
    search, 80–81
    use, 83–85

T

technology, ecology and,
    189–191
Teilhard de Chardin, Pierre,
    65, 66, 169

Third World cultures, 192
Thompson, D'Arcy, 78
Thorpe, W. H., 81
Tillich, Paul, 83–84, 151
tincture of opium, 72
together, growing, 148–153
tool-user society, 32–33, 58
totem and taboo, 35
trade, development of, 47
transduction, replicative
    growth by, 23
transformation theory:
    aims of, 6–7
    basic postulates of, 14–15
    behavior, 111–153
        enigmas of Man, 139–153
        growth model, 123–137
        patterns of human
            growth and motivation,
            111–122
    fundamental premise of,
        8–10
    meaning of, xiv, 4, 8–10
    meaning and direction,
        157–195
        achieving growth, 185–
            195
        evolution, 167–184
        philosophy and, 157–165
    origins, 3–107
        of behavior, 17–34
        evolution of man and en-
            vironment, 53–73
        overview, 3–16
        psychology from biology,
            75–107
        second nature, 35–51
    and physics, 199–220
        chemical growth, 210
        energy and growth, 199–
            202
        excitation levels of di-
            atomic molecule, 217–
            220

growth of molecules,
    205–207
microcosmos, 212–217
phases of growth, 202–
    203
polar covalent bonding,
    208–209
probability or inevitabili-
    ty, 210–212
replicative non-polar co-
    valent bonds, 207–208
tradition vs. change, 203–
    205
principles as general sys-
    tems theory, 197–198
transportation methods, im-
    provement in, 44

U

unicellular organism, 21
    animal growth forms, 27–34
    offspring of, 23
    that do not band together,
        27
University of Chicago, 180,
    185
University of Wisconsin,
    100
uracil, 180
use, system functions, 83–85
usefulness for growth, 55

V

values, human decisions and,
    157–158
Vesalius, 59
villages, development of,
    47
viruses, 19
    DNA and, 22

defined, 22
  genetic hybridization, 23
vision, power of, 81

W

Waddington, C. H., 158, 160, 161, 168
Wallace, Alfred Russel, 58, 176
Watson, James D., 5
Watson-Crick double-helix structure, 22

writing, development of, 58–59

Y

yucca moth and yucca plant, mutualism between, 29

Z

zoology-based concepts, human behavior and, 8
zygote, 21

About the Author

GEORGE T. LOCK LAND was born in Hot Springs, Arkansas. In 1951 he began a series of experiments in development of creativity, and since then has continued basic research work in multi-disciplinary science, creativity, motivation, and human behavior. He has served as a consultant to over a hundred major U.S. and international companies in the field of creativity, innovation, and change. He founded the Innotek Corporation, and is presently chairman of the Turtle Bay Institute in New York City.